THE AMERICAN REVOLUTION

In its Political and Military Aspects

1763-1783

BY

ERIC ROBSON

The Norton Libr

W · W · NORTON & COM

NEW YORK

FIRST PUBLISHED IN THE NORTON LIBRARY 1966

Published simultaneously in Canada by
George J. McLeod Limited, Toronto

Books That Live
The Norton imprint on a book means that in the publisher's
estimation it is a book not for a single season but for the years.
W. W. Norton & Company, Inc.

PRINTED IN THE UNITED STATES OF AMERICA

123456789

CONTENTS

Introduction by Sir Lewis Namier and Mr. T. H. McGuffie   iv

Author's Preface   vi

I   The Position in 1763   1

II   Why Revolution?   16

III   Why Independence?   43

IV   Attitudes in 1775   76

V   Why British Defeat? 1   93

VI   Why British Defeat? 2   123

VII   Why American Victory?   153

VIII   Changes of Plan, December 1777—June 1778   175

IX   The Conciliatory Mission, and the Expedition to St. Lucia, June–December 1778   200

X   The Results of the American Revolution   220

Bibliography   239

Index   245

Map of the American Colonies   19

INTRODUCTION

ERIC ROBSON, who died on May 14th, 1954, at the age of thirty-six, was a historian of great promise, well fitted for the work of which this book was to have been a first instalment. A student of Manchester University, he took, in 1939, a brilliant First in Modern History, with eighteenth-century British political and constitutional history for his Special Subject. His war service, which carried him to East and West Africa and to Burma, and which he concluded with a fine record and the rank of major, widened and deepened his historical interests: they now extended to the Empire and to military science. He thus came to be exceptionally well equipped to deal with various aspects of the second British Civil War, the American Revolution, and he made it his special study when, in 1946, he was appointed to a teaching post in Manchester University.

In 1951 he published *Letters from America, 1773-1780,* by a British officer on active service. A series of essays on military and constitutional problems during the American Revolution, printed in leading historical and military magazines, further established his reputation. In the book now published he tried to weld together work done in many fields: an attempt very worth while making even though the book, original and thorough where based on his own researches, could not cover the wide subject in a uniform, well-balanced manner—the subject is too vast and the book was to have been merely the beginning of a life's work. In the end even this has to appear without having received those last touches which only the author himself can give to his work. We have gone through the proofs as best we could, but it is not an easy task to deal with the incompletely finished work of an author to whom no questions can be addressed and with whom we could not argue where we differed from him. We therefore limited our intervention to a bare minimum, and have refrained from adding anything even where there are obvious gaps, or from making changes which we might have urged upon the author but which we did not feel entitled to make without his authorization.

Incomplete as the book may appear in certain aspects, it forms a solid piece of work and, it is to be hoped, the starting point for further work by others now that Robson cannot continue it himself. The book deals with human beings in action: they are alive and three-dimensional, not the mere stereotypes of superficial narratives. Problems are treated in their rich complexity, and military events are integrated with political developments: men, weapons, motives, higher direction, human frailties and strivings mingle in the well-known pattern of those years, which is re-drawn with the clearness of thorough study and the freshness of a new approach. It is just because Robson went deeper and tried to study problems and events at their source that it would have required many more years to cover the wide area in a more uniform manner. But it is a gain that at least this part of his labours had reached the stage of publication before he was suddenly cut off from their further pursuit.

L. B. NAMIER
T. H. McGUFFIE

London, 1955

AUTHOR'S PREFACE

MY GREATEST debt in many years' work and teaching on this subject is to Sir Lewis Namier, whose inspiration first introduced me to it. Many books on the American Revolution still contain no reference to his reading of eighteenth-century British history, which has been influential on periods remote from that age: these essays attempt, however inadequately, to remedy that omission.

Mr. Alan Hodge, Joint Editor of *History Today*, first suggested a book on this theme to me; for his advice, practical assistance, and interest, I am very grateful. I have to thank the editors and owners of *The Times Literary Supplement*, *The Listener*, *The Manchester Guardian*, and *History Today* for permission to reprint material which first appeared in their columns.

My thanks are due to Mr. R. R. Sellman for permission to make use of an adaptation from his 'Student's Atlas of Modern History'.

I have also to thank Captain Malcolm Wombwell, of Newburgh Priory, Yorks, for permission to quote from the Fauconberg Papers in his possession, and T. W. Freeman, Reader in Economic Geography in the University of Manchester, and Miss Burgard of that department, for assistance with the map.

ERIC ROBSON

I

THE POSITION IN 1763

The Peace of Paris in 1763, which ended the Seven Years' War, marks the culmination of the old colonial Empire: Great Britain had arrived at a height of glory and wealth such as no European nation had attained since the decline of the Roman Empire, a prosperity in large part due to her colonies. The very success of the war carried with it the germs of disintegration of the British Empire in North America. Victory removed the most powerful practical restraint upon the growth of separatism—the presence of the hostile French in Canada on the flank of the colonists—and gave free play to the tendency to separation inherent from the beginning of British colonisation in America in the seventeenth century. Colonies had been founded as the result of an escape rather than as a natural expansion: as John Adams pointed out, the Revolution began in 1620 (the date of the establishment of the Pilgrim Fathers' settlement at Plymouth); it was in the minds and hearts of the people from the beginning.

The colonists were not dispatched by government, but went out as a result of individual and private effort, seeking to escape from religious, political, economic and social conditions in Great Britain. Their motives were naturally various, but pre-eminent among them was the desire to secure freedom to worship God in their own way (which did not imply toleration of others) by getting away from the Anglo-Catholic policy inspired by Archbishop Laud; to flee from the political absolutism of the early Stuarts; to find the stability denied at home by rising prices, and stationary or falling rents; to secure land, the motive of many small-holders and agricultural workers displaced by enclosure. The early seventeenth-century emigrations 'skimmed the milk of bitterness in England' (hence the relative harmony of English society during the greater part of the eighteenth century) but they merely postponed, and removed to another continent, the final struggle with authority that was determined in England itself in the seventeenth century. A peculiarly seventeenth-century atmosphere envelops much of the dispute between Great Britain and the American colonies after 1763, particularly with the Puritan settlements of New England, the centre of the Revolution, which were as much a state of mind of controversial truculence as a mere group of states.

In 1763, all might yet have been well had not the British, at last free from European entanglements and impelled by their experience in the war, which had revealed many defects in the working of the old colonial system, set out to reform patent abuses, and enforce the working of that system in its entirety for the first time. It was a policy imperfectly conceived and foolishly applied, not only by George Grenville, its originator, but by his successors, and served only to emphasise the inferior status of the American colonists at a time when they were seeking more equal treatment with the people of Great Britain, and the removal of all restrictions on their freedom of action. This was particularly the case with regard to the development of the lands to the west of the colonies, now open to them. In this development the leading colonists wished their views to be taken into account in the imperial plans[1]—indeed, many of them, in Virginia especially, felt that these lands clearly belonged to their colonies, and hoped to make their fortunes there, a hope immediately thwarted by the Proclamation of October 1763.[2] All active and ambitious groups in the colonies increasingly considered British rule to be an unnecessary and incalculable restraint upon them, an obstacle in the way of successful maturity.

In another light, the Empire in 1763 was a business as much as a political concern, in which England played the part of managing director and principal shareholder, and in which the colonies brought profits into English markets, or filled some gap in the

---

[1] See Thacker, *Sentiments of a British American*, Boston, 1764.
[2] It reserved for Indians a large part of former French territory.

English economic system. Colonies which would not, or could not, play their part in this system were lightly valued, while those which showed the largest profit were the most jealously guarded in peace and war. As Adam Smith put it later, the sneaking arts of underling tradesmen were erected into political maxims for the conduct of a great Empire; a baleful spirit of commerce governed nations on the maxims of the counter. This hard unimaginative concept ignored the real basis of successful Imperial connection: affection and loyalty. It looked ever to the present gain; it overlooked colonial aspirations and needs; it took too much for granted.

The interest of trade prevailed over the interest of plantations with dire results. Mercantilism, implicit in the founding of the early colonies, became explicit in the acts of trade and navigation (the commercial code of the Old Colonial System) passed between 1660 and 1696, and reinforced in the eighteenth century. Colonial trade was regulated in the interest of Great Britain (and, as the British argued, for the benefit of all within that economically self-sufficient Empire) to render it commercially independent of the outside world. To soften the impact of economic regulation on these developing colonial communities, compensations were provided—bounties for the encouragement of certain products required by Great Britain, and otherwise obtainable only from foreign sources, such as naval stores and indigo—while virtual monopolies of the home market in other commodities were granted to colonial producers. Many sacrifices were demanded of English producers and consumers in return for the undoubted advantage derived from the possession of overseas settlements, including the prohibition of tobacco growing, which had been widespread in England in the seventeenth century. British merchants were as closely bound to obtain raw materials from the colonies as the colonies were bound to obtain their manufactured requirements from England. Moreover, the American colonies had benefited by the concentration of the British West Indian colonies on the production of sugar and its by-products, one of the pillars of the Old Colonial System: but for their commerce with the Caribbean possessions in fish, provisions and timber, the northern mainland colonies would have remained collections of poor farms and fishing stations. Colonial shipping also had been fostered, particularly that of New England: of 7,694 vessels engaged in British trade in 1775, it has been estimated that 2,342 were colonial-built.

Although the motives for emigration had been personal and mixed, there had been a commercial basis in every colonial venture. The Virginia Company (1606) is estimated to have expended £1,000,000 by 1621, and although it lingered on after the colony had become a Royal colony (in 1624) until 1632, it never paid a dividend. The Massachusetts Bay Company (1629) was only made possible by a group of merchants in London, who financed the emigration at a cost of £200,000 in that year. The transport of settlers, the provision of food, tools, fortifications and defences were expensive, and financial interests supporting them naturally expected a return on their heavy outlay. The willingness of individuals to invest was a major reason for the strict regulation of colonial trade that developed after 1660, both to safeguard a return on colonial ventures, and to prevent foreigners from reaping the benefit of British investment. As Bacon observed in his essay *Of Plantations,* the planting of countries was like the planting of woods: 'you must make account to lose almost twenty years' profit, and expect your recompense in the end.'

Trade regulations attempted to secure that end. But by 1763, many colonists were wondering whether the end would ever come. They wished to have the regulations lessened (a natural reaction after a period of war) and to participate more in the profits. In fact, through natural increase of population, and through development of natural resources, the northern mainland colonies had outgrown the closed mercantile system of the seventeenth century, just as Great Britain was shortly to outgrow a closed Empire by the first half of the nineteenth century, and for the same reason. By 1763, the British West Indian islands were unable either to take all the provisions which the mainland colonies had for disposal, or to supply their requirements in sugar, molasses and rum. Unable to find a market for their produce

within the Empire, and as a consequence unable to obtain legally
the specie with which to meet their debts to English merchants
and manufacturers, the mainland colonies wished both to broaden
the old colonial system by extending their markets outside the
confines of Empire, and to develop their own industries in order
to lessen their indebtedness. The balance of trade, estimated at
£50,000 in 1713 and £2 million by 1760, in favour of Great
Britain, which had to be settled by payment of gold and silver,
was by 1763 the major economic problem of the British Empire.

Gold and silver could be obtained legally by trade with the
British West Indies, or by the freight charges of colonial shipping,
but not in sufficient quantity to meet this increasingly adverse
balance. It could also be secured illegally by trade with foreign
possessions in the West Indies, or direct with the continent of
Europe. These breaches of the old colonial system, which had
been openly revealed during the Seven Years' War, and
their extension so much desired by the colonists, were anathema
to mercantile interests in England. They argued that they would
assist the economic development, and therefore the material
strength, of national rivals (a reason which never worried the
supremely self-confident colonists) and would hamper British
West Indian interests (well represented in British parliamentary
and governmental circles, as the American colonists were not).

Moreover, the supplying of French colonies during the war,
alone enabling them to continue resistance, and neutralising
British naval supremacy, smacked too much of treason to be
acceptable as a peacetime solution. As to the development of
colonial industry, this ran clean counter to official policy.
Throughout the eighteenth century, the Board of Trade had
insisted that the colonies should apply themselves to the production of 'such commodities as are fit to be encouraged in those
parts, according to the true design and intention of those plantations': development of industry, which would lessen colonial
dependence on this country, was not the colonial role. The
colonies might mine ore and turn it into iron, but they should
not make up iron into tools, weapons, or steel: this would hinder
what was by 1763 the predominant British concern, the export

of manufactured articles to the colonies. The conversion of raw material into finished articles was to remain the business of the mother-country: colonies should not aspire beyond providing the raw material. A stream of legislation sought to give effect to this aim. The Woollen Act of 1699 forbade colonial woollen goods to be sold outside the place or plantation where they were woven. In 1719, an act to forbid the manufacture of iron of any kind in the American colonies failed, but duties, not modified until 1750, were imposed on all colonial iron imported into England. In that year, pig and bar iron were granted free admission, but no mill or other engine for slitting or rolling of iron, or any plating forge or steel furnace, were to be allowed in the colonies. Despite these controls colonial industry developed and prospered.

From time to time some small measures of relief in direct trade were granted, but insufficient to satisfy the colonists or provide the real solution to their main problem. In 1729, South Carolina was permitted to export rice direct to all European ports south of Cape Finisterre, a concession extended to Georgia in 1734. (The market was mainly continental, and the detour through England required by the trade laws costly.) But the mercantile attitude to the major colonial aim, the widening of the system, was clearly revealed in the Molasses Act of 1733. This act, 'for the better securing and encouraging the trade of His Majesty's sugar colonies' (still the prime interest of merchant and politician alike), placed a prohibitive duty on the import of sugar, rum and molasses from foreign possessions into British colonies or Great Britain. The intention was disquieting, a failure to move with and meet the needs of the time, or to recognise the inevitable development of the mainland colonies, and the way in which they and the French West Indian possessions had become mutually dependent in their economic interests, through the failure of the British islands. It was this dependence which made prohibition of the trade, or enforcement of the Act, extremely difficult. Had the act been rigidly enforced, difficulties would have arisen immediately, for it made impossible, or illicit if carried on, an increasingly important part of colonial trade. The effect was apparent during the closing years of the Seven Years' War, when it was applied, supported by the use of the Navy to check breaches, and by its re-assertion in the Sugar Duties Act of 1764. Here was a leading cause of colonial discontent, which explains John Adams' comment that rum was an essential ingredient in the American Revolution.

The need to meet the adverse balance of trade caused acute financial difficulties in the colonies. It drained them of gold and silver at a time when increase of population and expansion of trade made barter inconvenient, and a plentiful supply of currency essential. The export of English coin to the colonies was not allowed, nor were the colonies permitted to mint coinage of their own. Various expedients were tried. North Carolina declared seventeen commodities legal tender, a practice followed elsewhere, as with tobacco in Virginia. Some colonies authorised 'lawful money' of their own, based on Spanish pieces of eight, which circulated widely. This money was over-valued in terms of sterling. A piece of eight, worth 4s. 6d. in terms of sterling, was valued at 4s. 8d. in Georgia and South Carolina, 6s. in Virginia and the New England colonies, 8s. in New York, and 7s. 6d. elsewhere. The issue of paper money, 'bills of credit', in almost every case with no effective backing, had begun as early as 1690 in Massachusetts Bay, and become general. In 1740, £100 sterling was worth £160 local currency in New York and New Jersey, £170 in Pennsylvania, £200 in Maryland, £800 in South Carolina, and £1,400 in North Carolina.

The evils of paper money inflation were common in all colonies long before the War of Independence revealed the heights to which the colonists could rise in this respect. Land banks were yet another solution of this problem—the attempt to found one in Massachusetts Bay in 1741, by ruining the father of Samuel Adams, may have played some part in later happenings. Here again the authorities relied on control and regulation. An Act of 1751 declared New England paper money illegal tender in debt payment, and in 1765 all further issue of paper money was prohibited. The Stamp Act (1765) and the Townshend duties (1767) both still stipulated payment in gold and silver. As Professor Hale

Bellot has suggested,[1] the British Parliament and the colonial assemblies increasingly represented rival economic interests. Pressure was put upon colonial debtors by English creditors to meet their debts in sound specie, while the British Parliament, in response to the wishes of those creditors, was opposed to measures of relief adopted by the debtor, whether by extended trade to secure specie, or by increasing their own manufacture.

The growing interest in colonies as markets rather than as sources of raw material, recently re-emphasised by Professor Harlow,[2] which became noticeable from 1763, served to increase this financial embarrassment. It implied that the colonies would be constrained permanently to buy more than they sold—an economic grievance which did a great deal to link colonial planters and merchants to colonial politicians. This new emphasis turned British attention from the West Indies to the mainland colonies; the controls and reforms necessary effectively to enforce British regulations for the first time on the mainland coincided with a desire in these colonies for greater freedom. The population of the continental colonies was doubling every generation, and the benefit of this market, 'a certain and constant vent to the home product', had to be reserved to England. The changed attitude was shown in the acquisitions made by the Treaty of Paris, the significant retention of Canada rather than of conquered West Indian sugar islands—Guadeloupe—primarily as an increasing market for manufactured goods. Increased production, caused by industrial changes in England, required an outlet beyond the capacity of the West Indies, and for which even the American colonies became too limited. In 1698, seven-eighths of England's colonial trade was with the West Indies, Virginia, Maryland, and the Carolinas, while the Middle and New England colonies, with Newfoundland and Hudson Bay, accounted for only one-eighth. By 1747 one half, and by 1767 two-thirds, of English exports to the colonies went to areas north of Maryland.

[1] H. Hale Bellot: *American History and American Historians*, London, 1952.
[2] V. T. Harlow: *The Founding of the Second British Empire, 1763-1793*, Vol. I, London, 1952.

This changed attitude, which led to what is often described as the Second British Empire, is visible some twenty years before the collapse of the First, and was given practical expression by the same men who proceeded to apply dynamite to the fabric of that edifice. Neatly demarcated epochs are rare in history: the Second Empire (if such a term has to be used) was much more a development from known ways than a distinct new departure. There was a continuous effort, rather than any breakdown of the First Empire, followed by a long period of apathy, neglect and negation, and then a swift re-awakening of interest by the third and fourth decades of the nineteenth century, which is the accepted version. There was no such generation of imperial standstill. 1763 marks the beginning of a critical and exceptionally formative stage in the evolution of the British Empire, which continued despite the loss of the American colonies. Great Britain had attained a commanding position not only in North America but also in India and on the ocean routes of world trade. Scientific and industrial development at home, with the possession of decisive superiority at sea, led a self-confident people (self-confidence was a patent cause of British miscalculations regarding the American colonists) to search the oceans for new markets in a sustained spell of maritime exploration unparalleled since the days of the Tudor seamen. The voyages of Byron, Wallis, Carteret and Cook, and the writings of Alexander Dalrymple, represented a conscious revival of an ambition to secure commercial predominance in the areas of the Pacific Ocean and the South China sea, from which England had been diverted in the seventeenth century by the alternative enterprise of founding settlements of her own people along the Atlantic seaboard of North America, and in the Caribbean. This duality between commercial and territorial dominion has always been present in British Imperial activity, an alternation between exchange of manufactures for exotic commodities in tropical or sub-tropical areas, involving intercourse with coloured races, and the foundation of British settlements. The revulsion against actual settlement was naturally accentuated by the quarrel with the Americans, but it was present before: its root cause was the fear that colonial communities would become industrial competitors. Unfounded jealousy often accompanies abounding self-confidence.

In the political sphere before 1763, old controversies remained, new ones were added. and no permanent solution of difficulties was reached. In 1763, when the British Government had time, capacity and power positively to apply the old colonial system, it was too late, and in any case it ignored political as well as economic development in the colonies. It overlooked the vital fact that during generations of neglect, the colonies had both organised a life of their own and achieved *de facto* self-government. The very remoteness and weakness of British control meant that control itself was lost sight of—as Chief Justice Oliver of Massachusetts Bay once stated: 'When Jove is distant, lightning is not to be feared.' Once the French menace from Canada was removed, only supreme self-restraint could have prevented a political rupture, and supreme self-restraint was not likely in that legalistic age. Sir John Dalrymple rightly told Lord George Germain in 1778 that it was 'the busy meddling officious practmatical I had almost said Parliamentary turn of England which has brought the present mischief upon us.'[1] The writing had been on the wall as early as the Civil War, when Massachusetts Assembly rejected the legislative authority of the British Parliament, because 'our allegiance binds us not to the laws of England any longer than while we live in England' Circumstances, the need for protection against the French, and the benefit of trade in the Empire, had caused allegiance to be continued, but now in 1763, the colonists, a self-reliant people, wished fully to control their own affairs, and saw no valid reason why they should not do so. The British case had also been stated in the seventeenth century, and remained unchanged: the preamble to the 1650 Navigation Act declared that colonies planted and settled by the people and by the authority of this country were, and ought to be, subordinate and dependent upon it, a thesis expressed in every colonial charter, and underlined in the Declaratory Act of 1766.

The most striking political development before 1763 was the position attained by the elected assembly in almost every colony.

[1] Historical Manuscripts Commission: *Stopford Sackville MSS.*, II, p. 103.

In theory, and in the British view, the duty of the assembly was to pass acts and vote funds, which the executive (to the British the dominant factor in colonial administration) would put into operation and distribute. In practice, and in the colonial view, the Assembly was dominant: it came to direct the executive, and to deprive it of any independence, by the power of the purse. As Governor Clinton of New York described it in 1752, the Assembly made officials sensible that the only way for them to prosper or to be rewarded was by neglecting their duty; by their performance of it, they would only suffer. The Assembly, instead of co-operating with Governor and Council, was 'a dead weight against the other branches of the legislature'. In every colony, it claimed the right to determine its own sessions, and to appoint its own officials, as for instance in the resolve of the Pennsylvania Assembly in 1707 'to have all government and powers in their own hands, the regulation of all courts, the nomination of all officers'. Successive British administrations insisted vainly that the assemblies make permanent provision for the salaries of colonial officials, especially the Governors. In 1763, only in Virginia, Maryland, North Carolina, Georgia and Nova Scotia were officials independent of the local assembly in this respect. Elsewhere, dependent on the assembly for their salaries, they were unable conscientiously to carry out their duty to the Crown. As a contemporary said, every governor had two masters: one who gave him his commission, and another who gave him his pay.

Having defeated the local prerogative, Governor and officials, the assemblies in 1763 were now prepared to challenge the British Parliament for equal rights, privileges and powers. Supreme in the colonies, they intended to secure the freedom of their authority from any external control. Both they and the Imperial Parliament set up claims to an unlimited authority: this boded ill for an equitable and well-defined Imperial relationship, which lacked the fundamental identity of interest. Here is the basic cause of the American Revolution or War of Independence: a demand for self-government which was not acceptable at that time in Great Britain, and was indeed still somewhat suspect when again suggested by Lord Durham in 1839. The real motives of the colonial leaders were shown in their reiterated claims that their assemblies were equal in status and power to the British Parliament, and in their constant endeavour to set limits on the supremacy of Westminster, provided as they were by the British with repeated opportunities after 1763.

Conflicting political ideas, not tea nor taxes, caused the secession of the colonial peoples from the British Empire. Colonial and British political thought and development had come to the parting of the ways. This was how Joseph Galloway, a leading Loyalist, saw it in 1775:[1] a dispute between the supreme authority of the State, and a number of its members, as to the limits of authority on the part of the former, and of obedience on the part of the latter. Canning rightly described the American Revolution as having been 'a test of the equality of strength between the legislature of this mighty kingdom, and the colonial assemblies'. It had been a leading principle wherever possible to turn all colonies into Royal colonies, principally to secure greater adherence to the laws of trade. New Jersey became a Royal colony in 1702, North Carolina in 1719, South Carolina in 1729, and Georgia in 1754. By 1763, all were royal with the exception of Connecticut and Rhode Island (corporate colonies), Maryland, Pennsylvania, and Delaware (proprietary colonies), Massachusetts Bay (a royal chartered colony on its peculiar constitution of 1691). Nevertheless, because of the position attained by the assemblies, this conversion availed the British purpose little. Lack of authority and conflict of purpose were clearly visible in 1763.

Already in 1748, a Swedish observer, Peter Kalm, had noted a certain coolness in the colonies towards Great Britain, a view confirmed in 1757 by William Knox, later under-secretary to Germain, on his arrival in Georgia. Kalm thought that 'commercial oppression' had made the inhabitants less tender towards England, and this coolness was increased by the many foreigners settled in the colonies—Dutch, German, French—as well as Scottish and Irish who had no special love for England. He believed loyalty was not to be expected from the native-born

[1] *A Candid Examination of the Mutual Claims of Great Britain and the Colonies*, Philadelphia, 1775.

colonials, whose ancestors had left England in resentment, and
for whom the 'narrow spirit of commercial gain' offered insufficient inducement to retain the connection. Above all, he
went on, 'some people are always discontented and love change,
and exceeding freedom and prosperity nurse an untamable
spirit'. He had been told publicly that within fifty years, the
English colonies in America might constitute a separate state,
entirely independent of Great Britain. In his opinion there was
only one reason 'why the love of these colonies for their metropolis does not utterly decline': the presence of the French on the
frontiers, and the protection of the coast by the Navy. 'The
English government has therefore reason to regard the French in
North America as the chief power which urges their colonies to
submission'. In 1763, these dangerous neighbours were neutralised
by the result of the Seven Years' War and this gave free play to
all the hitherto restrained separatist tendencies.

There was however one restraining factor not considered by
Kalm which more than any other reveals the folly of successive
British administrations after 1763. This was the want of union
among the colonies themselves, which had been displayed as
late as 1754 in the failure of any assembly to ratify Benjamin
Franklin's Plan of Union (agreed at the Albany Congress), the
last of many such schemes since 1643, to set up a central authority
for defence preparations against the French, to deal with Indian
relations, and land development. Diverse racial origin, religious
differences, conflicting material interests and particularism, seemed
to render the colonies incapable of acting together for a common
object however vital and necessary. America in 1763 was a
geographical expression. In each colony, and between them all,
were sectional differences which not even common opposition
to Great Britain after 1775 completely effaced. In each colony
there was a conflict between frontier and tide-water—the more
recently settled Western regions complained that representation,
the courts, and the administrative areas were rigged in favour of
the older seaboard settlements; a conflict between privileged and
non-privileged groups, large landowners against small or expect-
ant holders (the land problem has usually been the first touch-

stone of social cleavage in settlement colonies), property-holders against tenants and the growing number of wage-earners. Between the colonies, there were bitter frontier disputes, and the nineteenth-century division between North and South on the slavery issue was already present. Smaller colonies were naturally jealous of the larger: moreover, differences of soil and climate had sharpened the innate differences between the Puritans who founded New England and the more conservative Southern settlers. The War of American Independence had not only rid the colonies of British control; it had also seen the paying off of old social, economic and political scores against those of the colonial social élite who remained loyal. What was it in British policy between 1763 and 1775 which combined this mere chaos of uncemented states into a constitutional union? How much did both Britain and the Colonies themselves contribute to this result? In 1760, in the opinion of Morison and Commager,[1] a civil war within the colonies seemed more likely than a war for independence from Britain. This comment should be borne in mind throughout this period, in considering both British policy and colonial reactions to it.

The principle of the British Empire in 1763 therefore remained as it had been since the beginning of colonial expansion, but the practice in North America had become very different. Nowhere else had there developed a system of government that gave so much freedom of action and responsibility of self-regulation to the local units, and which yet sought at the same time to reconcile this liberty with the maintenance of centralised supervision and direction. In this freedom there lay what the British regarded as a weakness, an instability, which prevented the establishment of that unity which would alone ensure internal strength amidst the great diversity of establishments and interests. Not for the first time, the British could not leave well alone. The struggle between the rival claims was to be the dominant feature of the next twenty years. None of the mechanism evolved by the British to keep their Empire in due subordination was adequate to the task in

[1] S. E. Morison and H. S. Commager: *The Growth of the American Republic*, Vol. I, Fourth Edition, Oxford, 1950.

1763, particularly with the growing maturity of the colonies, and the disappearance of restraining circumstances. If subordination to London existed, and was accepted before 1763, it was a subordination based not upon force or 'tyranny', but upon colonial self-interest and convenience. Precisely the same motives inspired colonial action after 1763. The colonies had needed the encouragement and the protection afforded by the mother-country in their days of infancy and adolescence. Now, grown to man's estate, with foreign menace removed from their borders, and conscious of a new sense of security and strength, they determined, whether wisely or not is immaterial, to control their own destinies. Two contemporary writers saw this clearly. Dean Tucker of Gloucester commented in 1774: 'It is the nature of them all to aspire after independence, and to set up for themselves as soon as ever they find they are able to subsist without being beholden to the mother-country'.[1] Thomas Paine who, in *Common Sense*, in 1776, made independents of the bulk of the colonists, put it even more concisely: 'To know whether it be the interest of this continent to be Independent, we need only ask this easy simple question: Is it the interest of a man to be a boy all his life?'.[2]

[1] Josiah Tucker: *The True Interest of Great Britain set Forth*, London, 1774, p. 12.
[2] Quoted in M. C. Tyler: *The Literary History of the American Revolution, 1763-1783*, 2 vols., London, 1905, II, p. 43.

II

WHY REVOLUTION?

George III, in his own time, was accused by his opponents of attempting to subvert the system of government established by the Revolution, a charge translated by subsequent historians into one of attempting to subvert the system of responsible government.[1] The American colonists rebelled, as the argument runs, because they were the first to feel the full force of the King's assault upon liberty; their success prevented a similar effort being made in this country. Samuel Langdon, President of Harvard College, stated what became the opposition thesis as early as May 1775—that the plan of the British Government was to subjugate the colonies first, and then the whole nation, to their will. The Reverend Robert Bramley wrote to the third Duke of Portland on November 3rd, 1775, of 'a regular plan of despotism' establishing among us, of which the American measures were but 'one link in the chain'. According to Horace Walpole, commenting on events in March 1778, the evident tendency of the King's measures was to drive all the colonies into rebellion, that all might be punished and enslaved: 'I had as little doubt but if the conquest of America should be achieved, the moment of the victorious Army's return would be that of the destruction of our liberty . . . Would that Army, had it returned victorious, have hesitated to make the King as absolute as they had made him in America? Would they not have been let loose against the friends of liberty as mere rebels?'[2] In that same year, David Hartley, M.P. for Hull, a leading advocate of conciliation, saw 'a design to establish an

[1] R. Sedgwick (ed.): *Letters from George III to Lord Bute, 1756-1766*, London, 1939, viii.

[2] J. Doran (ed.): *Journal of the Reign of King George the Third, 1771-1783*, by Horace Walpole, 2 vols., London, 1859, Vol. II, pp. 240-1.

influential dominion, to be exercised at the pleasure of the Crown, and to acquire from America an independent revenue at the disposition of the Crown, uncontrolled and not accountable for to Parliament'.[1] Sir George Otto Trevelyan, whose books on the American Revolution are still standard reading, fostered this argument, drawn from the contemporary opponents of George III, and carried it even further. He described the Revolution as 'a defensive movement', undertaken in behalf of essential English institutions, 'genuine national self-government and real ministerial responsibility against the purpose and effort of a monarch to defeat the political progress of a race'.[2]

The realities of the working of the British Constitution in the eighteenth century, the absence of either genuine national self-government or real ministerial responsibility, have since been revealed by Sir Lewis Namier, Professor Richard Pares, and others; a careful reading of the manuscript sources of the reign of King George III similarly contradicts many of the absurd conclusions that have been drawn about that much maligned monarch's attitude towards the American colonies, and on the dispute between them and Great Britain. It was curious tyranny that permitted a steady growth of agitation through merchants' committees and committees of correspondence, Sons of Liberty, and similar groups, groups which did not shrink from violence whenever it seemed necessary, in large affairs like the Boston Tea Party, or in numerous smaller terrorisations and beatings of 'Tories'. Indeed, the attempted and unpopular reform of colonial administration in America between 1763 and 1775 was introduced with what now seems an amazing disregard of precautions, to which the key is weakness rather than tyranny. As Samuel Adams wrote in 1773, that Great Britain should continue to alienate the growing millions who inhabited North America, 'on whom she greatly depends, and on whose alliance in future time her existence as a nation may be suspended, is

[1] *Letters on the American War,* London, 1778, second letter. See also G. H. Guttridge: *David Hartley, M.P. An Advocate of Conciliation, 1774–1783.* Berkeley, California, 1926.

[2] G. O. Trevelyan: *The American Revolution,* 4 vols., London, 1928 edition, Vol. III, p. 161.

perhaps as glaring an instance of human folly as ever disgraced politicians'.[1]

Those who accept the charge of tyranny levelled against George III should consider, for example, his attitude to the request of Hillsborough, Secretary of State for the American Department, for stern measures to be taken in 1769 against Massachusetts Bay and New York. Hillsborough had proposed to the Cabinet on February 13th that the appointment of the Council of Massachusetts Bay, at that time elected, should be vested in the Crown, and that the passing or entering upon the Journal of the House of Representatives of that province of any note, resolution, or order, denying or questioning the power and authority of Parliament to make laws for the province should be *ipso facto* ground for the forfeiture of the Charter. The King, in a memorandum on these proposals, wrote that the nomination of the Council by the Crown might 'from a continuance of their conduct' become necessary, 'but till then ought to be avoided as the altering Charters is at all times an odious measure'. The second recommendation was 'of so strong a nature that it rather seems calculated to increase the unhappy feudes that subsist than to asswage them'.[2]

They should also ponder the position which is most clear between 1763 and 1775, that had the King wished to hold power and authority apart from the British Parliament, had he in fact held the idea of overturning the Constitution usually ascribed to him, the weapon was in his hands in the conception of a separate sovereignty in the colonies, outside Parliamentary control, which colonial leaders, who would have been his best, most obvious, and most willing allies, continued to suggest down to 1774. The opportunity existed, but was never taken. The colonial leaders believed that if the King could be made to see their argument that the colonies were governed under charters issued by him which gave them self-government, including the right of taxation (and that Parliament therefore had no power to

---

[1] Tyler, *op. cit.*, Vol. II, pp. 16–17.

[2] Sir J. W. Fortescue (ed.): *The Correspondence of King George III, 1760–1783*, 6 vols., London, 1927–8, Vol. II, Nos. 701 and 701A.

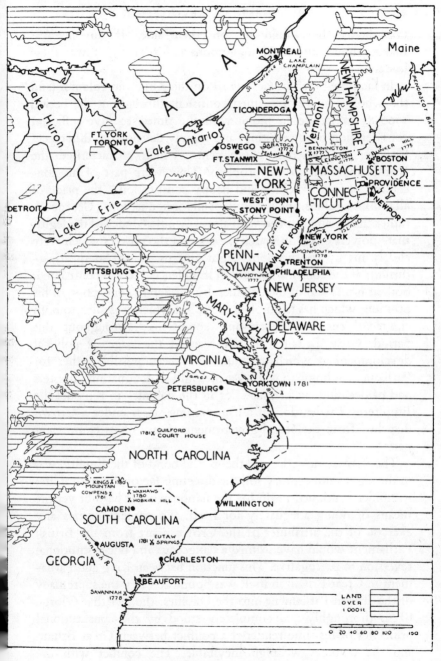

THE AMERICAN COLONIES

tax them), he would be on their side. If anyone was making unconstitutional suggestions before 1775, it was these leaders.

In fact, the views of George III on the American colonies (and the whole Empire) remained consistent throughout the period 1760–83: a failure to move with the times, to give sufficient consideration to the existing, and rapidly developing, differences between the different components, which characterised the British approach to the problem. They were part of his conception of 'our excellent and happy constitution', 'the pride of all thinking minds, and the envy of all foreign nations'. George III, rather than being imbued with a grossly inflated idea of the legitimate powers of the monarchy, exercised the powers which were clearly his by constitutional right and usage not in the overturning of the constitution, but in its defence. He was confronted, both at home and in the colonies, by a different conception of his position, which has triumphed since, but which was alien to both eighteenth-century theory and conditions. Throughout this period, Great Britain had not reached the stage of political development at which it would have been possible either for Parliament at home to take over the right of designating ministers and of deciding on measures, or in the colonies to remodel the Empire as a federation of self-governing states under a Crown detached from the actual government of any of its component parts.

The Crown, now the sole theoretical bond of the Empire, was in the eighteenth century still the directing factor in political life; its holder continued to do for the nation what it has not yet the means of doing adequately for itself. To contemporaries any exercise of the attributes of the Crown apart from the British Parliament would have seemed a dangerous and unconstitutional reversion to prerogative. This junction between King and Parliament in Great Britain in itself was bound to carry the supremacy of the British Parliament into the colonies; the fact that George III so thoroughly and completely stood by the constitutional principles of his time rendered a conflict between Great Britain and the colonies wellnigh inevitable. The conflict with the

American colonies was engaged in and conducted by George III and his ministers to uphold the supremacy of Parliament at Westminster. It was this, rather than the rights of the Crown, which was at stake. As Lyttelton put it in 1766, in opposing the repeal of the Stamp Act, 'this is no question of expediency; it is a question of sovereignty until the Americans submit to the Legislature'. The British, conceiving the Empire to be one unit—like one of Capability Brown's gardens, a tidy and symmetrical whole—were attempting to keep the colonists to their proper place in that eighteenth-century concept of Empire. It might not be the constitution as the Americans understood it, and certainly was not the constitution as they wanted it; nevertheless, it was the Constitution, pinching for the first time after 1763, because only then were the colonists brought face to face with its realities. Remoteness, and the absence of control caused by British distractions elsewhere, had mistakenly persuaded them that control by the mother-country no longer existed. Only when Parliament gave up the struggle—with General Conway's motion of February 27th, 1782, to declare impracticable the purpose of subduing the revolted colonies by force—did George III give up the 'battle of the Legislature', as he had described it to Lord North on September 10th, 1775.[1] 'The dreadful resolution of the 27 February last of the House of Commons', he wrote later in 1782, 'this has so entirely removed the real cause of the war to the utter shame of that branch of the legislature that it would be madness not to conclude peace on the best possible terms we can obtain.'[2]

This attitude of George III to the colonies is abundantly supported by evidence, hitherto mainly neglected. He stated it clearly to Dartmouth, Secretary of State for the American Department from 1772 to 1775, in that latter year. There was nothing he more earnestly desired, the King told him, than to remove the jealousies and quiet the apprehensions of his American subjects, and to see them reconciled to British government 'upon principles that may secure the permanent peace and tranquility

[1] Fortescue, *op. cit.*, Vol. III, No. 1709. See also Vol. IV, No. 2451.
[2] *Ibid.*, Vol. VI, No. 4004.

of the British Empire'. He considered it his first duty in the existing situation 'to maintain and support the rights of the Constitution of Great Britain'.[1] Dartmouth, regarded by many as a friend to the colonists, fully accepted and appreciated this viewpoint. He himself had told General Gage, Commander-in-Chief in North America, on June 3rd, 1774, that the sovereignty of the King in Parliament over the colonies required a full and absolute submission from them. 'The constitutional authority of this Kingdom over its colonies must be vindicated, and its laws obeyed throughout the whole Empire.' Not only its dignity and reputation but its power and very existence were concerned: 'should these ideas of independence . . . once take root, that relation between this Kingdom and its colonies, which is the bond of peace and power, will soon cease to exist and destruction must follow disunion'.[2] He repeated this to Gage on March 3rd, 1775, in terms which describe not only the attitude of the King himself but also that of the majority of the politically conscious nation in this country at that time. The King considered himself 'bound by every tye to exert those means the Constitution has placed in his hands for preserving that Constitution entire, and to resist with firmness every attempt to violate the rights of Parliament . . . and to encourage in the colonies ideas of independence inconsistent with their connection with this Kingdom.'[3]

Herein lay the fundamental cause of the American Revolution. It was further underlined by the Solicitor-General, Alexander Wedderburn, when he replied in 1775 to Burke's plan of reconciliation, and stated the official view. The power of Parliament was defied. A portion of the King's subjects, though they had not formally cast off allegiance, were in open rebellion: such an enemy 'in the bowels of the Kingdom' must be resisted, though manufactures be interrupted and commerce languish. 'The integrity of the Empire is more to be regarded then the accumu-

[1] Historical Manuscripts Commission, Fourteenth Report, Appendices, Part X. *Dartmouth Papers*, Vol. II, p. 283.
[2] C. E. Carter (ed.): *The Correspondence of General Thomas Gage*, 2 vols., New Haven, 1931–3, Vol. II, p. 165.
[3] *Ibid.*, pp. 187–9.

lation of wealth, the sufferings of individuals are nothing compared with the safety of the State.'[1]

George III was fully aware of the distress and misery caused by war, and was averse to the use of force until it became the only means of restoring the American colonies to that due subordination to government which was the prerequisite of constitutional order, and which alone could preserve liberty from degenerating into licentiousness.[2] In his view, obedience to law and government was the means the Constitution had wisely framed, not only to safeguard liberty but also to have grievances removed. He had told Grafton as early as October 27th, 1768, whilst discussing dispatches from Gage openly avowing 'the tendency of the town of Boston to cast off that constitutional dependency on the mother country', that such licentiousness must be curbed, yet he still insisted that policy should be motivated by 'a desire with temper to let them return to their reason, not with violence to drive them'. It was clear throughout to George III that if the Constitution were overthrown, 'anarchy, the most terrible of all evils, must ensue', and anarchy, ever present dread of eighteenth-century statesmen, was even more dangerous in the colonies than at home, because of the risk of foreign intervention. The King's main reason for approving the changes in the Massachusetts Legislature in 1774 was precisely that it would establish 'some government in that province which till now has been a scene of anarchy'. By then, especially after the Boston Tea Party, an attack on property, the sacred pillar of eighteenth-century society, something more than words was required. Mediation had only served to encourage the American colonists 'annually to encrease in their pretensions that thorough independency which one state has of another, but which is quite subversive of the obedience which a colony owes to its mother country'.[3] The present relations between this country and the Dominions have

[1] O. S. Reid: 'An Analysis of British Parliamentary Opinion on American Affairs at the close of the War of Independence', *Journal of Modern History*, XVIII, p. 221.

[2] Fortescue, *op. cit.*, Vol. I, No. 372. For the King's attitude to war, see *ibid.*, Vol. II, Nos. 841, 879, 1151, and Vol. IV, No. 2649.

[3] *Ibid.*, Vol. III, No. 1379, George III to Lord North, February 4th, 1774.

done nothing to lessen uninformed criticism of British policy before 1775, when such relations were hardly dreamt of, and are a
further striking example of the care which is necessary (but
hardly ever applied) not to read past happenings in the light of
present conceptions, particularly those of the reign of George III
in both political and imperial affairs.

The die was now cast: the colonies must either submit or
triumph. They must be mastered, or left to themselves and
treated as aliens. Since the inhabitants of the colonies were, in
the British view, subjects established in America, they came
under the control of the laws of Great Britain, and these they
must obey.[1] All known history pointed the course to take.
As Dean Tucker remarked in 1775, prejudices and prepossessions
were stubborn things, and in none more peculiarly obstinate
than in relinquishing detached parts of an unwieldy extended
Empire, 'there not being . . . a single instance in all history of any
nation surrendering a distant province voluntarily and of free
choice, notwithstanding it was greatly to their interest to have
done it'. As late as June 11th, 1779, the King remarked to Lord
North that he should think it the greatest instance among the
many he had met with of ingratitude and injustice if it could be
supposed that any man in his dominions 'more ardently desired
the restoration of peace and solid happiness in every part of this
Empire' than he did. 'There is no personal sacrifice I could not
readily yield for so desirable an object'. But, at the same time,
no desire to get out of the present difficulties would incline him to
enter 'into what I look upon as the distruction of the Empire'.[2]

At home, the King's view was equally clear: the most beautiful
combination that ever was framed must be preserved in its
pristine lustre, and in all its aspects. There also he was determined
at whatever personal cost to withstand those who were attempting to attack the Constitution, particularly the group led by
Rockingham (and later by Portland), and inspired by Charles
James Fox, with its peculiar ideas on nomination of ministers and

---

[1] See the letters from the King to North, September 11th, 1774, and February
8th, 1775, *ibid.*, Nos. 1508 and 1590.
[2] *Ibid.*, Vol. IV, No. 2649.

control of measures. The rights to choose Ministers and to decide on measures were the main rights claimed by George III to guarantee the independency of the Crown; they saved the monarch from becoming a 'cypher in the trammels of any self-created band', and as the election on 1784 showed, these rights, a matter of conscience with the King, were also supported by the majority of the politically conscious nation. Politicians today act on the principles enunciated by Fox and Burke, who were right in thinking that ultimately they must succeed. It is too often forgotten that those principles did not succeed in their own time, indeed were quite alien to that age. Fox himself was under no illusion as to what he was about. At the coming in of the Rockingham Administration in March 1782, he said, 'this Revolution which he brought about was the greatest for England that ever was; that, excepting in the mere person of a King, it was a complete change of the Constitution'.[1] Nor was George III. He wrote to Lord North on August 7th asking for active support next session from him, and from the 'country gentlemen who certainly have great attention for him, to come early and shew their countenance'. Then 'I may be enabled to keep the Constitution from being entirely anihilated, which must be the case if Mr. Fox and his associates are not withstood. Many strange scenes have occurred in this country, but none more so than the present contest, it is no less then whether the sole direction of my Kingdom shall be trusted in the hands of Mr. Fox'.[2]

George III was equally right in believing that there was nothing in the circumstances of his time which obliged him to concur in views which he thought 'so novel', and which were certainly less well founded in history than his own. The brief Whig success in 1782–3, caused more by circumstances, a unique national disaster, than by principle, has led many to antedate the continuous development of modern political concepts, and to mis-read the motives of George III. These were clearly expressed in a private and unfinished draft: 'it has been my lot to change so frequently Administrations and those out of place have ever laid the blame

[1] Historical Manuscripts Commission, *Carlisle MSS.*, p. 604.
[2] Fortescue, *op. cit.*, Vol. VI, No. 3872.

on me, that I owe it to myself to write an exact narrative of the principal transactions of my Reign . . . The only difference of conduct I adopted was to put an end to those unhappy distinctions of party called Whigs and Tories, by declaring I would countenance every man that supported my Administration and concurred in that form of Government which had been so wisely established by the Revolution.'[1]

As George III maintained throughout, there was in fact a wider basic background to the American Revolution than has been appreciated by either his contemporary or later critics. It was well described by Francis Bernard, Governor of Massachusetts Bay Colony, writing on October 22nd, 1765, to Richard Jackson, London agent for Pennsylvania, later Solicitor to the Board of Trade, a recognised expert on American affairs. He believed that Great Britain and America were got 'so widely different in their notions of their relation to one another', that if this fundamental question was not soon determined, their connection must be destroyed. Bernard expanded this to his friend, Lord Barrington, Secretary-at-War, on November 23rd, 1765:

All the political evils in America arise from the want of ascertaining the relation between Great Britain and the American Colonies. Hence it is that ideas of that relation are formed in Britain and America, so very repugnant and contradictory to each other. In Britain the American governments are considered as corporations empowered to make by-laws, existing only during the pleasure of Parliament, who hath never yet done anything to confirm their establishment, and hath at any time a power to dissolve them. In America they claim . . . to be perfect states, no otherwise dependent upon Great Britain than by having the same King; which having compleat legislatures within themselves, are no ways subject to that of Great Britain; which in such instances as it has heretofore exercised a legislative power over them has usurped it. In a difference so very wide who shall determine?[2]

---

[1] *Windsor Castle MSS.*, George III, Private I, 1755–82, F. 15, 672.
[2] E. C. Channing and A. C. Coolidge (ed.): *The Barrington-Bernard Correspondence*, Harvard, 1912, pp. 96–8.

As Bernard saw it, the 'patchwork government' of America could last no longer. For the first time, the British were faced with the abiding problem of Imperial relationship. The determination of a country reaching maturity to have all its own affairs under its own control, the first real expression of colonial nationalism, was met by an unyielding refusal to grant that equality which would have been contrary to the views held by almost all politically conscious classes in Great Britain on the relative position of mother-country and dependent colonies. If, as the British believed, sovereignty was indivisible, how could there possibly be more than one sovereign Parliament under the Crown, which could be only the Parliament at Westminster? That was how Ambrose Serle, secretary to Admiral Lord Howe, and to the Peace Commission, saw it in September 1776: 'considering G. Britain and America as one Empire, it is necessary for the common welfare that they shd. be governed by the same supreme power, and that America should even be obliged, if necessary, to submit to it, as much as any other part of the State; that we have a union of polity among ourselves, and that the young scion may not draw off the sap from or exhaust the old tree'.[1] The deepest American grievances were as much emotional as constitutional. Captain Evelyn, a British regular officer serving in Boston, sensed the origins of the American Revolution when he wrote to his father in February 1775 that the true cause of it was to be found 'in the nature of mankind': 'I think that it proceeds from a new nation, feeling itself wealthy, populous, and strong; and that they being impatient of restraint, are struggling to throw off that dependency which is so irksome to them'.[2]

Evelyn disputed the argument championed by General Gage, that the unrest was due to a settled plan and system, formed and prosecuted for some years past by a few ambitious and enterprising spirits: he thought this only a consequence of the other development, 'such a time being most apt for men of abilities, but

[1] E. H. Tatum, Jr. (ed.): *The American Journal of Ambrose Serle, 1776–1778*, San Marino, 1940, pp. 84–5.
[2] G. D. Soull (ed.): *Memoir and Letters of William Glanville Evelyn, 4th Foot, from North America, 1774–1776*, Oxford, 1879, pp. 46–7.

desperate fortunes, to set themselves forward to practise upon the passions of the people, foment a spirit of opposition to all law and government, and to urge them on to sedition, treason, and rebellion, in hopes of profiting by the general distraction'. Gage, on the other hand, was convinced that the movement for independence was a deep-hatched plot, laid in Massachusetts Bay to begin with, 'and adjusted with some of the same stamp in others for a total independence'.[1] Whatever the diagnosis, the result was the same—a stroke levelled at the British nation, on whose ruins the colonists, in the General's words, 'hope to build their so much vaunted American Empire, and to rise like a Phoenix out of the ashes of the mother country'.[2]

The first paragraph of the Declaration of Independence stressed the colonial desire for a 'separate and equal station'. The Americans were convinced, whether correctly or not is immaterial, that it was now more for their good to be independent of Great Britain; the British, also affected by human motives of selfishness and jealousy, were equally convinced that such a step meant the destruction of the British Empire, a commercial as much as a political concern. Jealousy of the rising wealth and prosperity of the American colonies, whose population relative to that of Great Britain was the equivalent of the whole white population of the Dominions today, was frequently noted by Benjamin Franklin during his long residence in this country as a colonial agent. Here was a question of power and prestige: whether Great Britain should continue the head of the greatest Empire on earth, or return to her original station as one of the lesser European powers.

Consider the assessment made by George III in 1779 when he replied to the suggestion put forward by Lord North that the advantages to be gained by success in war against the colonies could never repay the expense. This was 'only weighing such events in the scale of a tradesman behind his counter': the present contest was the most serious in which any country was ever

[1] See e.g. Carter, op. cit., I, p. 412, Gage to Dartmouth, August 20th, 1775, and II, p. 450, to Barrington, March 10th, 1768.
[2] Ibid., I, p. 412.

engaged. (He told Pitt in 1788 that the American War had been the most justifiable war any country ever waged.) He asked North to consider the immense train of self-evident consequences the contest with America contained. Should America succeed, 'the West Indies must follow them, not independence, but must for its own interest be dependent on North America; Ireland would soon follow the same plan and be a separate state, then this island would be reduced to itself, and soon would be a poor island indeed, for reduced in her trade merchants would retire with their wealth to climates more to their advantage, and shoals of manufacturers would leave this country for the New Empire'. In this situation, there was only one sensible line of conduct to follow: being ready to make peace when it was to be obtained without submitting to terms that in their consequence must annihilate the Empire, and meanwhile 'with firmness to make every effort to deserve success'.[1] The King reiterated this to North on March 7th, 1780. If this country should be as far lost to all ideas of self-importance as to be willing to grant independence to America, he would despair of it 'being ever preserved from a state of inferiority and consequently falling into a very low class among the European states'.[2]

There was also jealousy of a 'Western Empire', less and less the product of influence exported by the mother-country, and more and more that of influences growing out of the amalgamation of the various streams of emigration to North America, and of the vast unlimited frontier. In a situation so charged with human motives, the British, instead of insisting on their undoubted legal rights, would have done well to follow the advice of Horace Walpole that it was the kindest way of ruling men to govern them as they will be governed, not as they ought to be governed. This advice was taken up by Alexander Hamilton in his pamphlet, *The Farmer Refuted*, of January 1775: 'the best way to secure a permanent and happy union between Great Britain and

[1] Fortescue, *op. cit.*, IV, No. 2649. See also the King's Letters to John Robinson, October 31st, 1779, Add MSS. 37834, f. 174, and February 16th, 1780, Add. MSS. 37835, f. 99.

[2] Fortescue, *op. cit.*, V, No. 2963. Jefferson had predicted this to John Randolph in 1775.

the colonies is to permit the latter to be as free as they desire. To abridge their liberties, or to exercise any power over them which they are unwilling to submit to, would be a perpetual source of discontent and animosity. A continual jealousy would exist on both sides'.[1] Dominion, as Franklin once pointed out, was founded in opinion: if the British wished to preserve their authority, they must preserve the opinion the colonial peoples used to have of them and their justice. This point was made at greater length in 1765 in some notes by Richard Jackson, for a speech on taxes. He argued that no one could doubt the constitutional authority of Parliament to impose taxes of every sort on every part of the British colonies, because 'an universal legislature is a necessary part of every intire state', and Parliament was that universal legislature of those dominions. But though the Constitution gave that power to Parliament, it should be exercised with moderation, even abstinence, and Parliament, for its own sake, should not impose internal taxes on America, 'that the people of the colonys may from thence derive a confidence in the Legislature that is essential to the well being of Government'.[2]

Here another element entered. If the colonies were Great Britain's estates, who were these colonial tenants and labourers to challenge British authority to do what she liked with her own? This conception was rightly opposed by the first Continental Congress in September 1774: they pleaded their constitutional right as arising from their ownership of the land, a plea which however justified was unacceptable to the British at this time.[3] The British conviction of social superiority, visible also in those colonists who remained loyal, was a fatal stumbling-block to any attempt at mediation or negotiation. Samuel Seabury, 'The Westchester Farmer', gave away a great deal, and reflected the two contrasted societies, when he wrote in 1774 'if I must be enslaved, let it be by a KING at least, and not by a parcel of upstart, lawless committee-men'. As David Hartley put it to Franklin on July 22nd,

[1] Tyler, *op. cit.*, I, pp. 389–90.

[2] Carl van Doren (ed.): *Letters and Papers of Benjamin Franklin and Richard Jackson, 1753-1785*, Philadelphia, 1941, pp. 194–6.

[3] On this fundamental point, see Sir Lewis B. Namier: *England in the Age of the American Revolution*, London, 1930.

1775, 'the supercilious usurpation of authoritative parental rights over those whom God has made our equals, cannot fail to pervert reason at this outset'.[1] An observer in 1778 held that the 'abominable pride' of the British Peace Commissioners would make them demand greater terms than the Americans could allow: 'They never could bear to think us upon any equality with them, they know they cant subdue us. They cant love us, it is not in their nature.'[2]

At a time when the colonists were seeking the removal of restraints, a return to the loose system of administration which had prevailed before the Seven Years' War, and the opening of the land to the West, the British, impelled by their experience in that war, and freed from European distractions for the first time in the eighteenth century, set out to reform patent abuses, and really to administer their colonial system in all its aspects—by the use of the Navy against illegal trade, the extension of Admiralty courts to deal with offences against the Navigation Laws, the sending out of Customs officers to their posts, and the obtaining of a revenue from the colonies. It was a policy imperfectly conceived, and foolishly applied, which served further to emphasise the inferior status of the American colonies. Between 1763 and 1775, there followed a spate of legislation and regulation, too much history in too short a time, which persuaded almost every particular interest in the colonies to share in a general movement of irritation against Great Britain. British policy was concerned first with the form of the system of colonial defence, and the question of who should pay for it, which brought up the problem of the relative powers of Parliament and the local assemblies. Next came the stopping of illegal trade, the only means by which the colonists could meet their financial commitments to Great Britain. This goes part of the way to explain why the opposition to the claims and the policy of Great Britain originated with the better sort, and was truly aristocratical in its commencement, as Alexander Graydon pointed out long ago.[3]

---

[1] Guttridge, *op. cit.*, p. 247.
[2] *American Historical Review*, Vol. XXIX, p. 182.
[3] Alexander Graydon: *Memoirs of a Life chiefly passed in Pennsylvania,* Edinburgh, 1822, pp. 131–2.

The colonial 'aristocracy' and the merchants attained to wealth, but were, or felt themselves to be, shut out from the highest social distinction, and from positions of evident and open political power. Those who fancied they paid the piper even then liked to call the tune. A feeling that prevailing conditions limited and hindered economic activity, that their immediate interests were threatened by the new Imperial policy, is the reason why prosperous colonial merchants led an agitation against the legislation of 1764 and 1765, and helped to stir up discontent among the less well-to-do which these same merchants later found embarrassing. The working of economic motives to revolt among possessing classes normally inclined to support existing institutions is most clear among the aristocrats of tide-water Virginia.[1] Largely dependent upon a single crop, accustomed to a high standard of living, increasingly indebted to London bankers and merchant houses, they hoped to re-establish their position in the western lands, but were barred by the Proclamation of October 1763, a barrier confirmed by the Quebec Act in 1774.[2]

Whatever the results of the mercantile system may actually have been, the colonists believed the laws of trade to be heavily weighted in favour of the mother-country. Indeed, there are those who are prepared to argue that the real cause of the American Revolution lay in this sphere: 'The American Revolution was as much a revolt against the limitations and penalties that hindered free enterprise under colonial regulations with England as it was a struggle for political independence'.[3] What is certain is that economically, as well as politically, the colonies had outgrown the Old Colonial System: the attempt now made to fit them back into it by more effective control was too late, and ignored the multifarious development of the colonies. Great Britain failed to understand the situation, and adjust herself to it. Here was the main failure of British statesmanship, greatly assisted by the stupidity of the measures suggested or adopted after

---

[1] See above p. 2, and D. G. Mays: *Edmund Pendleton*, London, 1953, 2 vols.
[2] See Crane Brinton: *The Anatomy of Revolution*, London, 1953, pp. 34–5, 69.
[3] L. M. Hacker: *The Shaping of the American Tradition*, New York, 1947, Ch. XVII.

1763—the proposal to extend the episcopal system to the colonies, and the Stamp Act in particular. Were the colonies expected to accept, in an atmosphere still redolent of the seventeenth century, the very system many of their forefathers had emigrated to avoid? The taxation of legal documents and newspapers, hitting the most vocal sections of the colonial communities, those who daily talked and daily wrote, was a blunder of the first magnitude, bound to bring sharp and continuing criticism and opposition. Geography had worked hitherto against a united America: the jealous particularism of each colony had been a powerful obstacle to any common action, or any move towards independence before 1763. It was the absence of a common responsible authority in America which led Grenville to call in the authority of the Imperial Parliament.

Seen in this light, the outbreak of the American Revolution resulted from the folly of successive British administrations in persuading the colonies that their real interest lay in mutual co-operation. Even so, that co-operation was never complete—that explains much of the colonial showing in a war in which victory was the result of French financial and naval aid. In contrast to the majority of the Americans, who knew what they wanted—whether to be independent or to remain loyal or, most numerous of all, to acquiesce in whatever happened—English ministers between 1763 and 1774 fumbled and failed to adhere to any certain line of policy. Indeed, writing to Shelburne on August 12th, 1782, George III was of the opinion that from the beginning of the American troubles to the resignation of Fox in early July, this country 'has not taken any but precipitate steps whilst caution and system have been those of Dr. Franklin which is explanation enough of the causes of the present difference of situation'.[1] British confusion is described in a revealing comment made by Barrington to Bernard in 1767: 'there is the most urgent reason to do what is right, and immediately; but what is that right, and who is to do it?'[2] The actual steps taken were a series of advances and retreats, cajolings and menaces. This was best

[1] Fortescue, *op. cit.,* VI, No. 3878.
[2] Channing and Coolidge, *op. cit.,* p. 128.

summed up by Wedderburn, the Solicitor-General, in some un-published notes drawn up for a speech on American affairs in Parliament in 1775. Wedderburn thought that the cause of the American Revolution lay deeper than the Stamp Act or its repeal: it must have happened from the confidence assumed when fear of a foreign enemy vanished, and from a natural impatience which the inefficient colonial governments promoted, together with the several acts of the past ten years. 'The only crime we have been guilty of is the inconsistency of our policy ... That has encouraged the mutinous subjects and dismayed the well affected in America ... We have deceived the friends and the enemies of government. We have taught them the dangerous lesson that their turbulence had an influence upon our councils. Their resistance springs from the hope of our yielding not from any consciousness of our own strength.'[1] The fumblings and vacillations in British policy since 1763 hardly square with a supposed design to establish an absolute tyranny.

Confusion produced general weakness, as it always will, which was continually condemned by General Gage, another individual whose reputation has suffered unduly at the hands of historians. Gage told Barrington, on December 16th, 1769, that 'if you do not enforce your authority, you must give it up; by assuming an authority which you tamely see rejected and dispised, without supporting it, you only bring yourself into contempt'.[2] On September 8th, 1770, he accurately described the situation. 'I will not pretend to determine whether it was proper for you to yield or not' (a typical regular officer's comment) 'but you have done it with an ill grace, you have yielded by bitts and in such manner, as it appeared that everything was constrained, and extorted from you; such a conduct could not fail to encourage people here to commit every extravagance to gain their ends and one demand has raised upon another.'[3]

Even so, there were many in the colonies who wished to remain in the British Empire, given terms of equality, in order to inherit from the mother-country, who, in the natural order of things

---

[1] *Wedderburn Papers*, Ann Arbor, Michigan, Vol. II, i.
[2] Carter, *op. cit.*, II, p. 535.   [3] *Ibid.*, p. 557.

must surely decline and pass away some day, and also for purposes of trade. Franklin believed in 1773 that the colonials should carefully avoid all tumults and every violent measure, and content themselves with verbally keeping up their claims, and holding forth their rights whenever occasion required, 'secure that, from the growing importance of America, those claims will ere long be attended to and acknowledged'.[1] Thomas Jefferson wrote on August 25th, 1775, to John Randolph then in England that he hoped the returning wisdom of Great Britain would, before long, put an end to the unnatural content which had begun. He wished for a restoration of just rights, and then for reunion, since he would rather be 'in dependence on Great Britain, properly limited, than on any other nation on earth, or than on no nation'.[2]

The Declaration of Rights in 1774 proclaimed that from the necessity of the case, and in regard to the mutual interest of both countries, the colonies consented to the operation of such acts of the British Parliament as were *bona fide* confined to the regulation of their external commerce, for the purpose of securing the commercial advantages of the whole Empire both to the mother-country and its respective members. Franklin, in his final efforts to prevent civil war, offered as late as 1775 to have all of the fundamental trade and navigation laws separately re-enacted by each colonial assembly, provided the claim to the right of taxation was abandoned. This alone surely weakens the arguments of those who ascribe the outbreak of the American Revolution to economic reasons.

If there were any inexorable economic forces which were inevitably drawing the colonies towards revolution, they are difficult to detect now, and the colonists then were not aware of them. It was from these people that support came in 1775 for redress of grievances rather than for violent revolutionary action; they were prepared to wait to enter into their heritage. They failed to realise until too late that importunity would wring no further concessions, that Great Britain now meant to stand fast.

[1] C. van Doren (ed.): *Benjamin Franklin's Autobographical Writings*, London, 1946, p. 295.
[2] Dumas Malone: *Jefferson the Virginian*, London, 1948, p. 210.

The next question which arises is whether, given the conditions and concepts which existed in the third quarter of the eighteenth century, even first-rate statesmanship could have avoided the secession of the American colonies from the British Empire? Samuel Adams believed in 1770 that he was advocating a cause which must in any case soon have arisen; Franklin, commenting in 1789 on the plan of union submitted to the Albany Conference of 1754, would only go so far as to suggest that had it, or something like it, been adopted, the subsequent separation of the colonies from Great Britain might not so soon have happened.

On the British side, Chatham, one of the most far-seeing statesmen of the age, maintained until his death the undoubted supremacy of the British Parliament, and the impossibility of allowing American independence—this was the theme of his final speech in the Upper House—while Burke and Fox had no practical solution, though they produced plenty of high-sounding phrases. The Rockingham group stumbled on the repeal of the Stamp Act in 1766, forced to it by pressure of merchant interest rather than from conviction: thereafter their colours were nailed to the mast, and could not be hauled down. Nothing better reveals the forced nature of eighteenth-century divisions between Administrations as such and Oppositions as such than the Rockingham attitude towards the American colonies. As Lord Brougham later suggested, the course pursued by one group dictated that taken by the other: things to differ upon, as well as things to agree upon, must needs be found. The Rockinghams were thrown upon the 'liberal' side of the question, without which they could neither keep together nor continue to resist the ministry. 'Is any man so blind as seriously to believe,' Lord Brougham asked, 'that, had Mr Burke and Mr Fox been the ministers of George III, they would have resigned rather than try to put down the Americans.'[1] Power, not principle, was their aim, as it was the basic aim of every politician at this time—self was still in any faction the leading principle of action.

What minister would ever volunteer his advice to dismember

---

[1] Lord Brougham: *Historical Sketches of Statesmen who flourished in the time of George III,* 3 vols., London, 1839, Vol. I, pp. 303–4.

the Empire? The American War had been pursued for years before the word 'Separation' crossed the lips of any man in either House of Parliament; all the attacks upon the government were centred upon mismanagement of the war, not upon having started it. The official British solution to the problem, accepted by a large majority, was clear, and unacceptable to the colonists: the only real solution was held by a small minority of English radicals and dissenters, who, knowing no hierarchy in either religion or politics, could think of the colonists as congregations of brethren beyond the seas. There were occasional glimpses of the future. Franklin quite rightly objected to the claim of subjects in one part of the King's dominions to be sovereigns over their fellow subjects in another part of his dominions, and put forward a modern conception of Commonwealth, writing to his son, 'a thorough government man', on October 6th, 1773. He believed, 'from a long and thorough consideration of the subject', that the British Empire was not a single state, but comprehended many. It had the same King but not the same legislature: 'the Parliament has no right to make any law whatever, binding on the colonies . . . the King, and not the King, Lords and Commons collectively, is their sovereign . . . the King, with their respective Parliaments, is their only legislator'.[1]

As Sir Lewis Namier insists, so long as the King was a real factor in administration, before he was outside the British Parliament, and apart from it, the modern conception of the Crown as a royal symbol of paternal authority, divested of all executive power, was impossible. Neither the constitutional theory nor practice of Great Britain allowed of the application of Franklin's view, nor of similar schemes, at this time. The Americans almost equally failed to solve this problem of Imperial relationship apart from these few exceptions. The colonial maxims of 'natural rights' and 'no taxation without representation' were vague slogans, difficult of real definition. Would an offer of representation have provided any remedy for the real colonial grievance of inferiority? What sufficient representation could they have been given, and of what value would it have been

---

[1] C. van Doren (ed.): *op. cit.,* p. 295. See also pp. 307-9, 313, and 316.

in the British House of Commons? The House of Representatives of Massachusetts Bay, in its circular letter of 1768, framed in opposition to the Townshend Duties, repeated the resolution of the Stamp Act Congress, and made it clear that the people in that colony preferred taxation by Parliament without representation to any such taxation with representation, and in their own constitution later, only two States applied that 'sacred' principle.

The colonies were accustomed to granting taxes in their own assemblies, and wished to continue to so do, rather than have taxes or internal legislation imposed upon them from outside, a further mark of inequality which representation at Westminster would in no way have removed. In any case, distance alone would have raised almost insuperable barriers to efficient colonial representation at Westminster: indeed, Alexander Graydon thought that nature, by placing the Atlantic Ocean between Great Britain and the colonies, had thereby interposed an insurmountable bar to a much longer colonial connection on constitutional principles.[1]

'No taxation without representation' is not in itself an adequate explanation of the beginnings of the American Revolution, though it may have been a slogan capable of exciting people to action at this time. Its main effect was to lend additional emphasis to the real grievance, and to enlist sympathy in Great Britain, where sections of the community might respond to it—there was a close connection between the radicals in this country and the colonists. But it should not be taken for, nor allowed to obscure, the fundamental cause of the civil war in the British Empire in 1775; the demand for self-government and home rule, expressed in metaphorical terms by Graydon: 'when the nurturing season is past, the young of all kinds are left to act for themselves. Even man, by a law of his own pursuing, that of nature, has appointed a time for the enfranchisement of youth; and America had perhaps completed her years of minority'.[2] From 1763 to 1775, the colonists modified and altered their theories to suit both the circumstances and their needs—they made distinctions between internal and external taxation, and then denied all British right of taxation,

[1] Graydon, *op. cit.*, pp. 113-4.   [2] Graydon, *op. cit.*, p. 114.

though precedents abounded, and were accepted, as on every post day. The underlying purpose which conditioned their perpetual changing of ground was the determination to take control of their own affairs.

One further point requires consideration. The American Revolution was the result of two general movements in the colonies, the one concerned with Home Rule, the other with the question of who should rule at home. There were class divisions that even common opposition to British policy could not efface, differing in each colony, but present in all. In a number of colonies, the internal friction between different economic groups and social classes was quite as important as the friction between the colonies and Great Britain. These conflicting groups and classes —with careers closed to them, or advancement and progress difficult, or development blocked—made much of the external quarrel because they could the more effectively diminish thereby the power and prestige of the local ruling 'aristocracies', which was as much their aim as diminishing the power of the British government. It is this which explains the bitterness and ferocity towards the Loyalists, the paying off of old social, economic, and political scores characteristic of any civil war. Many of those wanting Home Rule cared little for the rights of the common man, for the democratisation of colonial politics and society: radical as regards American rights against Great Britain, they were conservative as regards internal American rights, with no wish to usher in either 'democracy' or social upheaval. They did not contest the idea of upper-class leadership; they merely wanted to replace a British with an American upper-class. The common people—the country artisans, small farmers, frontiersmen, mechanics—if properly reined could certainly be used as allies in the task of freeing the colonies from British rule, but the gentry were to reap the benefits. this was to be a safe and sane revolution of gentlemen, by gentlemen, for gentlemen, a conscious repetition of the Glorious Revolution of 1688.

As usual, things got out of hand. As John Adams later commented, 'The poor people themselves, who, by secret manoeuvres, are excited to insurrection, are seldom aware of the purposes for which they are set in motion or of consequences which may happen . . . and when once heated and in full career, they can neither manage themselves nor be managed by others'.[1] As the struggle went on, class hostility in the colonies increased. There was the impression that no taxation without representation should apply in the colonies as well as towards Great Britain (a widening of political rights); a growing feeling against profiteers and monopolists (a widening of economic rights); and an almost general spread of what Graydon best described as 'licentious levelling principles'—again a seventeenth-century expression—particularly powerful in Pennsylvania (a widening of social rights). In a quiet way for revolutions, that in America effected a very sensible spreading into smaller units of the ownership of property.[2]

Pennsylvania, by its constitution of 1776, was gravely suspect in all the other colonies as a standing example of what occurred when a revolutionary movement got out of the control of gentlemen. Here, in the only really radical constituted colony, the western farmers and Philadelphia artisans had united to defeat the eastern ruling class, and to reform the situation which had existed before 1775, when the capital and three eastern counties sent twice as many delegates to the Assembly as did the eight interior and western counties, and where the employed workers, the 'mechanics' of Philadelphia, were excluded from the poll by high property qualifications. Elsewhere, warned by this example, the conservatives carried the day against the widening of popular rights—as late as 1790 only one in every ten of the male residents of New York City owned sufficient property to vote for the Governor. As Benjamin Rush said in 1783, the American War was over, but that was far from being the case with the American Revolution: the conflict of tidewater with frontier, property holders with tenants and wage earners, landowners with landless, privileged with non-privileged groups, still had to be decided.

In both movements, external and internal, the Revolution was

---

[1] J. H. Stark: *The Loyalists of Massachusetts,* Boston, 1910, p. 48.
[2] See J. F. Jameson: *The American Revolution considered as a Social Movement,* Princeton, 1926.

the work of an active minority which persuaded a hesitant majority to a cause for which that majority had very little real enthusiasm. Professor Brinton has recently estimated that leaving out the avowed loyalists, and the very numerous indifferent or neutral, the group which actively engineered, supported, and fought the American Revolution was probably not more than ten per cent. of the population. The great majority were 'cowed conservatives or moderates, men and women not anxious for martyrdom, quite incapable of the mental and moral as well as physical strain of being a devoted extremist in the crisis of the revolution'.[1] It required careful organisation and management, the playing of the right grievance at the right time to keep the differing sections together, and to make particular interests and complaints general. This is how Graydon described the scene in 1776, wishing to correct the error of those who seem to conceive that year to have been a season of almost universal patriotic enthusiasm. 'This was far from prevalent . . . Among the lower ranks of the people, at least in Pennsylvania . . . the true merits of the contest were little understood or regarded . . . and as the oppression to be apprehended had not been felt, no grounds existed for general enthusiasm.' He thought the 'cause of liberty' fashionable, and great preparations were made to fight for it, 'but a zeal proportioned to the magnitude of the question, was only to be looked for in the minds of those sagacious politicians, who inferred effects from causes'.[2] From 1765, there had been a three-way struggle going on in the colonies, between the moderates (those merchants and prosperous landowners who began the movement by their agitation against the Stamp Act); the radicals (that by no means united group which finally put through the Declaration of Independence); and the conservatives (later loyalists who never really complained about the Imperial government). In this struggle, the radicals exhibited an extraordinary technical skill in the practical organisation of revolution, beginning with local committees of correspondence, and working up to Continental Congress. In this organisation, particularly during the first Continental Congress, the radicals won the decisive

[1] Crane Brinton, *op. cit.*, pp. 166–8.   [2] Graydon, *op. cit.*, pp. 131–2.

victory; they were able to work on the masses, and effectively stir up grievances, and achieve their aim of independence. The strength of the movement lay with the plain people, and they, though often critical of Congress, never turned to the British side. The mass were ready to go along with whichever group was successful, and the loyalists were at a disadvantage with zealous, active, organised opponents, because loyalty was a normal condition, negative and inactive.

III

WHY INDEPENDENCE?

The First Continental Congress in 1774 confined itself to the consideration of such colonial rights as had been infringed by acts of the British Parliament since 1763. This emphasises a point too often overlooked in the study of the American Revolution: it was not the original colonial system, but its reformation, by the new measures passed since the close of the Seven Years' War, which caused dissatisfaction, a dissatisfaction moreover which would not have deepened as it did had the French still held Canada. These new measures were responsible for the more critical attitude held towards the existing Imperial system by leading colonists, producing protests and final repudiation; they also gave full scope to hitherto quiescent forces in the colonies, which once awakened, could not be checked. The result of the Seven Years' War, as well as colonial conduct throughout it, made Great Britain less tolerant of colonial autonomy; the measures taken to control this autonomy, fostered by circumstances, and demonstrating that the 'age of reason' had not yet made its influence felt in this country, contributed to a movement in favour of virtual, if not actual, independence which previously had been an isolated, spasmodic dream.

The removal of the direct French menace, by the conquest of Canada, was of cardinal importance, because it destroyed the equilibrium of an unstable structure, and allowed full scope to centrifugal forces within that structure. It made independence possible: the decision as to when it would come was made by the handling of the situation by successive British administrations between 1763 and 1775. The British, thinking of the Empire as a whole, as one unit, and largely ignorant of colonial conditions, never gave sufficient consideration to the existing and rapidly developing differences between the component parts. The rigidity of their attitude was largely responsible for the culmination of the movement for independence in 1776. As John Jay suggested in 1821, it was by necessity rather than by choice that it did come about then—through the sheer inability of the British to realise that the changed political and economic conditions of the colonies demanded a revision of the relations between them and this country.

George Grenville, who, as First Lord of the Treasury, originated much of the new policy between 1763 and 1765, typifies the British treatment of the colonial question in terms of law, precedent and custom, divorced from reality. Unimaginative, obstinate, stiff, arrogant, Grenville was a master of form, his ideas 'such as might originate in the mind of a clerk in a counting house', and he showed an unbounded attachment to them. (Franklin described him as 'besotted with his stamp scheme'.) Great Britain, left unchallenged as the first Imperial power in the world, now determined to put the colonies in their proper place in the accepted eighteenth-century system. Ministers took up colonial affairs where, through European distractions, they had been left, without taking into account the inevitable developments which had transformed the colonies: the political and economic dependence which had been salutary and necessary when they were struggling communities was now out of place.

The stupidity of British measures appears in every phase of policy after 1763: it is this, not tyranny, which is their chief characteristic. The colonial people then persuaded themselves, and historians have copied them since, that there was a direct design in Great Britain to establish an absolute tyranny. Pendleton believed that the sending of the tea to Boston in 1773 was 'a preconcerted scheme' between the ministry and the East India Company, 'for the very purpose of producing the consequences which happened'.[1] Quite clearly, there was no such intent in the confused minds of British ministers, who, neither for the first nor the last time in British history, simply did not know their own minds. The tea was sent purely to relieve a financial crisis in the

[1] D. J. Mays: *Edmund Pendleton, 1721–1803*, 2 vols., Cambridge, Mass., 1952, I, p. 272.

affairs of the Company, with no realisation of its implication in conditions of which ministers were unaware. It is difficult to reconcile the evidence adduced for this contention of tyranny as the consistent motive of British policy with the fumblings and vacillations in that policy in this period, or with the experimental tariff of customs duties and taxation, levied, varied, and counter-manded by Grenville, Rockingham, Townshend, Grafton, and North. As Burke commented in 1774, in a passage overlooked by many who have followed his general picture, the British had never taken a connected view of the colonial problem, but pro-ceeded 'by bits and scraps, some at one time and one pretence, and some at another'. The absence of collective Cabinet responsi-bility made a connected policy difficult of attainment, and in any case policies are more often the result of accident than of rational thought; men in high positions can be, and often are, fools. As Horace Walpole put it, 'How little men are, though riding at what is called the top of the world'. They stumble on measures and methods without real understanding of what they are about, and because they are successful, they follow these same principles on future occasions; foresight and design are added after the event, either by the participants themselves or by historians. The colonial system of Great Britain, the freest Empire in existence, came nowhere near 'political slavery' at any time before 1775.

The majority of thinking men in the colonies knew that they enjoyed more liberty than colonies of any other power: only thus can the long pursuit of redress of grievances rather than a revolu-tion of government be explained. Jefferson recognised as late as August 1775 that he would rather be in dependence on Great Britain, properly limited, than on any nation upon earth, or than to no nation.

Next, and quite naturally, the British, in keeping with the accepted beliefs of mercantilism, attempted by improvements of the administration of the laws of trade, to obtain the maxi-mum commercial benefit from both the old established colonies and the territories newly acquired. These two main motives are clearly discernible in the Proclamation of October 1763 by the Board of Trade. This was intended to prevent colonial penetration of Indian territory: it limited trading with Indians to certain posts, and stipulated that licences for such trade were to be issued by colonial governors. The British did not intend to allow a mad rush westward—there was to be orderly progression along a definite line, controlled at every stage through these selected posts, in conformity to the symmetry so beloved in eighteenth-century England. There was to be no colonial ownership and settlement in this newly acquired area; surveys, private treaty and purchase of land there was prohibited. As Mr. de Voto has shown, this committed the British to the support of trade as against the colonial desire for land. It undertook to confine the colonies east of the mountains, and ran clean counter to the first visible expression on any large scale of the 'manifest destiny' of the colonists to expand westwards. The Board of Trade confirmed in 1772 the reasons behind this proclamation. It was to ensure that settlement should extend no further than British control could reach; also, the extension of the fur trade depended entirely on the Indians being undisturbed in the possession of their hunting grounds, 'all colonizing does in its nature, and must in its consequences, operate to the prejudice of that branch of commerce'. The trade in beaver pelts, which since 1763 had been the principal objective of Imperial competition and conflict in the north American continent, had a further significance for Great Britain.[1] Furs were the currency in the vast market for manufactured goods among tribes which were now incapable of supporting life without these goods, first introduced among them by the French. This merely reflects the changing purpose of colonial possessions, away from suppliers of raw material previously obtained from foreign sources to wide and expanding outlets for the developing industries of Britain, and explains the attention given to the mainland colonies rather than to the West Indies after 1763, though even in the West Indies the Free Port Act of 1766 had the same motive.

This restriction on westward expansion was contrary to the expectation and desire of many important figures in the colonies,

[1] Bernard de Voto: *Westward the Course of Empire*, London, 1953, pp. 90–1, 222, 228, 235.

though it is doubtful if the great mass of the colonists were yet conscious of their manifest destiny to push the western boundaries of their colonies as far as they had first been drawn in the original charters, the full extent of the land, west to the ocean. Nevertheless, amongst the great patricians there were some of considerable influence who wanted to settle what they looked upon as their empire. 'As both a dream and a fact the American Empire was born before the United States',[1] and an empire whose settlement had only been prevented previously by the presence of Indians and French. There was a tremendous land hunger, particularly in the Southern colonies, as the grant of land (200,000 acres) to the Ohio Company in 1749 showed, and large amounts of capital had been sunk with an economic as well as a personal reason. Virginia had already granted 2 million acres in the Ohio valley to promoters and speculators; $2\frac{1}{2}$ million acres were being sought in the Mississippi valley. The character of tobacco culture, sucking away the fertility of soil in an age that had only an elementary knowledge of fertilisation, called constantly for new land—only shifting cultivation (which many colonial peoples have practised till very recently) could ward off the early appearance of soil erosion. Its exponents were not likely to receive with pleasure the dictum of authority that if they wished to develop land, they should first fully work that behind the existing frontiers, whilst the land beyond the mountains would be developed under Imperial control, and the Indians, a constant thorn in colonial flesh, would be given Imperial protection (as later American history showed, a very necessary protection).

Until the middle of the eighteenth century and the appointment of a Superintendent of Indian affairs, the British had left management of Indian relations to the separate colonies. One of the purposes of the Albany Congress (1754) had been to secure an agreed combined colonial Indian policy, which had failed. During the Seven Years' War, mainly because of the fear of losing their lands to the British (a fear propagated by the French, and later confirmed), the majority of Indian tribes had either sided with the French or remained as neutral as was humanly possible for them,

[1] *Ibid.*, p. 228.

and in 1763, during the Pontiac rising (in one sense, the Mau-Mau movement of the century, the abandonment of everything the white man had brought, the restoration of primitive crafts, skills and religion), had caused further sorrow and devastation in the colonies—a rising which was only put down by the assistance of British regular troops. These traditional, and very real, enemies of the colonists were now taken under British care. From 1763 until 1768, the Board of Trade attempted to work out an Indian policy under Imperial control, which entailed great expenditure in the provision of posts, troops, and officials. Largely because of this, Indian relations were given back to the colonies in 1768, but still only under the restricted terms of the Proclamation. The British system of licences and military supervision broke down under a welter of private competition and inter-colonial rivalries —an indication that the 'new' colonial system worked no more efficiently in practice than the old.

Although the fear of a possible French attempt to recover a footing in North America must have been present, it seems clear that the real purpose behind the British decision to maintain permanently in the colonies a larger force than hitherto was to assure compliance with this new land and Indian policy—to staff the posts, and control movement. The British felt themselves on top of the world in 1763. They felt adequate to this task of efficiently taking in hand the colonial system (a view strengthened by the feeling which came from actual contact of many during the war with colonial people); they would have questioned the possibility of an almost immediate recovery programme begun in the French navy, as they disputed its ability even when completed. Reality even then had to be learnt the hard way. Whatever the reason for organisation of defence in 1763, an army of 10,000 men, twenty battalions, fifteen in the mainland colonies and five in the West Indies, was decided upon. The failure of colonial agreement on defence in 1754-5, and in the Indian rising (when Amherst called upon the colonies for assistance which never came, and only mastered the movement by keeping British regular forces on a war footing, despite instructions to reduce), suggested that the colonies could not be trusted to provide adequately in this respect—indeed the constant tendency of colonists to shirk the service of local protection and to expect the Crown to provide security had been a permanent feature of all colonial defence in the eighteenth century.[1]

On the prevailing theory of Imperial defence, the obligation of Great Britain to give protection did not extend to widespread permanent garrisons in time of peace, and defence against Indian raids was their legitimate responsibility, reluctant as the colonies had been to recognise this previously. Moreover, it was natural that Great Britain should require them to contribute to the cost of their defence, and to bear their fair share of the expenses of the Seven Years' War (financed to an excessive degree from credit), which had raised the National Debt by £55 million to £132 million. With this increase, there was little likelihood of remission of taxation in Great Britain, and administration looked about for relief and assistance. As a logical development from the events of 1754–5, British administrations increasingly supported the view that the only means of obtaining from the colonies their just share of this expenditure was through taxation by Parliament.

Voluntary union had failed at the Albany Congress; defence must continue, and the colonies must help. This solution had been suggested repeatedly—the Governor of Virginia, Dinwiddie, had proposed in 1754 that Parliament should levy a poll tax on the colonies to defray the expenses of war, to bring the colonial people to a sense of duty, to awaken them from their indolence to take care of their lives and property, and to compel assistance from the backward. The emergency of war had intervened, and forced immediate support from home; now the situation was easier, and the problem could be re-examined. The snag was that by 1763, with the French menace removed, there was even less likelihood of willing colonial help, particularly in measures which would check their autonomy—the probability was that only Parliamentary legislation could bring them to help to pay for the limitations imposed on their own movement westward, and the effect of Parliamentary taxation could not be accurately gauged.

[1] Sir H. W. Richmond: *The Navy as an Instrument of Policy, 1558–1727*, Cambridge, 1953, pp. 339, 352.

From the decision to impose it came the Revenue Acts of 1764-5, and the fundamental problems of the power of Parliament over the colonies, its ability to compel the colonies to contribute funds towards the support of an army whose necessity they did not accept, and over whose actions they would have no control.

Moreover, it contributed to the colonial feeling against a standing army, another facet of the still prevailing seventeenth-century atmosphere, particularly in the New England colonies. However much the colonies might disagree about taking defence measures for themselves against Indian tribes until forced to do so by calamity and necessity, that the British should do it for them at their expense was yet another sharp reminder of their inferiority, which helped to bring them together, to mature the awakening American consciousness, the rising colonial nationalism of this period. (They, as is natural with all participants in a victorious military effort, believed theirs to have been a major share in the result of the Seven Years' War.)

That war not only showed up the faults and weaknesses of the old colonial system (particularly in the illegal trade with French West Indian colonies), but further underlined the vital fact (which continued to be ignored by the British) that many problems had grown beyond the capacity of the legislature of any single colony, but still remained primarily colonial problems—Indian relations and the raising of men and money for colonial campaigns among them. Faced with an evident disinclination in the colonies to assume responsibilities commensurate with the benefits received, the British decided not to extend autonomy, not to wait for intercolonial co-operation, but to attempt to improve the old system, and make it work efficiently. The desire for preservation rather than change was fundamental in Great Britain in the eighteenth century—the colonial system, like the constitution itself, was a masterpiece to be reverenced and jealously guarded, to be drastically altered only under exceptional circumstances.

The use of the Royal Navy to check contraband trade, highly successful during the war, was authorised in a measure introduced by Grenville, and begun at once. Grenville next tackled the inefficiency of the Customs service—the customs houses of

Massachusetts Bay were collecting only between £1,500–£2,000 a year in duties at a cost of between £7,000–£8,000. Too many holders of posts remained in this country, employing to carry out their work poorly paid deputies whose salaries were so low that they were an obvious target for 'gifts' and bribes to overlook the evasion of regulations. In any case, until 1767 these customs officials came directly under the Plantation Board of the English Commissioners of Customs, who were too distant to exercise effective supervision. The solution· devised by Grenville, to order absentee officials in Great Britain out to their posts, was not likely, even had it been successful, to staff the colonial customs service with contented and satisfactory officials; it was no more than a temporary step to further reform, the need for which became evident from the inquiry instituted by Grenville in 1763 into the trade figures and customs receipts in each colony, and which the setting up of a separate Board of Customs in 1767 was intended to satisfy.[1]

These measures, accompanied by an extension of Admiralty Courts, with their suggestion that the Trade Laws were now to be really enforced, had a disquieting effect in the colonies. Hitherto the shoe had never pinched because the lace had been left untied; when the attempt was made to tie it, the foot had grown, and a different shaped and sized shoe was necessary. Thomas Pownall, a late Governor of Massachusetts Bay, one of the best informed persons on colonial affairs in this country, saw to the root of this matter in his comment in 1768 that if the British were determined to carry the Navigation Acts and other laws respecting the plantation trade into strict and literal execution, 'without reviewing and considering what the very different circumstances of the colonies now are from what they were when they were first settled . . . we must determine to reduce our colonies again to . . . mere plantations'. This period is an effective illustration of the way history is based on social psychology, though it is rarely considered from that basis, since it is more easy to remember and list events than to recall emotions.

[1] D. M. Clark: 'The American Board of Customs, 1767–1783', *American Historical Review*, XLV.

Yet increasingly since the middle of the eighteenth century, the emotions of the people more than anything else finally explain events. As well as knowing what happened, it is human feeling which most assists the historian to explain why things occurred. As an observer of Virginia planters wrote in 1775, 'they think little about the political dispute: indeed that part of the people never think till they feel'.[1] By 1763, not only did the colonial assemblies wish to be equal with the House of Commons; it was even more important that they should also appear to be equal, and this, which might have been settled by a political agreement (which would have been most difficult to reach as British reaction to the Declaration of Independence shows),[2] also challenged the fundamental economic basis of the colonial empire. Any sign of inferiority was bound to provoke outcry, whatever benefits the particular policy brought to the colonies. This is clearly discernible in their attitude to the Laws of Trade. The colonial system had its disadvantages, but these were more than offset by obvious benefits visible in general colonial prosperity. Before 1763, the colonial peoples did not disapprove of the laws of trade as a whole; from that date what they considered the results of the laws to be was more important than those actual results.

Despite the mutual advantages of the working of the mercantile system, by 1763 there were many grievances felt by particular interests on both sides of the Atlantic, and these grievances were heightened by the abnormal political temperature. Mr. Mays has shown recently that the motive for the alliance of a naturally conservative class, the Virginia planters, with the political radicals of the North was the virtual bankruptcy of the plantation system in Virginia before the revolution began—a bankruptcy for which the British were not responsible, but which made more acute the agitation over British fiscal and political policy, and which worked along with Parliamentary measures to convince Virginia where her real future lay.[3] There were many who believed with Washington that 'our whole substance does already in a manner flow to Great Britain'—a view later taken up by groups in opposi-

---

[1] Mays, *op. cit.*, II, p. 354, n. 24.   [2] See below, p. 74.
[3] Mays, *op. cit.*, I, Ch. XI.

tion at home. David Hartley argued constantly that this country gained enough from her colonial trade to compensate for the expense of administration and defence; that the colonists had in any case assisted Great Britain in these expenses, and that the wars from which the major part of the expenses had come had been waged in British as well as in Colonial interests. There were others in the colonies who believed that they were paying more for European manufactured goods and getting less for their colonial produce than they would under unrestricted conditions, that industries were regulated by a body over which they had no control and whose power seemed unlimited, and that the system too greatly favoured the metropolis.

On the British side were complaints about protections and bounties, the cheaper cost in the colonies of foreign produce shipped from Great Britain to the colonies with the duty repaid by the British taxpayer, grievances poignantly expressed by Adam Smith: 'Parliament, in attempting to exercise its supposed right, whether well or ill grounded, of taxing the colonies has never hitherto demanded of them anything which even approached to a just proportion to what was paid by their fellow subjects at home. Great Britain has hitherto suffered her subjects and subordinate provinces to disburden themselves upon her of almost the whole expense'—a natural reaction to the load of taxation and National Debt in this country after 1763. The main effect on colonial opinion was the psychological effect of any restriction: the inability of the colonies to impose duties on their imports from Great Britain emphasised again the limitations on their freedom of action and their inferiority of status, particularly galling to a people who had acquired independence in spirit before they proclaimed the physical fact. That this was the real complaint, and that economic reasons came far behind political causes in the outbreak of revolution, is shown in a number of ways. Notwithstanding occasional pious aspirations to economic independence, in the economic boycotts during this period, colonials were only induced with difficulty to forgo the satisfaction of purchasing British goods, and following British styles. As a lady in New York wrote to a friend in the country in 1765, it was a sore trial 'to resign the charms of dress and let a horrid homespun (which can become none but a country wench) take place of the rich brocade and graceful sattin'.[1]

The comprehensive indictment of Great Britain embodied in the Declaration of Rights contained only a passing allusion to the commercial system—'from the necessity of the case, and in regard to the mutual interest of both countries, we cheerfully consent to the operation of such acts of the British Parliament as are *bona fide* restrained to the regulation of our external commerce, for the purpose of securing the commercial advantages of the whole Empire to the mother country and its respective members'. Franklin, in his various schemes to produce a durable union in 1774, included a proposition that the Acts of Navigation should be all re-enacted in all the colonies.[2] But from 1763, with the addition of many more goods to the list of 'enumerated articles', restrictions were enlarged, and inferiority stressed. As the situation worsened, complaints from specific interests increased in number and volume, drawing many particular sections into the general opposition to Great Britain.

The Sugar Duties Act 1764 had a dual purpose—to aid in the re-shaping of the mercantile system, and to raise revenue 'towards defraying the necessary expenses of defending, protecting, and securing the British colonies and plantations in America'. It was the first statute distinctly to tax the colonies rather than to regulate trade: it reduced by half the 1733 Molasses Act Duty on foreign sugar and molasses, absolutely forbade the import of foreign rum, imposed new duties on supplies hitherto free of duty—coffee and indigo from foreign colonies, and wine from Madeira—and added iron and lumber from the northern colonies to the list of enumerated articles under the Navigation Acts. The duties were to be paid in specie—gold and silver—into the Treasury in London, a further drain on the inadequate stock of hard cash in the colonies. The major snag in this measure for the colonists was that it was

---

[1] E. B. Greene: 'New York and the Old Empire', in A. C. Flick (ed.): *History of the State of New York,* New York, 10 vols., 1933, Vol. III, pp. 133-4.
[2] C. van Doren (ed.): *Benjamin Franklin's Autobiographical Writings,* London, 1946, pp. 355-7, 385.

clearly intended to enforce it, whereas under the evasion and slack administration of the Molasses Act, foreign supplies of sugar had come in free of duty. This forcing back of the colonies into an outmoded system (since the British West Indies could neither meet mainland demand nor take their surplus provisions), cutting them off from the source of their wherewithal to meet the debts due to British merchants, was bound to cause trouble. Many historians have regarded it as a greater blow to rising colonial consciousness than the Stamp Act which followed it; whilst John Adams later stated he did not know why the Americans should blush to confess that molasses was an essential ingredient in American independence. There were several arguments put forward in 1764 that the more trade the colonies were allowed with foreign islands, the more British manufactures they would be able to take, but free trade of this kind was anathema to British commercial and political opinion.

At the introduction of this act, Grenville pointed out that it would not provide sufficient revenue to meet a fair colonial share of military expenditure, and he announced his intention to supplement it by a colonial stamp tax, giving the colonies a year in which to suggest alternative, possibly more agreeable, means of raising the revenue, which he declared to be his only object. A Stamp Tax had been in existence in England since 1664, and its extension to the colonies had been suggested on several occasions in the eighteenth century.[1] Only one practical alternative scheme, Franklin's plan of a General Loan Office, was submitted; the other suggestions made were a return to the old requisition system (the inefficiency of which had been sufficiently displayed in the war), and numerous angry petitions, which, since it was the custom of the House of Commons not to receive petitions against revenue bills, were rejected without a hearing. Colonial opposition to central taxation was now clear—an opposition later continued by the refusal of the separate states after 1775 to entrust it to Congress. Nevertheless, few in Great Britain, not even the colonial agents, realised the outcry that the Stamp Act, which received Royal assent on March 22nd and became effective from

[1] L. H. Gipson: *Jared Ingersoll*, New Haven, 1920, pp. 116–18.

November 1st, 1765, would provoke in the colonies. It passed the House of Commons with little opposition in a languid debate, and is hardly mentioned in the diaries or correspondence of this period. Part of the colonial attitude doubtless arose, as in the case of New York, because £115,000 of the extraordinary expenditure of that colony in the war (in all £291,000) remained unpaid, which was regarded as a major contribution already made, but there were more basic reasons which appeared during the controversy which ensued.

All legal and commercial documents, bills of lading, ships and merchant papers, pamphlets, newspapers, almanacs, cards and dice in the colonies were affected by this Act. Penalties incurred under it, as with the Sugar Duties Act, could be sued for in the Admiralty or Vice-Admiralty courts, outside colonial influence and control. The estimated yield, between £60,000–£100,000, of which a large part would come from the West Indies, was to be maintained as a separate fund, to be disposed of by Parliament for the defence of the colonies. The tax was intended to fall upon those best able to pay, the trading and merchant interests, but politically it was a fatal blunder—it hit the most vocal and influential sections of the community, the people who daily wrote (in newspapers, pamphlets) and daily talked (lawyers) to the public; in this it resembled the proposal which had wisely not been taken up: to establish an episcopacy in the colonies.[1]

John Adams believed that in the years immediately preceding 1775, apprehension of an American episcopacy contributed as much as any other cause to urge the common people to close thinking on the constitutional authority of Parliament over the colonies, since only an act of Parliament could establish an American bishopric. In Virginia, where the Church of England was still established, the Lower House described the idea in 1771 as a pernicious project. The influence of sermons was only just beginning to suffer under the rivalry of the printing press, but the churches and meeting houses still remained the social centres round which much colonial life gathered: the house, which

[1] S. E. Baldwin: *The American Jurisdiction of the Bishop of London in colonial times*, Worcester, Mass., 1900.

according to John Turnbull in *M'Fingal* in 1776 served Heaven but one day in the week, was 'open the rest for all supplies, of news and politics and lies'. Again, in an age where there were no cinemas, cards and dice in the taverns were a major pastime—every time they were used, the emblem of the tax was flaunted. These two Revenue Acts were estimated to bring in at their maximum £145,000 yearly, between one-half and one-third of the necessary cost of the forces which would never be required to serve except in North America or the West Indies. This yield meant an increase in taxes in the colonies, where taxes were low, of nearly two hundred per cent., and this at a time of the collapse of abnormal wartime prosperity: but the question to be asked is, whether this was to any degree incommensurate with colonial wealth? The money was to come from all the colonies, though the chief outlay and benefit was for the mainland colonies (an argument they refused to accept), and it still left Great Britain carrying the major part of the expenditure.

All these steps and measures since 1763 were intended to make the old colonial system, amended and reformed, really work. They all emphasised in concrete form that the colonies were not independent communities, but part of a larger political system, controlled by a remote power who now intended to assert its authority: an intention that ran counter to the autonomy which had been developed during the period of negligent administration forced upon Great Britain by distractions elsewhere. They clearly involved a diminution of colonial freedom of action, but it is ludicrous to contend that they introduced tyranny. It has more correctly been stated that the colonists made a stand not against tyranny inflicted (there had been none) but against tyranny anticipated—further measures threatening these already acquired autonomies, though even this mistakenly magnifies and distorts the intentions of British ministers. The Rhode Island lawyer who said (and was mobbed for his pains) that the colonial people brought the tax on themselves was nearer truth: these reforms and measures were undertaken because of a failure of colonial statesmanship, first to agree among themselves as to defence and Indian policy, and next to suggest alternatives to Imperial taxation—Grenville never denied the right of the colonial assemblies to tax themselves; he only called in the authority of the Imperial Parliament because of the absence of any responsible authority in the colonies prepared to take decisions, and because of the undying belief of the eighteenth century that government must be carried on. (There was grave fear of anarchy, the non-execution of laws.)

As Professor Brogan has suggested, colonial grievances were serious, but not maddening; some of the most important were prospective, not actual. The colonists felt that the kind of society that the vast, empty land was calling on them to build was certain to be impeded by the sluggish and inefficient bureaucracy of London, and by the elements of colonial society it favoured. Behind this feeling were a score of petty annoyances that, in the aggregate, added up to a decisive total—and in this lies the main accusation which can be brought against British handling of the situation between 1763 and 1775. Relatively small grievances left to rankle eventually produced remarkable results; consciousness of strength, as much as any present or future grievance, persuaded the colonists to rebel, to see if they could not do better for themselves.[1]

The Stamp Act led to the Stamp Act Congress in New York in October 1765, where twenty-seven delegates from nine colonies (Nova Scotia, New Hampshire, Georgia, North Carolina, and Virginia were unrepresented) met, and supported the Virginia resolution, first proposed by Patrick Henry, that the representative assembly of a colony alone had the right to impose taxes and other burdens on a colony. Here was the first intimation, followed by the circular letter in 1768 of the House of Representatives of Massachusetts Bay in opposition to the Townshend duties, that the colonies were really opposed to representation at Westminster: they wished to continue being taxed, if that was necessary, by their own representative assemblies.

These bodies not only claimed all the privileges of the House of Commons, but stretched them even beyond what they were imagined to be there—as Clarendon had noticed in the period of

[1] D. W. Brogan: *The Price of Revolution*, London, 1951, pp. 4, 122, 208.

the Commonwealth in England, the Puritan ancestors of many of the colonists had shown a tendency to become intensely aggressive in privilege, 'more imperious upon the apprehension of any discourtesies', than lawful or regular monarchs had formerly used to be.[1] At the heart of the contest between Britain and the colonies lay this issue of the control of finance: possibly the biggest result of the Stamp Act was that it crystallised the constitutional opposition to the British programme of Imperial reorganisation, and forced the colonists to formulate a theory of Empire that would accommodate itself to colonial conditions— it is significant that the various constitutional suggestions made to remedy the situation date from 1766. This congress, authorised by nothing in any colonial charter, nor by any instruction from London, sat eighteen days, 'a congress of committees', and produced an address to the King, a petition to both Houses of Parliament, and resolves setting out the rights of the colonies in their relations with Parliament, and their grievances.

There were those in the colonies who already saw that the measures most likely to cause the British to reconsider their approach would be economic. Washington believed that 'whatever contributes to lessen our importations must be hurtful to their manufacturers', and fancied that the merchants trading to the colonies would not be among the last to wish for a repeal of the Stamp Act, while Pendleton thought it essential to engage their interest for that purpose. It was the merchants who brought about that result early in 1766. As a British merchant wrote, the Stamp affair 'seemed to be the whole cause of the Parliament's meeting, by the King's speech. The trading part of the country and manufacturers seem all to be keen for a Repeal or a mitigation tho' at the same time condemn the behaviour of the Colonys'.[2]

Colonial business in Britain was coming to a standstill, and unemployment spreading; moreover merchants faced not only loss of markets, but non-payment of large amounts owing to them. Only the fear that repeal would show weakness, encourage disobedience, and set a fatal precedent, held back the earlier exercise of their influence. Burke claimed that the first Rockingham ad-

[1] Quoted Richmond, *op. cit.*, p. 98.   [2] Mays, *op. cit.*, I, pp. 167, 170, 173.

ministration adopted an entirely new attitude to commercial affairs, organised public meetings, consulted merchants, and acted on their advice. Had the merchants never influenced previous administrations? At this time, as the result showed, consultation was unfortunate, for these political innocents were no match for experienced mercantile interests. The elasticity which is the prime aspect of the Cabinet in the eighteenth century was stretched to the utmost by this ministry, the supposed pattern of constitutionalism—one, at Rockingham's house on December 31st, 1765, included a London merchant not then even a member of the House of Commons.

The repeal was accompanied by a measure which was far more popular in England, the Declaratory Act, copied almost word by word from the measure of 1719 setting forth the dependency of Ireland on this country, and annulling all resolves and proceedings of colonial assemblies tending to claim any authority in their respective districts independent of that of Great Britain. Parliament, the act declared, 'had, hath, and of right ought to have full power and authority to make laws and statutes of sufficient force and validity to bind the colonies and people of America subjects of the Crown of Great Britain in all cases whatsoever', which many colonists mistakenly believed was face-saving, a device for securing an honourable retreat from a position rendered untenable by their opposition.

Shelburne rightly contended that the Stamp Act should either be enforced or acknowledged as a mistake; whatever policy was decided upon should be followed through to the end. Shifting of ground and muddling from one expedient to the next could only bring British control into question. The Declaratory Act, as he stated to Chatham, kept alive an unfortunate jealousy and distrust of government throughout the colonies, ready to widen out to any provocation, such as given in the Townshend duties. The theoretical assertion of right might have been borne only if it had remained strictly theoretical, but in 1767 it again became a practical force and grievance. Frederick the Great perceived the British lack of policy when he said that it was a difficult thing to govern men at such a distance, but if Britain had intended conciliation, some of the measures had been too rough, whilst if subjection were the object, they had been too gentle. And Botetourt, Governor of Virginia, summed up the problem in 1769: he thought opinions of the independency of the legislature of the colonies had grown to such a height in them 'that it becomes Great Britain, if ever she intends it, immediately to assert her Supremacy in a manner which may be felt, and to lose no more time in Declarations which irritate but do not decide'.[1] Singleness of purpose in policy is a prerequisite of success at all times.

The Rockingham administration also modified the Sugar Duties Act, by repealing the duty on foreign molasses, and putting a duty of a penny per gallon on all molasses whether imported from British or foreign sources—thus showing their acceptance of revenue rather than trade regulation as the purpose of legislation—and introduced a Free Ports Act. This, hastily conceived and passed, was again the result of the influence of North American and West Indian interests working in co-operation.[2] Burke commended it, first, because the materials were provided and insured to British manufacturers, its least important effect, and next, because the interests of the northern and southern colonies, before that time jarring and dissonant, were understood, compared, adjusted, and perfectly reconciled. (As he himself later admitted, it is a general popular error to imagine that the loudest complainers for the public are the most anxious for its welfare.) Whately was nearer the truth when he described the problem as one which required the most mature deliberation, much previous enquiry, a watchful jealousy, and extensive provisions. In its main aspect, this Act was intended to obtain a wider market for the rapidly increasing manufacturing industries of Great Britain, caused, as an observer in 1775 expressed it, by 'the great improvements in machinery, by which the expense of labour is much diminished, and the perfection of the work increased; the cheapness of fuel, which is more universally diffused by means of internal navigation, and the more easy communication by land'. It legalised a

[1] Mays, op. cit., I, p. 255.
[2] Frances Armytage: The Free Port System in the British West Indies, 1766–1822, London, 1953.

trade with the Spanish settlements in South America which had long been practised, and connived at by Customs officials on both sides, though from its nature 'a thing not to be talked of aloud', as Savile described it in 1765, but which had been hampered by Grenville's officiousness between 1763–5.

The enforcement of the old colonial system prohibited the entry of foreign vessels into British ports, and made liable to seizure Spanish ships frequenting Jamaica, the centre of the trade. This act provided that small foreign vessels from neighbouring foreign colonies could be admitted into selected ports in the British West Indies, and allowed to import goods that did not compete with produce of the British colonies or of Great Britain, and export British manufactured goods. There were other motives besides those stressed by Burke—to continue the ancient trade with Spanish colonies, to meet the requirements of British colonists, to draw the North American colonies away from the French; but these were subordinate to the main purpose of larger markets.

The Free Port Act, a stage in the changing nature of the British Empire, described by Professor Harlow as the half-way house to the direct trade of the nineteenth century with a then independent South America, when Imperialism came to be at a discount, though empire itself, an empire of markets for British manufacturers, was at a premium. Increasingly the expansion of commerce replaced the extension of territory as the purpose of Empire. These measures, based on expediency and pressure rather than on conviction, placed the Rockingham group and their supporters on the colonial side in the future; their attitude was well described by Lord Brougham in a passage of deep significance for all students of eighteenth-century politics: 'observe how plainly the course pursued by one class dictates that to be taken by the other. There must be combinations, and there must be opposition; and therefore things to differ upon, as well as things to agree upon, must needs be found. Thus, the King is as hostile as bigotry . . . can make him to American liberty, and his ministers support him in the war to crush it. This throws the opposition upon the liberal side of the question, without which they can neither keep to-

gether nor continue to resist the ministry'.[1] The result of the
measures of the Rockingham administration not only meant that
the Imperial administrative system had been successfully defied in
its attempts really to work the colonial system, and its authority
undermined, brought into a contempt from which it never re-
covered, but also that the British were no further forward in their
search for revenue to meet the increasing costs of colonial expenditure, now about £400,000 annually. This was the purpose behind
the duties introduced in 1767 by Charles Townshend, Chancellor
of the Exchequer in the 'mosaic' administration headed, but in no
way controlled, by Chatham. This administration is an effective
demonstration of how, in office, the position rules the individual
—prominent members of it, Shelburne, Camden, Conway,
Grafton, had been champions of a more liberal attitude in 1765–6,
but their ideas and illusions succumbed under the actuality of
responsibility.

There had been some apprehension that colonial opposition
to direct taxation might widen to include indirect taxation
—to colonial customs duties imposed by Parliament, or to a
questioning of all laws of trade. Walpole feared in 1765 that
there might be a demand for the repeal of the whole of the
Navigation Acts, a potent historical basis in support of the
validity of Parliamentary authority over the colonies. This
demand not having been made, Townshend, with his unstable
facile cleverness, took the colonists at their word, and imposed
external taxes only, duties at colonial seaports on imported glass,
lead, paper, paint, and tea. As early as 1754, he had said he was
confident he could devise a plan for raising a colonial fund that
would be acceptable to the colonies; in January 1767, led away
in debate, he repeated this assertion, and committed the ministry
to raise a colonial revenue which would reduce taxation at home.
The very willing country gentlemen took Townshend at his
word, and the House of Commons reduced the English land tax
from four to three shillings in the pound, further increasing the
financial pressure on administration.

[1] Lord Brougham: *Historical Sketches of Statesmen who flourished in the time of
George III*, 3 vols., London, 1839, Vol. I, pp. 303–4.

The proceeds of these duties (effective from October 1767) were not merely to meet military expenses, but also to defray the expenses of civil government in the colonies, thus challenging the power of the purse held by the local assemblies: John Adams believed that if the salary of the Governor of Massachusetts Bay came to be paid by the Crown in this way, it would be 'the tragedy of American freedom'. Moreover there was to be further enforcement of the regulations. Writs of Assistance, established in England in 1674, extended to Royal colonies in 1697, were now authorised in every colony of whatever kind. These writs were general warrants, specifying no particular place, and no particular goods, directed to all, to allow and aid customs officers to break into vessels, warehouses, and dwellings in their search for smuggled goods. Their duration was for the life of the King and six months afterwards, a general authority to search everywhere, again outside the control of colonial assemblies. Next, revenue cases were to be tried in Admiralty Courts, which were now augmented, sitting without juries. A separate Board of Customs Commissioners with powers in the colonies similar to those exercised by the English board, was established in Boston. It set to work immediately. Income from duties rose to over £30,000 annually, penalties against smuggling yielded increased returns, and before the end of British authority in the colonies, over £257,000 was collected from these two sources. Finally, the Assembly of New York was prohibited from transacting any business until it complied with the Quartering Act of 1766, which extended to the colonies the provisions of the English Mutiny Act, and required them to provide British forces quartered there with barracks, fuel, bedding, candles, salt, vinegar, small beer, cider, or rum, and utensils for dressing victuals. These measures 'stole through the House' in London, but reawakened in the colonies the suspicion of British motives which had been prominent in 1765.

Their general result was a broadening of the colonial opposition, first suggested by John Dickinson of Philadelphia in his *Letters* of *a Pennsylvania Farmer* (1768), to the attitude that all taxation (external or internal) imposed by the British Parliament must be denounced as contrary to 'the rights of man' and the 'laws of nature'. On this vague foundation almost every kind of opposition could be based, and, as later events were to show, could be indeed very one-sided in its application. The Massachusetts Bay Assembly, which protested against the Townshend duties on these grounds, had no intention in 1774, at the time of the Quebec Act, of allowing freedom of worship to Catholics in Canada, nor of allowing freedom of opinion to Loyalists during the actual military struggle. The broadening of the colonial case went even further in that Washington in May 1769 was already considering resistance by arms if other means failed. These means were twofold. An attempt was made by the circular letter of the Massachusetts Bay Assembly to other colonial assemblies to unite the colonies against the duties, a move countered by instructions from London to all Governors to prevent their assemblies taking any action on receipt of the letter—that of Massachusetts Bay was dissolved for its refusal to rescind the letter, whilst that of Virginia suffered the same fate for actually receiving, and considering, it. Secondly, a non-importation agreement, started in Boston, spread to New York and Pennsylvania, but failed completely in the southern colonies: as New York merchants put it when the agreement was abandoned in 1770, other towns were more active in resolving what they ought to do than in doing what they had resolved. Even so, imports into New York, which had been worth £482,000 in 1767–8, dropped in the following year to £74,000; colonial economic retaliation clearly played its part in bringing about partial repeal in 1770. The main weakness of that weapon lay in the fact that its effectiveness depended upon those, the merchants, who stood to lose most by it.

One further important administrative change was made in 1768, the creation of an American Department of the British Government, under a third Secretary of State.[1] Lord Chesterfield stressed the need of such a department in 1766, when he said that if Great Britain did not establish a Secretary of State with full and

[1] M. M. Spector: *The American Department of the British Government, 1768–1782*, New York, 1940; and A. H. Basye: 'The Secretary of State for the Colonies', *American Historical Review*, Vol. XXVIII.

undisputed power over America, 'in a few years we may as well have no America'. The probability is that the appointment was made too late; in any case, the scope and powers of the new department were certainly never properly defined, and were a constant cause of jealous squabbling and interference from the older Secretaries. Thomas Pownall had suggested preference for another solution, that the President of the Board of Trade, the body in continuous contact with colonial business, should be given full responsibility, executive powers, and access to the King on colonial matters, but this idea was turned down for the same reason which rendered doubtful the success of the new Department: the giving of sole authority would not only arouse personal feelings but would involve a political and administrative re-shuffle in the major offices of administration. The institution of this department was a step in the right direction—like most of the others, late and hesitant—but even with sole responsibility and authority, the attitude in Great Britain was such that the eventual result would have been no different, for this required a totally changed conception of the status and purpose of colonial possessions.

Uneasy relations between Great Britain and the colonies continued, and came to a head in the Boston 'massacre' on the very day, March 5th, 1770, that Lord North asked Parliament to repeal the Townshend duties. At a customs post in Boston, with a guard of one officer and six men, threatened by a large crowd which refused to disperse, shots were fired by mistake, resulting in four deaths. The captain in charge and the soldiers were tried by a Boston civil court, defended by John Adams, and acquitted of the charge of murder. That 'outrages' had been committed by the troops in Boston and in other parts is no doubt true, but in the existing situation, these incidents were naturally exaggerated, and in the majority of cases, the probability is that the troops, acting under strong provocation, were the abused party. John Adams stated later that judgment of death against the soldiers concerned in the Boston incident would have been as foul a stain upon Massachusetts Bay as the execution of Quakers or witches anciently, and that, as the evidence was, the verdict of the jury was exactly right. A surgeon who attended one of the wounded deposed that he saw many things thrown at the sentry, and heard the people huzza every time they heard anything strike that sounded hard. He thought the soldiers a great deal abused, and never in his life saw them bear so much before they fired, which they did to defend themselves, and prevent themselves from hurt. A supporter of Rockingham, Lord Belasyse, accepted this. Writing to his father, Lord Fauconberg, May 12th, 1770, he believed the 'massacre' to be 'a long premeditated scheme of the people to drive the military from the town' (in which, incidentally, they succeeded), which, 'as the people first insulted the military near approaches rebellion and indeed it was mentioned by the Governor to them in that light, their answer to which, was, that they knew it was; but that they would sacrifice every thing that was dear to them before they would allow the troops to remain in the town'. The Boston 'massacre' in fact was the inevitable result of colonial resentment against troops who were a standing invitation for disorder.

The North administration, possibly influenced by economic pressure, once more tried conciliation. First, the Townshend duties, save that on tea, to keep up the right (and that only retained by one vote in the Cabinet), were repealed, Lord North stressing their two main defects from the British point of view. It was injurious to British commercial interests to impose taxes on British manufactured goods (he might have added, had he known he would be linked with this charge by later historians, that it was a curious form of tyranny); duties on articles manufactured here served as a most effective stimulus (especially in conjunction with non-importation agreements) to colonial production, and consequently to the development of colonial industries. Since the raw materials for almost all the products taxed existed in unlimited quantities in some, or all, of the continental colonies, the import tax on British manufactures of these articles could only operate as a protective tariff, an encouragement of colonial competition. Second, the American Department told colonial governors that the British Government had given up the idea of proposing any further taxes with the purpose of raising a revenue in the colonies. Third, no attempt was made to punish either Massachusetts Bay or South Carolina for their refusal to provision troops under the Quartering Act, in contrast with the treatment of the New York assembly in 1767. The resultant re-opening of trade, the breach visible between the colonial mer-chants and radical politicians in the colonies, led to better feelings —by July 1771 the British Government were considering a re-duction of the military establishment on the mainland to ten battalions. Was this the method of an administration intent upon establishing a military despotism over the colonies?

This better relationship was only superficial. What was really required in 1770 from the British Government was precisely what it could not make—a large constitutional gesture. If it intended to raise no further revenue by taxation, why keep the remaining duty on tea? The continued insistence on right, insisted upon by the majority of the politically conscious—an ever-present practical demonstration of the Declaratory Act—meant that the situation was left, as it had been before the Boston 'massacre', at the mercy of an incident which, once it occurred, might easily be beyond redemption. Distance alone could make it impossible for even first-rate statesmanship (which in the event was lacking) to grapple with the situation. It is a wise maxim of theatrical manage-ment that a play which has failed should be withdrawn before it is forced off the stage.

The incident came with the Boston 'tea-party' in December 1773. To meet a financial crisis in the affairs of the East India Company, the government allowed it to export its own tea in its own ships, for sale in the colonies through its own agents. Previously, the company had sold its tea in London to merchants who sold it in the colonies, but on this occasion it failed to choose as its agents those colonial merchants who had previously handled the trade. This not only produced the hostility to monopoly and special privilege which the colonists had inherited from their seventeenth-century ancestors (if a monopoly in tea were per-mitted, monopoly might spread to other commodities) but it brought the merchants back into co-operation with the radical politicians. Moreover, whereas previously East India tea had been liable to import duties both in England and the colonies, making it more expensive in the colonies than tea smuggled from Holland, it was now allowed a refund of the whole of the English import duty, which made it the cheapest tea available in the colonies. Cheapness would inevitably mean some sale, consequent payment of the remaining Townshend duty, and indirect acknowledgment of the right of the British Parliament to tax the colonies.

Tea ships had to return without unloading from New York and Philadelphia, but in Boston, violent action was taken by radical elements—some £15,000 worth of East India Company tea was thrown into the harbour. This attack on property, most sacred element of the eighteenth century, was fatal; there were many in the colonies who believed it required reparation, but distance, and the changed attitude of the British, eliminated its possibility.

The British now decided that as conciliation had failed, the time had come to assert, as well as declare, supremacy: there was to be no more of that 'fatal compliance' which had encouraged the Americans 'annually to increase in their pretensions'. There followed what the colonists described as 'the five punitive acts'— the Boston Port bill, which removed the Customs House and closed the port, one of the main sources of the livelihood of Massachusetts Bay; the modification of the charter of that colony, substituting a nominated for the elective council; the quartering of troops in Boston at local expense; the removal to England for trial of officials indicted by civil courts for murder in the suppression of riots; and the Quebec Act, which included among its provisions the grant of the land north of the Ohio river to Canada, making permanent there the banning of Westward expansion. The generous provisions of this last act, the first by which Parliament directly constituted a colony, were completely overlooked by the American colonists—the Address of the First Continental Congress conceived Canada to be so extended, modelled and governed that 'by being disunited from us, detached from our interests, by civil as well as religious prejudices, by their number swelling with Catholic emigrants from Europe, they might be fit instruments in the hands of power to reduce the ancient free Protestant colonies to the same state of slavery as themselves'. Seventeenth-century traditions (and exaggerations) die hard.

The first Continental Congress was a direct result of the British measures. The Virginia Committee of Correspondence, which was a committee of the Assembly in that colony, suggested to the other assemblies the calling together of an all-colonial congress, which met in Philadelphia in 1774, with delegates present from twelve colonies. Its most noticeable features was the growing cleavage between those who wanted a redress of grievances, and restoration of harmony with Great Britain, and those who wished to go further, and branch out on their own— a cleavage typified by the arguments of Joseph Galloway on the one side and Patrick Henry on the other, with his statement that government was dissolved, and the colonies left in a state of nature—a cleavage which continued down to the Declaration of Independence in 1776.

The contention of the first school was that they were forced by the British attitude into an independence they neither designed nor desired. If the King and the ministry restored rights that had been taken away, amity in their view could have been restored, and even if force were used, they believed only one campaign would be necessary to decide whether Great Britain would recognise colonial rights, or suppress the rising and punish the leaders. This attitude explains many of the cautious, tentative measures taken by the colonists—the proposal that New York, from its strategic position an obvious British objective, should prepare its defences was postponed before its final endorsement in May 1775, on the ground that conciliation would succeed; or the support for Artemus Ward as Commander-in-Chief, because he was familiar with the people and militia of the region (Massachusetts Bay) vitally concerned in that one campaign. Washington, on assuming command, believed he had merely to contain the enemy during the one campaign, and hoped to be back at Mount Vernon by the winter—and although by October 1775 he regarded all attempts at conciliation as futile, the limited terms of enlistment, and the volume of supplies commissioned, give practical expression of the belief in Congress of this view. Its declaration of July 6th, 1775, setting out the causes for taking up arms, insisted that it was not from ambitious designs of separating from Great Britain, and establishing independent states. Until 1776, independence, in the sense of separation from the Empire, was not really considered by a majority of the colonial leaders. In January 1776, John Page, writing to Colonel Woodford of the second Virginia regiment, advised against the burning of Norfolk, 'for it is possible matters may be accommodated in a short time, and, in that case, we shall have done ourselves a great injury to no purpose'[1]—a potent plea against any 'scorched earth' policy. The change came slowly, under pressure of circumstances, and also as a result of the publication of Thomas Paine's *Common Sense* in January 1776, which, as someone in South Carolina put it in March, 'hath made Independents of the majority of the country'. The supporters of the second school were prepared to wait, to allow events to advocate their cause for them, and in general were averse to the holding of a congress, which might temporise, and avoid the break which was their real aim, and which the momentum of events did much to secure.

The first Congress certainly began with the hope of defining those principles which would establish the rights and liberties of the colonies, while yet maintaining the Imperial link—the personnel of both this and the Second Congress were in the main middle-aged property owners and professional men, not likely enthusiastically to advocate rebellion,[2] while the delegates of four colonies had the purpose of harmony with Great Britain expressed in their instructions. Nevertheless, the growing radical strength was the marked feature of the first Congress—it was that which defeated the first of several plans advocated by Joseph Galloway of Pennsylvania for an American legislature, a Grand Council of members, elected by the colonial assemblies.[3] This body, acting as an inferior branch of the British

[1] Mays, *op. cit.,* Vol. II, p. 83.

[2] See Lynn Montross: *The Reluctant Rebels,* New York, 1950, pp. 248–50; and C. P. Nettels: *George Washington and American Independence,* Boston, 1951, Ch. VI.

[3] J. P. Boyd: *Anglo-American Union, Joseph Galloway's plans to preserve the British Empire, 1774–1788,* Philadelphia, 1941.

Parliament, was to deal with all matters of general colonial concern (a development of Franklin's earlier plan at Albany in 1754), while the colonies retained full authority over their own internal matters: it was also to discuss and approve proposed acts on colonial matters sent over from Great Britain, before they became law. On its executive side there was to be a Resident-General, possessing a veto on the acts of the Grand Council, nominated and appointed by the King.

The Congress also produced a Declaration of Rights in October, which showed its desire to go back to the mystical Golden Age before 1763, and which acknowledged the British right to regulate trade—colonial assemblies, it realised, could not exercise this control, since in trading matters they were but parts of a whole, and there must be a power to preside over, and preserve in due order, that economic connection. Addresses to the people of Great Britain, to the inhabitants of Canada, and a petition to the King were also made, but the most important practical achievement was the Continental Association, a repetition of the tactics of 1765-6, which had persuaded British merchants and commercial interests to press for the repeal of legislation that offended the colonies.

This new Association, largely the desire of the Southern colonies, laid down that non-importation of British goods was to begin on December 1st, 1774, non-exportation of colonial resources and raw materials on September 10th, 1775. More important still, it laid down penalties, and established administrative and judicial organs to enforce this economic boycott, which had a double result. They became the administrative machinery of revolution, the Committee of Safety in every town and county, chosen by those qualified to vote for representatives in the legislature, and they crystallised the issue: anyone not complying could be openly denounced as a traitor to the colonial cause. 'When it shall be made to appear, to the satisfaction of a majority of any such committee, that any person within the limits of their appointment has violated this association, that such majority do forthwith cause the truth of the case to be published in the Gazette; to the end, that all such foes of the rights of British America may be publicly known and universally contemned as the enemies of American liberty.' English imports into New York dropped from £437,937 in 1774 to £1,228 in 1775, into Maryland and Virginia from £528,738 in 1774 to £1,921 in 1775; but despite petitions from manufacturing centres in Great Britain, there were already signs of the widening of trade to other countries, which became the real source of the anti-imperialism of the first part of the nineteenth century.

Exports to Spain, Italy, and the East Indies increased by more than £1 million during this same period. Charles Irving, writing in September 1775 to Dartmouth, Secretary of State for the American Department, noted the 'present flourishing condition' of 'the manufactures in general': 'this great consumption of our commodities on the Continent', 'a ready market in most parts of Europe'. Irving presumed that it was owing to this that the interruptions of commerce with America had been little felt. With trade flourishing elsewhere, the more the colonists stressed to so-called illegal and unconstitutional encroachments of Parliament, the less responsive became the British merchants, and the less successful were the colonists when they made their appeals to the King and to Parliament: they should now be made to realise their place in the Imperial system. Only the hard reality of unsuccessful attempts to put down rebellion and French intervention in the war brought the British to face facts—and even then, in the Conciliatory Mission of 1778, the limit of British concession, there was still the fatal insistence on dependence. On that rock of Imperial sovereignty the North American empire foundered.

Meanwhile, the effect of the Association in the colonies was to develop the basis for independence. The production of local goods mounted, with every colonial occupation receiving encouragement. Every one concerned in industry in the colonies stood to profit by the political situation, and self-interest buttressed patriotism. The First Congress therefore, as it turned out, served more the purpose of joining the colonies together, and of strengthening the cause of independence, than of effecting a reconciliation with Great Britain. The actual steps which led to independence soon followed. The brush at Lexington (April 19th,

1775) surely meant that even if the British succeeded, things could never be the same again—although when Ticonderoga was occupied in May, Congress voted an exact inventory of captured supplies taken that they might be safely returned 'when the restoration of the former harmony between Great Britain and these colonies, so ardently wished for by the latter, shall render it prudent and consistent'. As Paine saw, by referring the matter from argument to arms, a new era was opened, and a new method of thinking begun. The period of debate was closed, and arms as the final arbiter would decide the contest.

The British Prohibitory Act (Sept. 21st, 1775) was rightly seen by John Adams as an Act of Independency—by declaring the colonies outside Royal protection, it recognised their separate station. On March 23rd, 1776, Congress declared colonial ports open to the trade of all nations and territories, save those subject to Great Britain, and on April 4th, the acts of Trade and Navigation were swept away with the authorisation of direct imports from foreign countries of non-British goods. On May 15th, all forms of British authority in the colonies were abolished. The Declaration of Independence, dedicated to the proposition that all men were created equal, and to the practice that some were more equal than others, was the completion of these earlier measures, and the practical demonstration of Paine's demand in *Common Sense* (for which Congress in 1785 voted him 3,000 dollars) for clear-cut, unconditional independence. Apart from its philosophical quality, the Declaration had important practical consequences. It enabled the colonies to secure recognition as belligerents from neutral countries, to demand for colonial prisoners of war the treatment accorded to regular forces, to obtain foreign alliances, to prosecute Loyalists legally if not justly, and seize their property. Prior to the Declaration, the moderates among the Loyalists had still defended the colonial cause, though disagreeing with its methods; after it, they were forced to become supporters of the Imperial policy. With bullet and bayonet reasoning in full sway, as Edmund Pendleton put it, 'those who are not for, are against us'.

In Great Britain also, the Declaration clarified the situation. It was a solid obstacle even to the most ardent advocate of a peaceful settlement. There were few, even among the groups in opposition, who were willing to purchase the friendship of America at the price of such a concession. The war had raged for years before mention of separation was made in either House of Parliament. All the attacks upon administration centred upon the ill-treatment of fellow subjects and mismanagement of the war rather than on its justice: the opposition suggested they would be both better rulers and generals, but with exactly the same object in view— to prevent the last of calamities, separation and independence of the American colonies. It is clear that the action taken against the colonies was supported by the bulk of conscious political opinion in this country. Governor Hutchinson was fully persuaded in August 1774 that 'there never has been a time when the nation in general was so united against the colonies'; Gibbon commented to a friend in May 1775 that 'in this season and on America, the Archangel Gabriel would not be heard'; Franklin himself, writing to David Hartley in 1780, disputed the latter's assertion that people wished for peace. 'You, my friend, have often persuaded me, and I believed it, that the war was not theirs, nor approved by them. But their suffering it so long to continue, and the wretched rulers to remain who carry it on, makes me think you have too good an opinion of them.'[1]

The war was supported until all hopes of eventual success disappeared, and disasters and expense became constant: independence was accepted only through pressure of events, through hard reality. Even so, it remained distasteful. 'To speak openly,' wrote George III to Pitt on October 20th, 1788, 'it is not the being considerably weakened by illness, but the feeling that never have day or night been at ease since this country took that disgraceful step, that has made me wish what years I still have to reign not to be drawn into a war.'

[1] Guttridge, *op. cit.*, p. 256.

IV

ATTITUDES IN 1775

The attitude of the colonial merchants has been the most important topic of recent consideration.[2] There seems little doubt that but for the ill-advised attempt of Lord North's administration to assist the British East India Company to monopolise the tea market at the expense of colonial merchants, the great influence of the trading class, certainly in the Northern colonies, would have been on the side of Great Britain: in the south, where merchants largely acted as factors for British mercantile houses, there was a desire to become individual traders set up on their own which political independence would forward.

A majority of the merchants joined with the radical politicians to defeat the purpose of the Tea Act, but few became fervent supporters of independence and separation from the British Empire, where their profits and interests were concerned: they wished to achieve an agreed relationship between the colonies and Great Britain which would continue to their common advantage, the prosperity and the strength of all its component parts. Many of those merchants who remained connected with the politicians did so only to attempt to control the radical elements. Every merchant who feared anarchy and was concerned for the safety of extensive property interests, had too great a regard for law and order and trade to be swept off his feet by the desire for liberty, especially as interpreted by the lower classes, whose services they used to augment their own wealth (the genesis of class and social

[1] See G. H. van Tyne: *England and America*, Cambridge, 1927, for general essays on this topic.

[2] H. M. Schlesinger: *Colonial Merchants and the American Revolution*, New York, 1918; L. A. Harper, 'The effects of the Navigation Acts on the Thirteen Colonies' in R. B. Morris (ed.): *The Era of the American Revolution*, New York, 1939; *The English Navigation Laws*, New York, 1939, and 'Mercantilism and the American Revolution', *Canadian Historical Review*, Vol. XXIII; O. M. Dickinson: *The Navigation Acts and the American Revolution*, Philadelphia, 1951.

conflicts in many colonies). The balancing point in the final decision largely depended on whether their wealth was easily removable or not, and on the choice between ostensible and immediate or long-term interests. Over two hundred merchants left Boston with the British in March 1776, while those who remained, both in Massachusetts Bay and elsewhere, were generally passive spectators of the struggle. They retained the economic and political convictions that had animated them between 1763 and 1775, and were an important element in the conservative counter-revolution that led to the United States Constitution of 1787. Harper's conclusion is that the relationship between mercantilism and the American Revolution depends on an analysis of the extent to which the colonies were exploited, and of the skill with which they were regulated (in particular, the measures in force as a result of the changed policy begun in 1763). His analysis of the economic effects of mercantilism fails to establish exploitation as a real cause of revolution, but insists that the deplorable regulatory technique of successive administrations was vital, especially since it further emphasised political dependence as a means to securing commercial benefit for Great Britain.[1]

The colonies were forced by events after 1763 to formulate a theory of Empire that would accommodate itself to colonial conditions, whereas the British were content with the Imperial system, as re-shaped by the reforms then introduced: they looked on it as part of the perfect British Constitution.[2] Only when the break-up drew near did suggestions advocating changes begin to appear. Several theories were put forward by colonial writers, to which perhaps undue weight has been given, for there exists little evidence to show whether these schemes ever gained the support of the majority of political opinion in the colonies, which would have been essential for their practical acceptance there, quite apart from their reception in Great Britain. Both the marked lack of thought given to the problems of Imperial relationship when conditions were more stable between 1770 and 1773, and the concentration on restoration of harmony with this country in 1774-5, suggest that these fascinating intellectual exercises were as

[1] Harper, L. A., see bibliography.   [2] See above, p. 56, 57.

much removed from colonial, as from British, opinion. Nevertheless, they show a permanent characteristic of the American people, that every problem must have an immediate, cut-and-dried solution, whereas the later evolution of dominion status shows that much more than ten years is required to make generally acceptable fundamental changes of this nature in any system of government. As Franklin saw when he discussed his ideas with Lords Camden and Chatham in 1775, 'they seem'd to think the Idea ingenious, but the Mode so new as to require much attentive thought before a judgement of it could be form'd'.[1] The colonists objected to the claims of subjects in one part of the King's dominions to be sovereign over their fellow subjects in another part of his dominions; 'The sovereignty of the Crown I understand,' wrote Benjamin Franklin, 'the sovereignty of Britain I do not understand . . . We have the same King, but not the same legislature.' As Sir Lewis Namier has insisted, neither the Imperial nor the constitutional problem of the eighteenth century could have been solved in the light in which the overwhelming majority of the politically-minded public in this country considered them at the time; but George III has been blamed ever since for not having thought of parliamentary government and Dominion status when constitutional theory and the facts of the situation as yet admitted of neither. Only after responsible government as we know it had arisen in this country did Dominion status within the British Commonwealth become possible.[2]

The idea that the British colonies in America were united to the Empire only through the Crown appeared in 1766 in Richard Bland's *An Enquiry into the Rights of the British Colonies*; it was suggested by Joseph Hawley of Massachusetts Bay, and by Benjamin Franklin, and became common coin for commentators on the nature and extent of government by the seventies.[3] Bland argued that a legislature (Parliament) exclusively that of Great

[1] Van Doren, *op. cit.*, p. 345.

[2] Sir Lewis Namier: 'King George III. A study in personality', *History Today*, Vol. III, September 1953.

[3] R. G. Adams: *Political Ideas of the American Revolution*, Durham, N.C., 1922, re-issued 1939; C. F. Mullett, 'English Imperial Thinking, 1764–1783', *Political Science Quarterly*, XLV.

Britain could have no jurisdiction over territories not part of Great Britain. The King had subjects other than those represented at Westminster, the descendants of those to whom the Crown had granted permission to move to new territories under stipulations made by it, and not by Parliament, which had no right of interference in the internal affairs of these lands. Bland considered Virginia an equal partner with Great Britain in the British Empire, made up of separate co-ordinate Kingdoms. Hawley advanced the view that the true plan of government pointed out by reason and experience was 'to let the several parliaments in Britain and America be (as they naturally are) free and independent of each other . . . And as the King is the center of union . . . the various parts of the great body politic will be united in him; he will be the spring and soul of the union, to guide and regulate the grand political machine'. Franklin repeated in 1769 that 'their only bond of union is the King'. The colonies were outside the realm of England, they were not parts of the dominions of England, 'but of the King's dominions'. The British State was only the island of Great Britain, the British legislature the proper judge only of what concerned the welfare of that state. He told his son in October 1773, that from a long and thorough consideration of the subject, he believed 'that the Parliament had no right to make any law whatever, binding on the colonies; that the King, and not the King, Lords, and Commons collectively, is their sovereign; and that the King, with their respective Parliaments, is their only legislature'.[1] James Wilson put forward the same view in his *Considerations of the legislative authority of the British Parliament,* written in 1770 and published in 1774, but he saw the difficulty caused by the 'inextricable association' of the King with the administration in Great Britain which was the greatest barrier to reform in this period. Before the King was outside the British Parliament and apart from it, the modern conception of the monarch as a royal symbol, divested of all executive power, was not feasible.

As Richard Price rightly commented in his *Observations on the nature of Civil Liberty* in 1776, 'the truth is that a common relation

[1] Van Doren, *op. cit.,* p. 295.

to one supreme head; an exchange of kind of offices; ties of interest and affection, and compacts are sufficient to give the British Empire all the unity that is necessary'. But the argument could not be followed to its logical conclusion, since the constitutional ideas and practice of Great Britain, the controlling power, did not yet allow of their application, nor did most colonial writers press their ideas further than home rule, with continued Parliamentary supervision of wider Imperial affairs, particularly in trade. It was home rule, colonial control over their own internal affairs, that was the fundamental principle of the American Revolution.⁵ As James Madison described it, 'the colonies were co-ordinate members with each other, and with Great Britain, of an empire united by a common executive sovereign, but not united by any common legislative sovereign. The legislative power was maintained to be as complete in each American Parliament, as in the British Parliament, and the royal prerogative was in force in each colony by virtue of its acknowledging the King for its executive magistrate, as it was in Great Britain, by virtue of a like acknowledgement there. A denial of these principles by Great Britain and an assertion of them by America produced the Revolution'.

The few men who accepted these notions in Great Britain were radical thinkers, mainly dissenters, who, knowing no hierarchy in either religion or politics, were able to conceive of the colonists as congregations of brethren beyond the seas. Granville Sharp in *A Declaration of the Peoples' natural right to a share in the Legislature* (1774) argued that the true method of connecting the colonies was not by Parliament but by the King. The King and the legislature of every separate colony were the only proper and constitutional rulers of it—he believed that such a commonwealth might become the prototype of a world organisation. John Cartwright, in *American Independence, the Interest and Glory of Britain* (1775), saw colonial governments as independent governments, which should have complete powers of legislation in taxation, trade and manufactures. Between these sister kingdoms, there should be treaties of alliance, a friendly league of free and independent states. The King would be separately the King of each of the constituent nations of the league, and protector of the whole against foreign powers. Colonial rights and status should be acknowledged and declared, an idea re-emphasised by William Pulteney in his *Thoughts on the present state of affairs with America, and the means of conciliation* (1778).

Apart from these proposals of a Commonwealth, other suggestions centred on some kind of federal system, based on the theory that it was possible to limit the jurisdiction of Parliament, and to give certain powers to legislatures which would however still remain subordinate. In these schemes attempts were made to work out colonial representation at Westminster, and the division of powers—all hotly contested by those in authority, and all lacking the wide support and interest necessary for their acceptance. Lord North himself by 1782 was of the opinion that peace was necessary, 'even if it can be obtained on no better terms than some Federal alliance, or perhaps even in a less eligible mode',[1] whilst Shelburne had this kind of alliance in mind from 1778. David Hartley expressed his support in the same year. He 'would cement the two countries together by a mutual nationalization in all rights and franchises to the fullest extent. We are derived from the same stock; we have the same religion, the same manners, the same language, the same temper, the same love of liberty and of independence, and if we must be seemingly divided, let there be at least an union in that partition'.[2] What Hartley most objected to were the allegorical terms of parent and children: 'if we must have allegorical terms, let us change them for brethren and friends. The duties annexed to the terms of brethren and friends in private life would naturally lead us to the contemplation of these duties between Great Britain and America; which would make a fine and everlasting bond of affection and mutual interest; but the supercilious usurpation of authoritative parental rights over those whom God has made our equals, cannot fail to pervert reason at the outset'.[3] (It was a perversion of long standing which had produced disastrous results.)

The British view was held by no one more strongly than the

---

[1] Fortescue, *op. cit.*, Vol. V, No. 3503.
[2] Guttridge, *op. cit.*, pp. 258–60.   [3] *Ibid.*, p. 247.

King himself, which added further difficulties to those seeking to achieve a solution on new lines, difficulties caused by both personal and constitutional reasons. As his governor saw him in 1758, George III had 'spirit . . . and does not want resolution, but it is mixed with too much obstinacy . . . He has great command of his passions, and will seldom do wrong, except when he mistakes wrong for right; but as often as this shall happen, it will be difficult to undeceive him, because he . . . has strong prejudices'. This foresaw precisely what occurred in the American Revolution. In the struggle between Parliament and the colonial assemblies, not of his making, George III completely identified himself with the cause of the British Parliament, and obstinately persevered in the struggle to its fatal end. As Sir Lewis Namier has said, 'egocentric and rigid, stunted in feelings, unable to adjust himself to events, flustered by sudden change, he could meet situations in a negative manner only, clinging to men and measures with disastrous obstinacy'. He had a conception of his own position which nothing in his long reign altered: his duty was to maintain the British Constitution, or the State would be ruined, falling into a very low class among the European nations. First and foremost, he put the good of the country, whose rights and interests he intended to preserve.

The views of George III on the American colonies and the Empire remained consistent throughout this period, a part of his unchanged attitude to the constitution throughout his reign— 'the most perfect of all human formations', 'the admiration of all ages'—an honest man, he was striving to do what he conceived to be his duty. As he wrote to Grafton, in October, 1768, 'the superiority of the mother country over her colonies must be supported'—with the hope that they would return to a reasonable acceptance of their position, entertained until 1774, when more active measures became necessary to achieve this end. Even so, he did not want 'to drive them to despair but to submission', which he was sure would come about by coolness and an unremitted pursuit of the measures that have been adopted'.[1] Submission was essential: 'where violence is with resolution

---

[1] Fortescue, *op. cit.*, Vol. III, No. 1563.

repelled it commonly yeilds, and I owne though a thorough friend to holding out the olive branch I have not the smallest doubt that if it does not succeed that when once vigorous measures appear to be the only means left of bringing the Americans to a due submission to the mother country that the colonies will submit'.[1] It is only fair to the King to point out that these views were supported by people with knowledge of the colonial people and of colonial conditions. Indeed he may have drawn his conclusions from them. It was the opinion of Gage, who was in London early in 1774, that 'they will be lyons whilst we are lambs but if we take the resolute part they will undoubtedly prove very meek';[2] whilst Haldimand considered in August 1775, that nothing but force would bring them to reason, and that until they had suffered for their conduct, it would be dangerous and weak to listen to any propositions they might put forward. As to the colonial views on a change in the Imperial constitution, it was the King's belief 'it would be better totally to abandon them than to admit a single shadow of them to be admitted'.[3]

The longest and clearest exposition of the King's views was made on June 11th, 1779, in a letter to North, discussing a motion of Sir William Meredith for an address to the throne to direct measures for restoring peace with America, which was to be moved that day. The King wished to convey his ideas 'on so very serious a subject on paper, as it will enable him at any time to recurr to this when he wants to know my ideas on the subject'. The King could not accept the motion on peace, nor the suggestion made at that time that William Eden should be employed as a private negotiator with Franklin to achieve that end: 'no inclination to get out of the present difficulties which certainly keep my mind very far from a state of ease, and incline me to enter into what I look upon as the distruction of the Empire'.

He disputed North's arguments on the expense involved, which could never be repaid by what was secured if the war was successful: 'it is necessary for those in the station it has pleased Divine Providence to place me to weigh whether expences though very

[1] Ibid., No. 1595.   [2] Ibid., No. 1379.   [3] Ibid., No. 1647.

great are not sometimes necessary to prevent what might be more ruinous to a country than the loss of money'. He went on to consider the real basis of the colonial claim, and its consequences: 'whether the laying a tax was deserving all the evils that have arisen from it, I should suppose no man could alledge that without being thought more fit for Bedlam than a seat in the senate'. Step by step, the colonial demands had increased: 'independence is their object, that certainly is one which every man not willing to sacrifice every object to a monetary and inglorious peace must concurr with me in thinking that this country can never submit to'.[1] The King repeated these sentiments to the members of the Efficient Cabinet on June 21st (the first of the two recorded occasions during the war he presided over that body, both concerned with possible reduction of the British Empire). He then stated that before he would even hear of any man's readiness to come into office, he would expect to see, signed under his hand, that, 'he is resolved to keep the Empire entire, and that no troops shall be consequently withdrawn from thence, nor Independence allowed'.[2]

'To keep the present constitution of this country in its pristine lustre,' and in all its aspects, was the King's object throughout: when North's waverings increased early in 1782, George III reiterated his objection to a separation from America: 'no consideration shall ever make me in the smallest degree an instrument in a measure that . . . would annihilate the rank in which the British Empire stands among the European states'. In the years which followed, it was his repeated consolation that any evils which might result from the recognition of independence, 'the loss of so essential a part of the English constitution', 'the downfall of this once respectable Empire', could not be laid at his door. He wrote on November 19th, 1782, to Townshend,[3] Home Secretary in the Shelburne administration, 'Parliament having to my astonishment come into the ideas of granting a separation to North America, has disabled me from longer defending the just rights of this Kingdom, necessity not conviction has made me

[1] Fortescue, *op. cit.*, Vol. IV, No. 2649.
[2] *Ibid.*, Vol. III, No. 2674.   [3] Lord Sydney

subscribe to it'[1] (an attitude shared by Shelburne). 'I should be miserable indeed . . . did I not also know that knavery seems to be so much the striking feature of its inhabitants that it may not in the end be an evil that they become aliens to this Kingdom.'[2] When asked by Fox in August 1783, whether it would be agreeable to him to receive a Minister from the United States, the King replied that it would never be agreeable, and added that he would have a very poor opinion of any Englishmen 'that can accept being sent as a minister for a revolted State'.[3] On the proclaiming of a definitive peace on Tuesday, September 9th, 1783, the King was glad it was on a day he would not be in town, as 'this completes the downfall of the lustre of this Empire; but when religion and public spirit are quite absorbed by vice and dissipation, what has now occurred is but the natural consequence; one comfort I have, that I have alone tried to support the dignity of my Crown, and feel that I am innocent of the evils that have occurred, though deeply wounded that it should have happened during my reign'.[4]

The attitude of those representatives of Great Britain who had been in actual contact with the colonial peoples throughout this period, and who were also to be the main agents in the struggle which ensued—the armed forces—are best set out in the correspondence of General Gage,[5] who only differed from his colleagues at the end in recognising the ability and purpose the colonial peoples could bring to military action. Gage assumed temporary command of the troops in North America during the absence of Amherst, granted leave in 1763, and was given more permanent status as Commander-in-Chief in November 1764. He held this command, an increasingly important position as the chief connecting link between the colonies and the home government,[6]

[1] Fortescue, *op. cit.*, Vol. VI, No. 3984. [2] *Ibid.*, No. 3978.
[3] *Ibid.*, No. 4441. [4] *Ibid.*, No. 4470.
[5] C. E. Carter (ed.): *The Correspondence of General Thomas Gage*, 2 vols., New Haven, 1931-3. All later references in this section, unless otherwise stated, are to this work.
[6] C. E. Carter, 'The significance of the Military office in America', *American Historical Review*, Vol. XXVIII, and 'The office of Commander-in-Chief' in Morris, *op. cit.*

until he was recalled in 1775, with only one leave of absence to London from mid 1773 to May 1774, to report on conditions in the colonies. Gage constantly warned ministers of the worsening position, and deplored the lack of policy, the bringing of authority into disrepute—'what as an Englishman and a servant of the Publick', he wrote to Lord Barrington, Secretary-at-War, on October 7th, 1769, 'I can't see go on without being hurt . . . After all, unless laws are supported and enforced, it's needless to make any; repealing some laws, and altering others because the Americans will not obey them, is a sure way to engage the Americans to disobey every law that is inconvenient to them, and to regard the Legislature in a light, I shall not venture to name'.[1] He firmly believed that Great Britain should not only assert but 'also support that supremacy which she claims over the members of the Empire, or she will soon only be supreme in words, and we shall become a vast Empire composed of many parts, disjointed and independent of each other, without any head'.[2]

Gage's attitude on the function of the colonies was set out in a letter to Hillsborough, Secretary of State for the American Department, in 1770, discussing the possibility of colonisation in the Illinois country.[3] Gage could see none of the advantages arising from it which nations expected when they sent out colonists into foreign countries. Settlement there could give no encouragement to fishery; though the country might afford some kind of naval stores, the distance would be too great to transport them; and for the same reason, they could not supply the sugar islands with lumber and provisions. As for the raising of wine, silk and other commodities, the same could be said of the present colonies, without planting others for the purpose at so vast a distance. Necessity would force any settlers there 'to provide manufactures of some kind for themselves: and when all connection, upheld by commerce, with the Mother-Country shall cease', it might be suspected that an independency in government would soon follow. Gage argued there was room enough for the colonists to spread within the present limits for a century to come. They were already

[1] Carter, Vol. II, pp. 526–7.   [2] Ibid., Vol. II, p. 603.
[3] Ibid., Vol. I, pp. 277–8.

almost beyond the reach of law and government; neither the
endeavours of administration nor fear of Indian tribes had kept
them properly within bounds. 'It is apparently most for the
interest of Great Britain, to confine the colonists on the side of
the back country, and to direct their settlements along the sea-
coast, where millions of acres are yet uncultivated.' He saw no
other use in colonies, and certainly did not envisage them as
launching grounds of new independent communities: the part of
the military was 'to protect the settlements, and keep the settlers
in subjection to the Government'.

Though Gage was not a great soldier, he was competent, had
a first-rate grip of administration, and an awareness of the problem
with which Great Britain was faced in North America. He saw
clearly the result of the disappearance of a direct French menace
from Canada: 'the difficultys in carrying on the service in North
America, increase very fast . . . the people in general begin to be
sensible, that they are not obliged to do, what they submitted to,
in times of danger.'[1] He reported farsightedly on the consequences
which this entailed: the colonial peoples 'never declared their sentiments of independency so openly before, and they state their
grievances (if in reality they have any) in such a way that I do not
see how it will be possible to relieve them. They push matters so
closely to the point that the subject seems to be, whether they are
independent states, or colonys dependent on Great Britain'.[2] The
question was not the inexpediency of the Stamp Act, nor colonial
inability to pay, but its unconstitutional nature, contrary to colonial
rights; for which attitude Gage blamed the lawyers, 'the source
from whence the clamors have flowed'. Their aim he expressed to
Barrington in 1768. The people in England could never be such
dupes as to believe that the Americans had traded with them so
long out of pure love and brotherly affection: 'if they do not
smuggle manufactures from other countrys, they must take them
from Britain, or go naked'. That they would build up their own
industries as soon as they were able, 'in spite of your laws to
prevent them', was certain, just as they would struggle for
equality and independence. 'From the denying the right of

[1] *Ibid.*, Vol. I, p. 49.   [2] *Ibid.*, Vol. II, p. 304.

internal taxations, they next deny the right of duties on imports, and thus they mean to go on step by step, 'till they throw off all subjections to your laws. They will acknowledge the King of Great Britain to be their King, but soon deny the prerogative of the Crown, and acknowledge their King no longer than it shall be convenient for them to do so.'[1] If this diagnosis was correct, Gage thought that British policy should be to help to keep the colonies weak as long as possible, and avoid everything which would contribute to increase their strength. Emigration from this country should be strictly limited, and any new settlements peopled from the old ones, 'a means to thin them, and put it less in their power to do mischief'; regiments in the West Indies should be recruited from North America for the same reason.

He noted 'the language of Billinsgate', 'strange pretensions', 'seeds of anarchy and licentiousness . . . thick sown through the colonies', and was particularly concerned by the increasing feeling both in, and against, the British forces. While taking every precaution that the troops might not become objects of resentment, he wrote of the disorders in Boston in 1770: 'The officers and soldiers are Britons, and the people found no advocates amongst them. It was natural for them, without examining into the merits of a political dispute, to take the part of their country; which probably they have often done with more zeal than discretion'.[2] This not only made it more difficult to maintain discipline, but increased the irritation of the troops themselves, whilst it hindered Gage in two practical ways—the getting of sufficient supplies from the colonists, and the concentration of a force for use in an emergency. At the end, he again returned to his main theme: Great Britain should not only assert, but also support, her supremacy. He believed in the existence of a plot to secure independence, begun in Massachusetts Bay, 'and adjusted with some of the same stamp' in other colonies. Its supporters amused people in England 'called the Friends of America', as well as many in the colonies, with feigned professions of affection and attachment to the parent state; they pretended to be aggrieved and discontented only on account of taxation. But, in Gage's opinion, they had

[1] Carter, Vol. II, p. 450.   [2] *Ibid.*, Vol., I, p. 249.

irritated administration in every possible way, and poisoned the minds of the people, ripening them for insurrection. In 1775, 'they would still deceive and lull the mother country into the belief, that nothing is meant against the nation, and that their quarrel is only with the ministers'—a fallacy and deceit he trusted would be seen through.[1] He himself had been convinced from 1774 that 'forcible means' were the only solution—and he differed from the majority of military opinion in the colonies in asserting that the force used must be a considerable one, 'for to begin with small numbers will encourage resistance and not terrify; and will in the end cost more blood and treasure'.[2] Though the colonists were not held in high estimation by the troops, 'yet they are numerous, worked up to a fury, and not a Boston rabble, but the freeholders and farmers of the country'. A check anywhere would be fatal, and since the first stroke would decide a great deal, 'we shou'd therefore be strong, and proceed on a good foundation before anything decisive is tried'[3]—most sensible advice which was never taken, since Great Britain rarely acts until necessity obliges. The crisis Gage had long seen approaching had arrived: the cause he was supporting was in rags, but he, a perfect regular soldier, was still keeping up appearance. When the struggle began, he insisted that, 'we can rely on nothing but our own force to procure even decent terms of peace, and that, if it was ever necessary to obtain peace thro' the means of war, it is highly so in the present juncture'.[4]

People (and the ministry) still believed the Americans would not seriously resist if put to the test, and Gage's consistent refusal to admit this was one of the reasons for his recall. Advice that the conquest of the colonies would not be easy; that it would be effected only by time and perseverance, and strong armies attacking in various quarters, was not what the British either expected, or wanted, to hear. No ministry likes to be told forcibly, in such terms as Gage employed, that it has misread any situation; that troops were sent out too late, that the rebels were at least two months 'before hand with us', that 'we are here, to use a common

---

[1] *Ibid.*, p. 412.   [2] *Ibid.*, p. 381.
[3] *Ibid.*, pp. 371–2.   [4] *Ibid.*, p. 422.

expression taking the bull by the horns, attacking the enemy in their strong parts'. 'Everybody had judged of them from their former appearance, and behaviour, when joyned with the King's forces, which has led many into great mistakes.' Government must realise, if it ever were to be successful, that its opponents were 'now spirited up by a rage and enthusiasm as great as people ever were possessed of, and you must proceed in earnest or give the business up'.[1] Did Gage in fact despair of adequate measures being taken by those in authority, and think that ministers would succumb to the proposition that blockade alone would achieve the British purpose? The British were to find that an attitude of tranquil superiority was of no use in meeting people 'raised to such a pitch of phrenzy as to be ready for any mad attempt they are put upon',[2] nor was the pious hope justified that the Loyalists (who were swept under by this 'phrenzy') would exploit the internal divisions in the colonies for them.

Sufficient differences existed among the colonial peoples for use of skilful diplomacy to weaken a largely enforced union: the mixed nature of patriot motives, which explains why several decades of continued effort and growth were necessary to give the United States a clear sense of national purpose, was never exploited during the struggle, and was rarely taken into consideration in the making of policy. Richard Oswald, a British peace commissioner in 1782, who owned land in both North America and the West Indies, did extensive trade with the southern colonies, and had lived six years in Virginia, was frequently consulted by members of the North administration on the conduct of the war. He consistently urged the breaking up of the colonial union by detaching one or more of the southern provinces, through an appeal to sectional economic interests. Thus, on February 9th, 1775, Oswald explained to Dartmouth that the needs of the southern colonies differed from those in the north because of an economy based on slave labour, and the existence of an influential 'aristocracy' with 'great family connexions'. He believed that by convincing these families that their interests were not the same as those of the 'mob of northern

[1] Carter Vol. II, pp. 686–7.   [2] Ibid., Vol. I, p. 380.

yeomen', that 'dispicable rabble of rioters', that 'confederacy of smugglers' in New England, Virginia would withdraw, and renounce the trade combination. In 1779 and 1781, Oswald again offered plans for the conduct of the war, based on a detachment of the southern colonies because of economic self-interest,[1] and because 'the better sort of People, having so sensibly felt the oppression of the lower Rabble, who now domineer over them, will certainly join in taking every method of bringing them into order'. (Revolutions, as Professor Brogan has remarked, grow in ways their begetters did not foresee or consciously wish for.)

What Oswald overlooked, and it is typical of every British approach in this period, were the hard facts of reality: the influence of economic self-interest was unlikely to reduce the ardent desire for political independence (with its social and economic implications for all classes) fostered by its actuality since 1776. Here was the root of the conflicting attitudes in 1775 as seen by Alexander Graydon: 'the discussion of the points in controversy only served to put the parties further asunder. To the Americans it disclosed the disadvantages of a dependence on a power so remote as that of Britain, and so oppressed by a weight of debt . . . Interest, which made resistance popular with us, made compulsory measures popular with them. It was this collision that, at this time, severed the two countries; though nature, which had placed the Atlantic Ocean between them, had thereby interposed an insurmountable bar to a much longer colonial connection on constitutional principles'.[2]

Franklin, commenting later on the failure of the colonial assemblies to ratify his plan of union put forward at Albany in 1754, would only go so far as to say that had it, or something like it, been adopted, the subsequent separation of the colonies from Great Britain might not so soon have happened: that separation came when it did was due to the handling of events between 1763 and 1775. In 1775, Great Britain and the colonies had got so widely different in their notions of their relation

---

[1] W. Still Robinson, Jr. (ed.): *Richard Oswald's Memorandum, 1781,* Charlottesville, Virginia, 1953, pp. 43–52.

[2] Graydon, *op. cit.,* pp. 113–14.

to one another that, in the existing conditions, separation or conquest were the only possible alternative solutions. A new order came out of what really began as a resistance movement. Nor, as inhabitants of colonies today are again finding out, does the acquisition of independence bring the expected end of all their troubles, but rather the real beginning of them—with no outsiders to blame, or to take the burden of undesirable responsibilities, there is greater need than ever before for the undertaking of duties, and the working out and practical acceptance of the fundamental principles of society, rights and national policy. In that sense, the American Revolution is still not complete.

V

WHY BRITISH DEFEAT? 1

Battles are so admirably fought after everything is over',
Major-General Robert Long wrote to his brother in
December 1811, 'and the science of after-thought is so
overwhelming that there is no standing against it'.[1] Afterthought,
and judgment by modern standards, have strongly influenced
the description of the War of American Independence by the
majority of historians: their attitude to the British conduct of the
war can be summed up in the charge of incompetence, and the
problems the British faced have been either overlooked or
rapidly dismissed. All the disadvantages from which the British
commanders suffered, explains a recent historian of England in
the eighteenth century, 'do not entirely account for the British
disasters'.[2]

An examination of these disadvantages leads to a different conclusion—that the scales were weighted against the British from the
beginning, and that only a staff composed of men of military
genius, backed by a decisive and imaginative government in
London, could have secured a British victory in this war. Men of
considerable talent, and of much goodwill and conviction, failed in
what was an impossible task. What then were the disadvantages
under which the British laboured, and what was their effect?
First, the terrain on which the war was fought confronted the
British with a kind of warfare to which they were unaccustomed,
and for which they were only partially trained. Just as the events
leading up to the outbreak of military operations reveal a British
failure to grasp political realities, so in the military struggle that
ensued the British showed a similar inability to adjust themselves
to strategical and tactical circumstances. Captain Sir James Murray

[1] T. H. McGuffie (ed.): *Peninsular Cavalry General, 1811–1813*, London,
1951, p. 156.
[2] V. H. H. Green, *The Hanoverians, 1714–1815*, London, 1951 edition, p. 358.

commented in November 1775, that to subdue by force of arms a country of several thousand miles in extent, almost entirely covered with wood, was not an easy operation, even were there no inhabitants at all; 'but when we consider that there are no less than 3,000,000 exasperated to the last degree and enflamed to the highest pitch of enthusiasm', there were already too many instances of what that enthusiasm had been capable of producing not to be very doubtful of the event.[1] He wrote after the engagement at Brooklyn Heights, August 1776, of country which for the Americans was 'entirely after their own heart, covered with woods and hedges, from which they gave us several very heavy fires'.[2]

During the advance made from Canada under Burgoyne in 1777, Ensign Hughes wrote of the country around Ticonderoga that 'in many places, the mountains were so steep we were obliged to pull ourselves up, and let ourselves down, by the branches of trees'; the road, 'running round the bottom of steep rocks, was so very crooked that we seldom saw 300 yards before us'.[3] Major-General the Marquis de Chastellux speaking of Freeman's Farm and Bemis Heights remarked that he avoided the term 'field of battle', for these engagements 'were in the woods, and on ground so intersected and covered that it is impossible either to conceive or discover the smallest resemblance between it, and the plans given to the public by General Burgoyne'.[4] Lieutenant Thomas Anburey probably came nearest to the truth when he described all the country traversed in that 1777 campaign as 'peculiarly unfavourable in respect to military operations',[5] a view expressed a year earlier by an American officer, Colonel William Irvine, when engaged in the campaign against Canada: 'nature perhaps never formed a place better calculated for the destruction of an army'.

[1] See E. Robson (ed.): *Letters from America, 1773–1780*, Manchester, 1951, p. 17.   [2] *Ibid.*, p. 33.

[3] E. A. Benians (ed.): *The Journal of Thomas Hughes, 1778–1789*, Cambridge, 1947, pp. 14–15.

[4] H. B. Carrington: *Battles of the American Revolution, 1775–1781*, New York, 1876, p. 338.

[5] T. Anburey: *Travels through the interior parts of America*, 2 vols., London, 1789, Vol. I, p. 424.

[6] Justin H. Smith: *Our Struggle for the Fourteenth Colony*, 2 vols., New York, 1907, Vol. II, p. 414.

General Howe laid especial stress on the nature of the country in his detailed explanation of the conduct of the campaign: almost every movement of the war in North America was an act of enterprise, dogged with innumerable difficulties. A knowledge of the country, intersected as it everywhere was by woods, mountains, water, or morasses, could not be obtained with a sufficient degree of precision necessary to foresee and guard against the obstructions that might occur—and the inhabitants were 'entirely ignorant of military description'.[1] Major-General Charles Grey confirmed that little or no knowledge could be obtained by reconnoitring, and thought it the strongest country he ever was in, the best calculated for the defensive—every one hundred yards might be disputed, and in every quarter of a mile was a post suited for ambuscades.[2]

The southern colonies were no better. Robert Biddulph remarked of the country round Charleston, South Carolina, in October 1780 that it was 'very ill-calculated for war'—unhealthy, intersected with creeks and swamps, without good water, and a most changeable climate.[3] Tarleton described the difficulties encountered and surmounted by both sides in the Carolinas from the climate and the country, 'which would appear insuperable in theory, and almost incredible in the relations'.[4] He told General Clinton, April 10th, 1781, that North Carolina was the most difficult of all provinces in America to attack, unless material assistance could be got from the inhabitants, 'the contrary of which I have sufficiently experienced', on account of its great extent, the numberless rivers and creeks, and the total want of interior navigation.[5] As an A.D.C. to the Comte de Rochambeau expressed it, the country of America was unconquerable[6]—even in some cases by the natives themselves. (Clinton's position, June 27th, 1778, near Monmouth Court House was decided by Washington to be too strong to be assailed with any prospect of

---

[1] Lt.-General Sir William Howe: *Narrative*, second edition, London, 1780, p. 6.   [2] *Ibid.*, p. 38.

[3] 'The Letters of Robert Biddulph': *American Historical Review*, XXIX, p. 96.

[4] Carrington, *op. cit.*, p. 582.   [5] *Ibid.*

[6] Shelburne MSS., Ann Arbor, 34 p. 2. John Trevor to C. J. Fox, April 16th, 1782.

success.)[1] Invading a country like the U.S.A. has rightly been compared with hurling a hammer in a bin of corn—a few kernels are hurt, but the hammer has to be withdrawn quickly, or lost.[2]

The effect of this on the British is quite clear: prompt communications and concerted action were largely out of the question in this country; the timidity and slowness of advance, with both Burgoyne and Cornwallis, was excused as much by the absence of roads and the nature of the country as by American opposition, and every mile advanced weakened the force—Tarleton viewed the British victory at Guilford Court House in March 1781 as the pledge of ultimate defeat. The country was wholly unsuited to the art of war as conceived and practised in Europe. Lord George Germain, Secretary of State for the American Department, 1775–1782, had clearly stated the dilemma in 1775: 'the manner of opposing an enemy that avoids facing you in the open field is totally different from what young officers learn from the common discipline of the army'.[3] Charles Lee saw this when he thought it very possible for men to be clothed in red, to be expert in all the tricks of the parade, to call themselves regular troops, and yet be totally unfit for real service: he agreed that the British troops had been excellent in America during the Seven Years' War, but not until they had absolutely forgotten everything which rendered regulars quite irresistible.[4] Instead of completely adapting their methods to these changed conditions, the British continued to attempt to force the rebels to an action 'upon terms tolerably equal . . . the object of every campaign during this war', as General Clinton, who succeeded Howe as Commander-in-Chief in 1778, expressed it in May 1779. As with the French in the war in Indo-China, the British in the War of American Indepen-

[1] Carrington, *op. cit.*, pp. 418–21.

[2] S. E. Morison and H. S. Commager: *The Growth of the American Republic*, 2 vols., Oxford, fourth edition, 1950, Vol. I, p. 424. Volney, who travelled throughout the U.S.A. in 1796, thought the whole country 'one vast wood'— he scarcely passed for more than three miles together on open and cleared land, and difficulties of communication were still such that a detour of several hundred miles by river and sea was preferable to an overland journey of fifty miles, *ibid.*, pp. 302–4.

[3] Historical Manuscripts Commission, *Stopford Sackville MSS.*, II, p. 2.

[4] Quoted by Tyler, *op. cit.*, Vol. I, pp. 398–9.

dence had to find some way of utilising their superiority in personnel and armaments: it was like trying to hit a swarm of flies with a hammer. For both, it was relatively easy to conquer territory; the difficulty came in holding it—hence the desire to use Loyalists (or Viet Nam troops) for occupation, so freeing regular forces for offensive duties.

The Americans succeeded in avoiding a decisive general action on ground that would have favoured the British, whose attempts to follow out European tactics were proved murderous at Bunker Hill, which began like a parade for inspection of knapsacks and full equipment for campaign service, though by the time of the final assault, knapsacks were unslung, and every needless encumbrance thrown away. Washington was averse to general action; he told Congress on September 8th, 1776, that on their side the war should be defensive: 'it has even been called a war of posts; we should on all occasions avoid a general action, and never be drawn into a necessity to put anything to the risk'. As he saw it, it would be presumptuous to draw out the young colonial troops into open ground against their superiors in number and discipline. This would be to risk a good cause upon a very unfavourable issue.[1] This belief and practice continued—he withdrew from Princeton when challenged in January 1777 from 'the danger of losing the advantage we had gained by aiming at too much'. As every defender ought, particularly one who yet lacked belief in the ability of his forces to stand up to the enemy in a general engagement, Washington rightly concentrated on skirmishing with the enemy, harassing them continually, and removing food and supplies from their reach.[2] This was how he began operations against Howe once more in September 1777, and how he resumed them after Brandywine, where poor intelligence of difficult ground had been a major factor in drawing him into an action. Early in 1778, he continued to stress the same theme—'remaining quiet

[1] There is much on this subject, as for everything else connected with Washington, in the invaluable biography by the late D. S. Freeman, of which 4 volumes are at present published in this country—Vols. III and IV, London, 1951, deal with the war to the beginning of 1778. See Vol. IV, pp. 234, 357.

[2] On this, see also A. W. Greene: *The Life of Nathaniel Greene*, 3 vols., New York, 1867-71, Vol. I, p. 336.

in a secure, fortified camp, disciplining and arranging the Army, till the enemy begin their operations, and then to govern ourselves accordingly'.[1] This positional warfare was eminently suited both to the nature of the terrain and that of the American forces. Admittedly, it left the initiative to the British, but they were not as insistent as Clinton represented them in undertaking it by a general engagement. The British caution, and their fidelity to the European art of war, was strengthened by Bunker Hill—as Lord Percy put it, the army was so small that it could not afford even a victory if it was attended with any loss of men.[2] Indeed, around New York in 1776, Howe hoped to avoid storming the works on Harlem Heights by outflanking the American positions, thus drawing Washington out into the open, and engaging him— which was the reason behind the move to Throg's Neck in October.

Howe confessed that 'as my opinion has always been, that the defeat of the rebel regular army is the surest road to peace, I invariably pursued the most probable means of forcing its commander to action', but with one proviso, 'under circumstances the least hazardous to the royal army; for even a victory, attended by a heavy loss of men on our part, would have given a fatal check to the progress of the war, and might have proved irreparable'.[3] This explains another British disadvantage. Being predictable is a cardinal sin in war. As Murray observed after Brooklyn, 'our former method of beginning always at the wrong end had given them some reason to suppose that we should land directly in front of their works, march up and attack them without further precaution in their strongest points'.[4] The success of tactics more suitable to American conditions, as in the flank march on Long Island in August 1776 ('the possibility of our taking that route', wrote Murray, 'seems never to have entered into their imaginations'),[5] persuaded the British once again to do nothing else. All Howe's later operations in 1776 were flanking operations, avoiding the assault of heavy works, and he began his activities against Philadelphia in precisely the same way—Brandywine was

[1] Freeman, op. cit., Vol. IV, p. 631.   [2] Ibid., Vol. III, p. 505.
[3] Narrative, p. 19.   [4] Robson, op. cit., p. 36.   [5] Ibid.

one of the best examples of this manoeuvre on record, and was successful partly because of American lack of reconnaissance, and ignorance of the ground. But had the Americans realised what was afoot, the circumstances at Brandywine were so similar to those existing on the eve of the Battle of Long Island that the result should have been vastly different.[1]

The British, hidebound by their European backgound, never improvised sufficiently. Howe, despite his reputation as a leading exponent of Light Infantry, followed exactly the art of war in Europe in the eighteenth century—the occupation of posts and cities, constant manoeuvring, fighting as few major battles, and losing as few men as possible; the assault upon Fort Washington in November 1776 was an exact replica of European conditions. As Major Thomas Bell had put it, 'battles have ever been the last resource of good Generals; a situation where chance and accident often baffle and overcome the most prudential and able arrangements, and where superiority in numbers by no means are certain of success, is such as is never entered into without a clear necessity for so doing. The fighting a battle only because the enemy is near, or from having no other plan of offence, is a direful way of making war'.[2] General Clinton showed exactly the same disposition to hold fast to what was gained already, and to be in no hurry to add to it unless a particularly favourable and sure opportunity should occur. He believed he merely had to hold what he had, and wait for America to collapse—and there were repeated signs between 1776 and 1781 that this might happen.

Nevertheless, the main enemy army remained the real objective of the war, and Howe had clearly come to see this. Reporting to Germain the great encouragement given to the rebels by the operations at Trenton and Princeton on January 20th, 1777, he realised the war could only be terminated by a general engagement, but did not see how to obtain it, 'as the enemy moves with so much more celerity than we possibly can'.[3] It was here that improvisation could have helped. The key to mobility in the

---

[1] See Freeman, *op. cit.*, Vol. IV, p. 487.
[2] *A Short Essay on Military First Principles*, London, 1770.
[3] Freeman, *op. cit.*, Vol. IV, pp. 362–3.

eighteenth century was to move light, fettered neither by cum-
brous equipment nor an elaborate supply system, and this was
rarely attempted by the British. The attitude of the inhabitants
of the colonies rendered it increasingly impossible for them to
move in this way. Despite the positive assurances given Howe
in 1777 and Cornwallis in 1781 that on the approach of a British
Army a great body of the inhabitants would co-operate with it,
very few actually asserted themselves in any way whatever. The
British Army had therefore to move as a completely self-sup-
porting unit, as little dependent as possible on either country or
inhabitants. Sergeant Lamb's comment on Saratoga was that the
British had too few men to oppose the enemy's rifle corps, and
that the insufficiency of trained men was the reason for the use
of Indians. 'There is an indisputable necessity of having Indians',
wrote Anburey, 'unless we had men enough of our own trained
up in that sort of military exercise, as our European discipline is
of little avail in the woods.'[1] Line regiments were deprived of
their best men to form Light Infantry to meet this need—a most
ruinous drain on them—and the loss of such *corps d'élite,* as at
Cowpens in 1781, was almost equivalent to the loss of the whole
Army.

All such improvisations were reluctantly made since they
offended against the British attachment to the eighteenth-century
art of war, which received its first effective shock in the War of
American Independence. Here, with riflemen and their like, was
introduced a new ideological element, characteristic of later wars
—in Lamb's description, 'a sort of implacable ardour and revenge,
which happily are a good deal unknown in the prosecution of war
in general'.[2] This posed another problem for the British, typified by the comment of William Carter on Bunker Hill that
'never had the British Army so ungenerous an enemy to oppose;
they send their riflemen five or six at a time who conceal themselves behind trees etc till an opportunity presents itself of taking

[1] Anburey, *op. cit.,* Vol. I, p. 297. See my 'British Light Infantry in the
eighteenth century: the effect of American conditions', *Army Quarterly,*
January 1952.
[2] R. Lamb: *Memoir of his own life,* Dublin, 1811, p. 174.

a shot at our advance sentries, which done they immediately retreat. What an unfair method of carrying on a war!'[1] Without improvisation, and adaptation to American conditions, the British were not in a position to assume an offensive with either vigour or success, and this had drastic results both on their own, and on Loyalist, morale.[2] The British Army was numerically unequal, and strategically and tactically unfitted, to the demands made upon its services: it was unable to meet the full contingencies of active operations. The withdrawals of the British, like that from Philadelphia to New York in 1778, announced that the Loyalists would be left to their own resources and to the merciless vengeance of the patriots in destruction of property, annihilation of business and personal misfortune: the key to their activity was British power to support and protect those who remained loyal, and positive proof of assured victory and permanent predominance was never forthcoming. The sailors saw this before the soldiers. Vice-Admiral Arbuthnot put it to Germain on October 10th, 1779: if we could not properly maintain posts after we had got possession, 'we had better not attack them, for I believe it will not be possible to persuade that the people will give any assistance';[3] and Rodney saw the war in America on December 22nd, 1780, as now turned to a war of posts, 'and unhappily for England, when they have taken posts of infinite advantage, they have been unaccountably evacuated without one good reason assigned'.[4]

Some of the most troublesome difficulties raised by the War of American Independence concerned supply and communications; indeed, on both sides, this war is an outstanding example of how all great military decisions depend ultimately on the administrative factor, and a knowledge of what is, and what is not, possible. As the First Lord of the Admiralty expressed it in a paper read in the Cabinet in September 1779, to suggest the proper modes of distressing the enemy was not very difficult, but to find the means of carrying those measures into execution, was not

[1] Freeman, *op. cit.*, Vol. III, p. 505.
[2] See E. W. Sheppard: *The Study of Military History*. Aldershot, 1952, pp. 116, 123.
[3] Historical Manuscripts Commission, *Stopford Sackville MSS.*, Vol. II, p. 147.
[4] To Germain, *ibid.*, p. 192.

easy: 'it is to little purpose to form plans without at the same time pointing out the manner of securing their success, therefore it will be necessary to lay down not only what ought but what can be done'.[1]

This war demonstrated that the principles and practice of military movement and administration were the crux of generalship—a point too often overlooked by the British, who usually enter war with an almost complete lack of preparation, and have to rely on an inherent capacity for improvisation and detailed organisation. Most stratagems are easily thought of, but are only executed by intelligent and careful preparation: irregular enterprises require just as much preparation as any other operation of war. As Rommel wrote in his notes on desert warfare: before the fighting proper, the battle is fought and decided by the quartermasters. Recognition of this fundamental would alter several verdicts of the military historian, particularly in this war: it explains why sustained and successful pursuit, the only means by which the full fruits of victory can be garnered, has been one of the rarest of military operations in the past, and remains problematical in the future. Effective supply and administration is a first condition of success, and a governing and limiting factor of strategy.

Past campaigns in the American colonies had relied to a great extent on local supplies; now the British had to fend for themselves. Lord Rawdon posed the fundamental question in January 1776 when he said the Americans could not last out beyond that campaign, 'if you give us the necessary means of carrying on the war with vigour'.[2] General Grant restated it to Admiral Byron on July 25th, 1779: 't'is not enough to put soldiers ashore in order to make them usefull to the King's service—they must be provided with what is necessary for their support and subsistence'.[3]

The British Army's base was the sea, and the navigable river leading from it—in themselves a limiting factor in the conduct

---

[1] G. R. Barnes and J. H. Owen (ed.): *The Private Papers of John, Earl of Sandwich, 1771–1782* (Navy Records Society, Vols. LXIX, LXXI, LXXV, LXXVIII), 4 vols. London, 1932–8, Vol. III, p. 165.

[2] Later 1st Marquess of Hastings. H.M.C. *Hastings MSS.*, Vol. III, p. 167.

[3] Colonial Office Manuscripts, C.O. 318: 5, 369.

of operations. Its position has been compared to that of a projectile fired by a powerful gun, the British fleet, whose range and power alone placed the target within reach.[1] Supply from Great Britain to America was precarious: during the winter of 1775-6, of forty transports from home, only eight reached Boston. The remainder either fell victim to colonial privateers, or were swept to the West Indies by the prevailing north-west winds. After the intervention of the French in 1778, supply became even more hazardous. Britain's only hope of carrying on the campaign depended upon her ability to keep intact her sea communications. Had the French at once secured American bases, and concentrated on interrupting British lines of communication, it seems probable that shortage of supplies would have compelled the British to withdraw.[2] Fortunately, in true eighteenth-century style, France from the beginning preferred to concentrate her forces in the Caribbean, for the purpose of acquiring West Indian islands. For the better part of two years, British transports and supply vessels made their way to New York with relatively little interference. When Washington at last secured the active support of a strong French fleet in 1781, it was decisive in ending the war on the North American Continent, and in sealing American independence.

The eighteenth-century system of government in Great Britain was in any case ill-suited for the conduct of war.[3] Even when ministers had agreed upon definite measures, the ordinary routine of administration encumbered action; there was a lack of co-ordination between departments, and in the supervision of preparations. Co-ordination was essential if expeditions were to be prepared and dispatched with speed; its absence meant delay and inadequacy. The practice of each department of government being separate and self-contained, and the minister in charge responsible directly only to the King, rendered more difficult the

[1] Sheppard, op. cit., pp. 24, 61.

[2] See G. S. Graham, 'Considerations on the War of American Independence', Bulletin Institute Historical Research, XXII, May 1949, and his Empire of the North Atlantic, London, 1951.

[3] See my 'The Expedition to the Southern Colonies, 1775-1776', English Historical Review, October 1951, in particular, pp. 53 8

carrying into effect of a vigorous policy—such a system could not grapple adequately with either the problems of strategy or those of organisation, supply, and transport. The successful execution of plans depended upon an efficiency of organisation and a degree of co-operation which did not exist between departments, and this became apparent during the War of American Independence to many of those most deeply concerned. The military and naval commanders in America felt the effects—and defects—of this system in the uncertain arrival of reinforcements, stores, and supplies: nothing was ready in time. Planning and execution of military operations in the colonies became increasingly impossible until supplies had arrived and were therefore assured. Howe reported to Germain on August 6th, 1776, that he had a sufficient force to begin operations, but lacked camp equipage, particularly kettles and canteens, 'so essential in the field; and without which too much is to be apprehended on the score of health, at a time when sickness among the British troops was never more to be dreaded, from a due consideration of their importance in the prosecution of this distant war'.[1] Stores for the 1777 campaign left England only in March, and did not arrive at New York until May 24th, and had still to be distributed in America—a fact which David Hartley made great use of when refuting, in his third letter on the American War in 1778, the contention that the groups in opposition had strengthened the hands of England's enemies and had acted traitorously. 'Was it owing to them that the campaigns of 1776 and 1777 were not opened till August or September, and that the armaments did not sail in the spring from English ports till . . . they should have been landed in America? . . . the very statement of these things is a sufficient refutation.'[2] (Opposition then, as now, refused to admit practical difficulties.) Dr. Johnson's comment on the fate of North could be applied to the Government—he would not say that what he did was always wrong, but it was always done at a wrong time.

General Gage told Dartmouth as early as July 1775 that his difficulty was not in getting out of Boston, but the fact that there were 'no rivers for the transportation of supplys, and hand carriages

[1] C.O. 5: 93, 461.   [2] Guttridge, op. cit., p. 251.

are not to be procured'. Advantages could not be taken of
victories 'thro the want of every necessity to march into the
country',[1] a difficulty which also rendered inconclusive the
successes of Cornwallis in 1780 and 1781. As Gage put it, victories
would bring no advantage but reputation. Howe similarly complained in April 1776 that 'their armies retiring a few miles back
from the navigable rivers, ours cannot follow them from the
difficulties I expect to meet with in procuring land carriage.'[2]
He justified his movement by sea in the following year to Pennsylvania because 'the communications for provisions through such
an extent of country could not possibly be maintained with the
force then under my command'.[3] The reason for Howe's delay
in proceeding from Head of Elk to Brandywine, and in occupy-
ing Philadelphia, was the need to replace the horses lost during
the long voyage for want of forage, and to secure waggons.

Charles Stuart noted in July 1777 that in a country with indifferent and scanty land communications, inability to provide
supply had 'absolutely prevented us this whole war from going
fifteen miles from a navigable river'.[4] Where operations had to be
carried on without the aid of rivers, the result was usually disastrous, and always offered a favourable opportunity to the Americans. In most cases, the British were then dependent upon horses:
to make feed unavailable paralysed them, and rendered wellnigh
impossible transportation of baggage and cannon. To keep forage
from the British became a major American operation which in
turn caused the British to form larger and larger foraging parties
to secure the essentials of movement.

The 1777 expedition of Burgoyne from Canada particularly
illustrates the British problem in this field. Schuyler made the
route from Skenesborough to Fort Edward as nearly impassable
as human operations could, by felling large trees, destroying
bridges, diverting small streams and choking creeks to impair
advance. Burgoyne's force had to build over forty new bridges

---

[1] Carter, *op. cit.,* Vol. I, pp. 409, 418.
[2] Historical Manuscripts Commission, *Stopford Sackville MSS., op. cit.* II,
p. 30.   [3] *Narrative, op. cit.,* p. 16.
[4] E. Stuart Wortley: *A Prime Minister and his son,* London, 1925, pp. 112–13.

as well as repair old ones, and at one place, had to lay a timber causeway of two miles before it could move on. Ensign Hughes believed that 'our long stay in Skenesborough to make a bad road scarcely passable, fit for carts etc. and in procuring a sufficient quantity of carriages etc. . . . was a primary cause of the miscarriage of Burgoyne's expedition'.[1] Anburey commented that for every hour that the General could devote to contemplating how to fight his army, he must allot twenty in contriving how to feed it.[2] His army could only with difficulty be victualled from day to day, and there was no prospect of establishing a magazine in sufficient time to pursue his early successes—it was this difficulty which was behind the expedition to Bennington, a great depôt for corn, flour, cattle, reputed to be guarded only by militia. When the supply line behind him snapped, Burgoyne had no hope: every mile of his advance had been an added mile of long and tenuous lines of communication—rivers, narrow lakes, forest tracks—and he could penetrate no further south. The climax, so beloved to an amateur dramatist, was upon him, but not one he would have staged of his own volition.[3] This supply problem was never satisfactorily solved by the British: hence their relative immobility, 'tethered by their supply lines to the coast',[4] and the continuing stress placed on the Loyalists—to keep the country open behind the fighting troops in a terrain where all were opposed or equivocally neutral until proof of ability to retain advantages was shown.

The Americans seemed to understand the mobility and flexibility given by the Navy better than the British military commanders, possibly because of their fear of the results of its use. There is no doubt that the Navy should have been able to provide the Army not only with secure communications but also with the power to create diversions, support local loyal forces, and commence operations in different areas within its reach. Washington continually harped on this theme: the ability the British had to

[1] Benians, op. cit., p. 11. See also Carrington, op. cit., pp. 318–28.
[2] Anburey, op. cit., I, p. 384.   [3] He was an amateur playwright.
[4] W. B. Willcox: 'British Strategy in America, 1778', Journal of Modern History, XX, No. 2, pp. 98–9.

concentrate secretly in superior force, deliver a surprise attack on any part of the American lines in complete protection, and disappear before American troops could arrive. As early as July 10th, 1775, he told R. H. Lee that the enemy were able to proceed to 'any point of attack, without our having an hour's previous notice of it', if the General kept his own counsel, and to meet this threat, 'we are obliged to be guarded at all points, and know not where, with precision, to look for them'[1]—a fact which General Gage never seems to have appreciated. General Charles Lee described it even more picturesquely to Washington in April 1776: 'the circumstances of the country, intersected by navigable rivers, the uncertainty of the enemy's designs and motions, who can fly in an instant to any spot where they chose with their canvass wings throws me . . . in this inevitable dilemma . . . I can only act from surmise and have a very good chance of surmising wrong.'[2]

The flexibility which was possible was shown by Clinton's arrival, after the expedition against the southern colonies, to take part in the Long Island campaign in 1776, in Joseph Reed's description, as if he had dropped from the clouds,[3] and even more by the American marching and countermarching during Howe's voyage to the Head of Elk in 1777.[4] In this last case, the advantage was let slip. Howe's six weeks' voyage of 300 miles, which with prevailing winds became nearer one thousand, and a march of fifty miles by land brought him to a place less than one hundred miles by land from where he started, and with the enemy in position to meet him. From the head of Delaware Bay, where he first went in, to that of Chesapeake Bay, where he eventually landed, was twelve miles by land, but as Howe went by sea, three hundred miles round a peninsula one hundred and fifty miles long—the only real justification he could have made was that he was conducting a war of nerves, the 'constant perplexity and the most anxious conjecture' recorded by Washington.

---

[1] Freeman, *op. cit.*, Vol. III, pp. 489, 506–7.
[2] *Lee Papers,* Collections of the New York Historical Society, 4 vols, New York, 1872–5, Vol. I, pp. 376–7.
[3] Freeman, *op. cit.*, IV, p. 145.   [4] Freeman, *op. cit.*, IV, p. 445.

What was insufficiently realised by the Americans then, and by historians since, was the weakness of the British Navy in 1775, and the mutual friction and mistrust between army and navy, both then and later. In 1775, a much reduced fleet (from the usual post-war economy drive) had been sent out, short even of its low peace complement of men, and further impaired by sickness and by its commander, Admiral Graves. It is probable that Howe would have evacuated Boston before the spring of 1776 had he had sufficient vessels to move both men and material at one voyage in the autumn of 1775, but this was not possible. When all these facts are taken together, it is clear that 'the means of carrying on the war with vigour' stipulated by Rawdon[1] were rarely forthcoming, and insufficiency bred inaction, which spread widely. By 1780, visiting North America from the West Indies, Rodney, reporting to Sandwich on the manner in which the war was carried on, observed 'there appears to me a slackness inconceivable in every branch of it, and that briskness and activity which are so necessary, and ought to animate the whole, to bring it to a speedy conclusion, have entirely forsaken it.'[2]

Mass conscription, which was to render casualties of comparatively less importance, had not yet been thought of. In consequence, numbers of men and their safeguarding were a prime consideration, which from the beginning imposed caution on British commanders. Here again, European practice, and the art of war in the eighteenth century entered: in an age of precise linear tactics, three to five years of intensive drill were believed necessary to turn out an accomplished soldier, and since all manufactures depended on hand labour, every item of arms and equipment had a significance not easily understood in an age of mass production.

Until this war, preservation of a force was the first eighteenth-century object, the results of its action secondary. This was particularly so with the British, whose army was the only one at the government's disposal: once lost, it could not be replaced. The

[1] See above p. 102.
[2] G. B. Mundy: *Life and Correspondence of Admiral Rodney*, 2 vols. London, 1830, Vol. I, pp. 428–9. He had also noticed a similar lack of spirit in Plymouth dockyard in December 1779, *ibid.*, p. 215. See also his comment on January 1st, 1782, Vol. II, p. 179.

belief was that nothing spoilt an army as much as war: it was too perfectly trained and exercised, the result of too much national effort, to be risked. The feeling of the average commander was like that of the owner of a new car on a wet day, unwilling to go out into the rain and mud, and prepared to wait for ideal weather and conditions to display the power and the grace of his property. Burgoyne prided himself after Saratoga that 'my army would not fight, and could not subsist; and under these circumstances I have made a treaty that saves them to the State for the next campaign'.[1] Howe quite rightly described his army as 'the stock upon which the national force in America must in future be grafted',[2] the capital of a business concern which must not be frittered away. All risks had to be reduced to a minimum, and defeat avoided at all costs, even if that meant the sacrifice of reasonable chances of victory, which a bolder conduct might have turned to good account. British commanders rarely went beyond the most active conduct consistent with safety: indeed, they could only do so at their own peril. This caution was shown repeatedly in the first three years of the war.

In the action against Brooklyn Heights in August 1776, instead of a final frontal attack, Howe relied on siege, although he believed assault would have carried the rebel lines. 'As it was apparent that the lines must have been ours at a very cheap rate by regular approaches, I would not risk the loss that might have been sustained in the assault'. He went on to remind the committee of the House of Commons examining him that the most essential duty he had to observe was not wantonly to commit the troops under his command when the object was inadequate; that any considerable loss sustained then could not be repaired easily or speedily. 'I also knew that one great point towards gaining the confidence of an army (and a general without it is upon the most dangerous ground) is never to expose the troops, where, . . . the object is inadequate. In this instance, from the certainty of being in possession of the lines in a very few days, by breaking ground, to have permitted the attack in question, would have been in-

[1] Historical Manuscripts Commission, *Stopford Sackville MSS.*, *op. cit.*, II, p. 78.   [2] C.O. 5: 93, 461.

considerate, and even criminal'.[1] At the time, this decision was fully approved by officers under Howe's command; it was in fact normal procedure. A correspondent of the Earl of Huntingdon, from New York on September 25th, 1776, thus expressed it: '. . . the general's plans are well laid, and, so far as he has gone, he has succeeded happily: that everything is at stake and that one daring attempt, if unsuccessful, would ruin our affairs in this part of the world, and the difficulty of getting troops, and such troops, is so great that we ought not to hazard our men without the evident prospect of accomplishing our purpose'.[2]

Or take the account of that operation given by Lieutenant-Colonel F. Mackenzie in his diary on October 26th, 1776. The cautious conduct of General Howe in all the actions of the campaign 'is generally approved of'; and although many are of the opinion that he should have followed up at once the advantage gained on August 27th, 'yet it must be allowed that it was extremely proper in him to consider what fatal consequences might have attended any check which the Army might have received in the first action of the campaign. He has therefore conducted every enterprize in that cautious circumspect manner, which, altho' not so brilliant and striking, is productive of certain and real advantages, at the same time that very little is set at stake. Great Britain has at an immense expense, and by great exertions, assembled an Army from which the nation expects an entire suppression of the rebellion, it would therefore be the height of imprudence in the Commander in chief, by any incautious or precipitate conduct, to give the rebels any chance of an advantage over it.'[3]

Howe stated his main principle when he wrote of Whiteplains (October 28th, 1776), 'if I could by any manoeuvre remove an enemy from a very advantageous position, without hazarding the consequences of an attack, where the point to be carried was not adequate to the loss of men to be expected from the enterprise, I should certainly adopt that cautionary conduct, in the hopes of

---

[1] *Narrative, op. cit.*, pp. 4–5.
[2] *Hastings MSS., op. cit.*, Vol. III, p. 186.
[3] *The Diary of Frederick Mackenzie, 1775–1781.* 2 vols., Cambridge, Mass., 1930, Vol. I, p. 89.

meeting my adversary upon more equal terms'.[1] And even when the Americans at Valley Forge in the winter of 1777–8 were unable to stir because of shortage of shoes, clothing, and provisions, Howe argued that that did not 'occasion any difficulties so pressing as to justify an attack on that strong position during the severe weather.'[2] Charles Stuart summed up both the policy and the difficulties when he wrote to Bute in June 1777 that 'our General must make his movements with great expedition and caution, for if he makes the least faux pas Great Britain, with the most strenuous exertions, can not be sure of finishing this war in two years'.[3] This turned out an optimistic forecast, to which Admiral Gambier, writing to Sandwich July 6th, 1778, added, 'our army as they are is healthy, brave, and zealous; but an army must constantly be recruited. Twelve hundred leagues with its natural difficulties demand a solemn thought—the means and expense'.[4]

Apart from the depressing effect which this caution and inactivity had in time upon morale, the shortage of men and difficulty of supply explain the disastrous reliance placed on Loyalist support throughout the war in an attempt to relieve regular troops for vital operations, as well as to keep open the country behind them. This reliance on a broken reed entailed a dispersion of effort which Frederick Mackenzie accurately described as a 'capital error' in the conduct of the war. 'Under the idea of having numerous friends in every province who would declare themselves and act with us, if we showed ourselves in it, we have extended our operations throughout most of them; by which means we have not been in sufficient strength in any one, and have found those to oppose us in all, who could not by any means have been brought to act against us in any particular province which we might think proper to make the seat of the war'.[5]

In 1776, the British had troops in Nova Scotia, New York, New Jersey, South Carolina, and in the last month also in Rhode

---

[1] *Narrative*, p. 7.   [2] *Ibid.*, p. 30.
[3] Stuart Wortley, *op. cit.*, p. 94.
[4] Barnes and Owen, *op. cit.*, II, pp. 299–300.
[5] Mackenzie, *op. cit.*, II, p. 525.

Island; in 1777, in Nova Scotia, Rhode Island, New York, New Jersey, Pennsylvania, and Connecticut; in 1778, in Nova Scotia, Rhode Island, New York, New Jersey, Pennsylvannia, and Connecticut; in 1779, in Nova Scotia, Rhode Island, New York, Connecticut, Georgia, and South Carolina; in 1780, in Nova Scotia, New York, New Jersey, New Hampshire, Georgia, Virginia, North and South Carolina; in 1781, in Nova Scotia, New York, New Hampshire, Georgia, Virginia, North and South Carolina—apart from those in East and West Florida, and Canada throughout the war. This lack of concentration made it impossible to drive a firm wedge into the rebellion at strategically vital centres, and to operate in force against the main rebel army, which should have been the major objective of each offensive. Economy of force has always been a cardinal principle of war: to concentrate and use every available soldier in the area, and for the operation, which was the main one, leaving only the bare minimum for necessary but secondary tasks. Secondary aims, instead of being left to be accomplished at leisure, became primary in this British policy.[1] It was also an undoubted advantage to the Americans, who were given a much longer indulgence at the hands of the British than they had any right to expect. Instead of operating against a weak, hastily organised force, and suppressing the rebellion, the British waited—in the belief that the American army would fall to pieces of itself, as for example in December 1776 when the term of enlistment of the bulk of that army expired. It was this refusal to take the initiative which allowed the Americans eventually to get an army together, and to launch out on optimistic operations which gave them experience of incalculable importance. As Washington said to Governor Cooke of Rhode Island, 'enterprises which appear chimerical often prove successful from that very circumstance. Common sense and prudence will suggest vigilance and care when the danger is plain and obvious, but where little danger is apprehended, the more the enemy is unprepared'.[2] Their vigorous activity at Trenton and Princeton, December 1776–January 1777, coming at a time when the British (and many others) expected their disbandment, re-

---

[1] See Sheppard, *op. cit.*, pp. 4–6.   [2] Freeman, *op. cit.*, III, pp. 512–13.

moved the panic which had struck the Middle Colonies, and was a great factor in raising an army for 1777. By July of that year, British inactivity and American vigilance had compelled Howe to withdraw from New Jersey—a declaration to the whole world, as John Hancock saw it, that the conquest of America was not only a very distant, but an unattainable, object.

It is a sound maxim in war to be clear about one's objective— all the rest will follow, given sufficient resources and activity. Until 1778, this was ignored by the British who were uncertain about their main motive. Was it to conciliate, or to subdue, the Americans; negotiated peace or war? This lack of determination meant immediate loss of initiative. Too vigorous a policy would ruin the chance of a settlement whilst too lenient handling of the rebels could only encourage them. It seems clear that had an energetic policy been followed from the start by pouring troops and supplies to the decisive points, by isolating the main areas of disaffection, and by dealing decisively with each one, the rebellion could have been crushed before France entered the war. There was not in these years one overriding plan to which all else was to be subordinated. The British were hoping to heal and settle, as well as to conquer, and imagined that by their very appearance the rebellion could be put down as suddenly as it had broken out —hence their neglect of what should always accompany the maintenance of the objective, sufficient resources readily available for its attainment. To pursue approaches for peace while using to their utmost extent the soldiers and ships which were provided were in reality two incompatible aims—and it was this misconception which frustrated the undoubted advantages with which the British opened operations against the colonies, and hindered them in action against their small, unorganised enemy.

General Howe did not at first believe there was any incompatibility in his position: he referred to this subject several times in his defence of criticism in 1779. If victory was to be followed by reunion, victory must be won with as much gentleness as war permitted. He was convinced that in endeavouring to conciliate the rebels by taking every means to prevent the destruction of the country instead of irritating them 'by a contrary mode of proceeding', he was acting for the benefit of the King's service. 'Ministers themselves . . . did at one time entertain a similar doctrine, and . . . it is certain that I should have had little reason to hope for support from them, if I had been disposed to acts of great severity'.[1] He continually denied that his civil commission as a peace commissioner was inconsistent with his military command, and that his mind was more intent upon bringing about a peace by negotiation than by force of arms. He insisted that what had determined his choice of alternatives in every case had been his duty 'of weighing the risk of ruining the cause I was engaged in by a considerable loss of troops'.[2] In other words, where the British failed was in their political appreciation of the situation in the Colonies, in refusing to see that a rebellion inspired by the purpose of securing national independence was not the kind of opposition to be reduced to terms. This presently became evident to Howe: he and his brother soon saw 'that the leaders of the rebellion were determined, from interest if not from principle, to prevent a reconciliation with Great Britain'.[3] Much more important, as Howe had hinted, the misconception also involved a failure on the part of the British to furnish proper means—in men, ships, and material—for full prosecution of war. By 1778, when their minds cleared, it was too late, for with the entry of other, national enemies, this shortage could never be put right. Moreover, with these national enemies, and with the positive assurances which came from both Clinton and Cornwallis, 1779–1781, that the colonies would soon rally to the royal cause, the ministry saw no reason to ship large reinforcements or supplies, again causing their commanders to miss many favourable opportunities. This lack of objective, and lack of sufficient force, is one of the major lessons to be drawn from the War of American Independence.

There were those who saw at the time that there should be no hesitation and tenderness, that the British should make up their minds, and hit hard in the most effective place. Gage understood the situation which faced him: he contradicted the contemptuous

---

[1] *Narrative*, p. 9.   [2] *Ibid.*, pp. 31–2.   [3] *Ibid.*

view the British had of the Americans, who were not the despicable rabble too many supposed them to be, but spirited up by zeal and enthusiasm. He advised the ministry from the beginning that there was no hope in conciliation, that the rebels were bent on independence. As early as October 1774, he argued for an army at least 20,000 strong in order 'to get this business over': 'foreign troops must be hired, for to begin with small numbers will encourage resistance and not terrify; and will in the end cost more blood and treasure'.[1] On June 12th, 1775, he wrote to Lord Barrington, Secretary-at-War: 'things are now come to that crisis, that we must avail ourselves of every resource, even to raise the negroes, in our cause. People would not believe that the Americans would seriously resist if put to the test . . . I have long since given my opinion . . . employ sufficient force in the beginning . . . nothing is to be neglected of which we can avail ourselves. Hanoverians, Hessians, perhaps Russians may be hired, let foreigners act here . . .'[2] The response of the ministry to Gage's suggestions had been quite different. Despite the probability that force—particularly naval force—would be necessary to execute the Boston Port Bill and its companion measures, the supplies for 1775 granted two thousand seamen less than for the previous year. Lord George Germain, before he entered the ministry, was opposed to this policy: he wrote[3] that as there was no common sense in protracting a war of that kind, he would be for exerting the utmost force of this kingdom to finish this rebellion in one campaign—a view shared by many serving officers.

Captain Evelyn argued in August 1775 that the 'good people of old England', if they meant to continue masters of America, should 'lay aside that false humanity towards these wretches which has hitherto been so destructive to us . . . they must permit us to restore to them the dominion of the country by laying it waste, and almost extirpating the present rebellious race, and upon no other terms will they ever possess it in peace.'[4] Charles

[1] Carter, *op. cit.*, I, p. 381.   [2] *Ibid.*, II, p. 684.
[3] *Stopford Sackville MSS.*, *op. cit.*, I, p. 137.
[4] G. D. Scull (ed.): *Memoir and Letters of William Glanville Evelyn, 4th Foot, from North America, 1774-1776*, Oxford, 1879, pp. 64-5.

Stuart commented on February 4th, 1777, on the Brooklyn engagement in 1776, when Sullivan surrendered, and Washington was obliged to retreat, that it 'had all the appearance of a successful one, and if we had followed our fortune and prevented their Army from escaping we shou'd have ordered, not woo'd them to make terms'.[1] Lt.-Colonel Harcourt stated the truth on May 31st, 1777, when he wrote that America was never to be regained without making an absolute conquest of her, and that all overtures had failed, except upon a footing of independence.

Charles Grey believed that too much refinement and altercation with such men as Washington had been used already: there was but one mode, the sword, of settling anything effectually with them (June 1st, 1778).[2] Frederick Mackenzie recorded in his diary, September 26th, 1778, the results of the change of plan in the war made in that year. 'Had it been pursued after their rejecting the offers made by the first commissioners, the rebellion would have been at an end before this; but the mistaken lenity of Government has prolonged the war, and brought the nation into the present dangerous crisis.'[3] This opinion was also held by George III, who, despite his critics, could acutely assess military realities. He wrote to John Robinson on March 5th, 1777, that if the Howe brothers would act 'with a little less lenity (which I really think cruelty, as it keeps up the contest), the next campaign will bring the Americans in a temper to accept of such terms as may enable the mother country to keep them in order; for we must never come into such as may patch for a year or two, and then bring on new broils; the regaining their affection is an idle idea—it must be the convincing them that it is their interest to submit'.[4] This the King repeated to Lord North on October 28th, 1777: he hoped Lord Howe would turn his thoughts 'to the mode of war best calculated to end this contest as most distressing to the Americans, and which he seems as yet carefully to have avoided; to me it has always appeared that there was more cruelty in pro-

[1] Stuart Wortley, *op. cit.*, p. 98.
[2] E. H. Tatum (Jr.) (ed.): *The American Journal of Ambrose Serle, 1776–1778*, San Marino, 1940, pp. 300–2.
[3] Mackenzie, *op. cit.*, II, p. 398.   [4] Add MSS., 37833 f. 137.

tracting the War than in taking such Acts of vigour which must bring the crisis to the shortest decision'.[1] In any case, as William Johnstone Pulteney suggested to Germain in December 1777, ability for negotiation was 'the gift of nature to very few men'; however high the Commissioners stood in the class of military men, it was very much doubted if they were likely to succeed in the other line.[2] Their very use did not suggest sincerity, while it limited their efficiency and their possibilities as commanders, whose main purpose it should have been to subdue rebellion. To conduct both peace and war at one and the same time was almost beyond human capacity. The plan of subjugation did not proceed upon a consistent view. There was neither uniform rigour nor uniform kindness, and the mixture of both qualities produced a neutral effect—'neither the impression of fear, which subjugates by force; nor the impression of love, which blinds by affection'[3] —in fact, a continuation of that indecisive handling of political relations between 1763 and 1775, which had contributed greatly to bringing on the war.

The general effect of this confused and double policy was important. First, on those Americans who remained loyal. Even those who were the keenest supporters of continued allegiance were bound at first to show an equivocal neutrality; only British success and apparent ability to retain any advantage gained could induce inhabitants of disputed areas to confess their loyalty. Actions then, as now, spoke louder than words. General Robertson might believe that two-thirds of the people were loyal at heart, twice the proportion constantly affirmed by John Adams, but they waited for the British to help them, and looked for vigorous action before they committed themselves—hence the lack of organisation and energy among them; the failure of the British

[1] Fortescue, *op. cit.*, III, No. 2072. As he put it to the Younger Pitt, January 25th, 1784, 'if we mean to save the country, we must cut those threads that cannot be unravelled. Half-measures are ever puerile, and often destructive'. *Pitt MSS., Chatham Papers*, P.R.O.

[2] *Stopford Sackville MSS., op. cit.*, II, p. 83. See also George III to Sandwich, September 13th, 1778, *Sandwich Papers, op. cit.*, II, p. 163.

[3] Robert Jackson: *A Systematic View of the formation, discipline, and economy of armies*, London, 1804, pp. 130–3.

to take effective action convinced the weakhearted to remain neutral, or acquiesce in support of the rebels. The Loyalists were strongest in New York, and next in Pennsylvania—John Adams thought these colonies were so nearly divided that if New England on the one side, and Virginia on the other, had not kept them in awe, they would have joined the British. In the case of New York, there was a clear historical reason for this attitude—it was one of the smaller colonies, whose leaders before 1775 had felt its population and resources unequal to the burdens imposed upon it by its geographical position. It was no accident that in 1775 the sentiment of loyalty was stronger there than in any other Northern Colony, nor that so many of the leading provincial families were loyalists, who looked to England for protection.[1]

The results of following the conciliatory point of view were generally disastrous. On the advice of the Commander-in-Chief and Governor of Canada, Sir Guy Carleton, the British Government sent an army of around ten thousand men to Quebec, rather than to the centre of the strategic theatre, for operations in 1776. Even at Quebec, they could have been used with decisive effect. Carleton trapped the retiring American forces in 1776 with superior numbers, and then failed to exploit the confusion of the retreat. Instead of annihilating them he let them escape, imagining that by such magnanimous restraint (the Declaration of Independence was not yet signed) he might yet reclaim 'His Majesty's deluded subjects', by showing them 'the way to mercy is not yet shut'. By July 3rd, the rebel army had reached the safety of Crown Point on Lake Champlain, which would otherwise have been at the mercy of the British, and with it the bulk of the lake boats, essential to reach Albany on the Hudson River.[2] This half-hearted action repeated Carleton's mistake of the previous year, when he had announced that 'lest a consciousness of past offences should deter such miserable wretches from receiving that assistance which their distressed condition might require', if they sur-

[1] See A. C. Flick (ed.): *History of the State of New York,* 10 vols., New York, 1933, Vol. II, p. 242.
[2] Quoted G. S. Graham: *Empire of the North Atlantic,* London, 1951, p. 84.

rendered, they should be cared for in hospitals, and when re-
covered, would be free to return to their homes.[1] Howe believed
late in 1776 that the moderate forbearing of the Army was bringing many to return to allegiance: he declared that in New Jersey
it 'had very nearly induced a general submission'.[2] But, as
Washington said at the same time, the Howes were Commissioners to dispense pardon to repenting sinners—who in the
majority colonial view were neither sinners nor repentant;
anything other than a settlement according to their supposed
rights had no chance of success, and this the Howes were not
empowered to give.

Mackenzie revealed the inevitable effect when he wrote on
November 17th, 1776, that the rebels had no right to expect the
mild treatment they met with, but in this, as well as in everything
else since the beginning of operations, 'the British humanity has
been conspicuous'. He noted many as of opinion that if Howe
had treated the garrison of Fort Washington with the severity
which might have been inflicted on them by the laws of war, 'it
would have struck such a panic through the continent, as would
have prevented the Congress from ever being able to raise another
Army. They say we act with too much lenity and humanity
towards the rebels, and that 'tho it is praiseworthy, and might be
supposed to be the most likely means of bringing them back to a
sense of their duty, yet it will prove bad policy in the end; for
they now oppose us as long as they have the power, and when they
fall into our hands, instead of being treated as rebels taken in
arms against their Sovereign, they find they have nothing more
to dread then the common sufferings of prisoners of war'[3]—a
humanity Mackenzie himself approved.

Several opportunities were missed at that time of striking hard
at a force which was almost disintegrating, with time-served men
taking their departure despite all appeals to remain: instead,
there were such measures as the Proclamation of November 30th,
1776, calling on all bodies of armed men to disperse, all congresses

[1] S. G. Fisher: *The Struggle for American Independence*, 2 vols., Philadelphia,
1908, I, p. 418.   [2] Quoted, *ibid.*, I, p. 552.
[3] Mackenzie, *op. cit.*, I, pp. 110–11.

and conventions to desist from treasonable acts, with full pardon for treason for all those who reported to designated officials, civil and military, within sixty days, and took a simple oath of allegiance—which also implied sixty days in which no operations would be attempted. It was the response to this proclamation which caused Howe to extend his lines for the giving of protection to include Trenton, rather than making Brunswick the left and Elizabethtown or Newark the right, of the line—with disastrous effects before the end of the year. Similarly, Howe explained his inactivity at the end of 1777, and gave as his reason for not making any attack on Valley Forge, that 'a check at this period would probably counteract His Majesty's intentions of preparing the way for the return of peace by the bills proposed'. The conflict between these two motives of lenity and effective conduct of military operations meant that British plans in America were blunted by division. The choice which really faced the British from the beginning, but was not realised until 1778, was either to provide large reinforcements, and make a great effort, or to evacuate—to get on, or get out—but to the latter, the views of the King and the majority of the politically conscious were an insuperable obstacle, and when the choice was made, because of the entry of France into the war, it was too late for the former alternative to be put into operation. The fundamental mistake was the failure to appreciate the real character of the issue; to believe that the leaders in the Colonies could be reduced to terms, without resounding military disaster.

Lt.-Colonel Harcourt wrote of the Americans on March 17th, 1777, that though they were ignorant of the precision, order and even of the principles by which large bodies moved, yet they possessed many of the requisites of good troops—extreme cunning, great industry in moving ground and felling of wood,[1] activity and a spirit of enterprise upon any advantage. He noted that though the British Army had once treated them in the most contemptible light, they now saw them as a formidable enemy.[2] Colonial morale and Colonial forces were built up, while the

---

[1] Thomas Paine once compared them with 'a family of beavers'. Freeman, op. cit., IV, p. 571.   [2] Ibid., p. 380 n.

spirit of the British declined. As Charles Stuart put it, the rebels both got 'the notion of victory' and became habituated to the military profession.[1] Even Howe reported to Germain, on July 7th, 1777, that the war was now upon a far different scale with respect to the increased powers and strength of the enemy than in the previous year.[2] The changed attitude of Frederick Mackenzie is typical. In 1776, he had approved of the cautious conduct of General Howe in all the operations of that year;[3] by August 1778, he was severely critical of his former idol. 'Lines, if briskly attacked, are generally carried. It was the opinion of almost every officer in the British Army, that if we had attacked the rebel lines at Brooklyn, immediately after the rebels were driven into them on 27th August, 1776, we should have carried them with a small loss, and captured the whole of the rebel troops on Long Island.'[4]

It was hindsight indeed! Still, almost all officers came to be critical of delay and inactivity. J. Mervin Nooth wrote from New York, November 23rd, 1779, that nothing surely could be more shameful than perfect inactivity through the whole summer and autumn. Not a single attempt had been made to annoy the enemy, although, exclusive of sick, there had been twenty thousand men in arms in the neighbourhood of that city.[5] Among the troops, lowered morale was visible in increasing desertion and indiscipline, growing discontent and boredom (not countered by welfare such as troops to-day enjoy). On July 6th, 1777, Mackenzie reported a soldier of the 43rd Foot shooting himself (the third case that summer), and several desertions, some of them by men of good characters who were not suspected of such an act. He quite correctly ascribed this to 'our having remained so long in a state of inactivity'. The soldiers had nothing to do but mount guard once in three or four days, and nothing was attempted against the enemy by which their minds might be engaged. 'If we were to undertake little enterprizes against the enemy, in which we could run no risque, it would employ the minds of the soldiery give them something to do and to talk of, fit them for the undertaking

[1] Stuart Wortley, op. cit., pp. 101-2.   [2] C.O. 5: 94, 524-5.
[3] See above p. 110.   [4] Mackenzie, op. cit., II, p. 336.
[5] Historical Manuscripts Commission, Verulam MSS., p. 127.

and execution of those of a more arduous and serious nature, and would at the same time teach the young soldiers and give them confidence. Such enterprizes would also prevent the enemy from undertaking anything against us, and would harass them greatly. A contrary conduct invites them to make attempts, makes them insolent on finding they may be effected with impunity, and tends much to dispirit our own men.'[1] But the British refused to take advantage of things which ought to have operated in their favour.

[1] Mackenzie, *op. cit.*, I, pp. 146–7.

VI

WHY BRITISH DEFEAT? 2

Morale

If Lord Montgomery's thesis that morale is the greatest single factor in war be accepted, it was singularly lacking on the British side in the War of American Independence, and this absence did much to determine the eventual results. With the hopes of early victory frustrated by confused direction, the reaction was severe. There was growing criticism of inactivity and mismanagement, and increasing want of confidence in the commanders. Short periods of recurring optimism at the beginning of each campaign were soon replaced by despondency. The Generals quarrelled between themselves, attempting to throw the blame for delays and reverses upon others; this want of harmony and confidence spread to the junior officers and the ranks. Commanders themselves, dubious of the justice of their country's cause and its ability to assert and maintain it, disheartened those upon whose exertions they depended. For, as Greene pointed out to Thomas Jefferson in 1780, officers were the very soul of an army: one might as well attempt to animate a dead body into action as to expect to employ an army to advantage, when the officers were not perfectly easy in their circumstances, and happy in the service.[1]

Troops should always be set tasks which they can accomplish, and should be provided with everything which might assist them in that task; operations for which troops are not ready or trained, and which are likely to end in failure, should not be undertaken, except in dire emergency. The British constantly believed anything could be achieved against such opponents, and yet rarely allowed their troops to achieve it—so throwing

[1] Quoted Carrington, *op. cit.,* p. 530.

away the greatest fostering influence of confidence and morale, victory. And when they did operate, they too rarely fully prepared or fully supplied their troops. How could such leaders win victories, if their hearts and their spirits were not in the cause? How could the morale of the men be high with such feelings in their leaders? Lord Howe wrote to Germain on September 25th, 1775, of a letter from his brother, in these words: 'He professes his plan to be of greater compass than he feels himself equal to direct . . . If Government is unable to furnish the force he suggests, estimated in his opinion at the lowest amount, he then thinks it better policy to withdraw the troops entirely from the delinquent provinces, and leave the colonists to war with each other for sovereignty, the certain consequence, he judges of their determined separation from the Mother Country . . .'[1] Ambrose Serle regretted, on May 16th, 1777, the desponding speeches set about by people whose business it should be rather to encourage than dishearten men; he could not but doubt 'of the spirit of those officers, who take the field with any uncertainty respecting the justice of their country's cause, or its ability to assert and maintain it'.[2] Captain James Murray, an officer full of zeal when he went out to America early in 1776, sincerely wished by September 1777 that it was all over, 'a barbarous business and in a barbarous country. The novelty is worn off and I see no advantages to be reaped from it'. By August 1778, he was contemplating accepting a majority in the newly formed Edinburgh Regiment (80th Foot) at home; 'one motive I think must influence every man in such a situation, the prospect of getting away from this unhappy country and receding from the sight of the disgraceful situation to which a succession of the most unaccountable mismanagement has now reduced us, for my own part I am thoroughly disgusted'. And writing from St. Lucia in March 1779, he stated that nobody 'will stay that can avoid it.'[3] Charles Stuart drew the same picture, writing from America on October 7th, 1778: 'hardly one General officer who does not declare his intention of going home, the same with officers of all ranks who,

[1] *Stopford Sackville MSS.*, *op. cit.*, II, p. 9.
[2] Tatum, *op. cit.*, p. 224.   [3] Robson, *op. cit.*, pp. 48, 57, 64.

could they procure leave, wou'd be happy to leave the army . . .
this want of spirit staggers the resolution I had of returning, lest I
shou'd incur the imputation that ought to fall upon their unmanly
pusillanimous behaviour'. Was there any wonder that he later
reported his regiment 'all desponding'?[1] And, near the very end,
Mackenzie thought on September 22nd, 1781, 'our Generals and
Admirals don't seem to be in earnest about this business',[2] whilst
Robert Biddulph commented on March 12th, 1782, that we had
but few officers who were really anxious for the service, 'the
generallity call it a Bore, a word unknown I believe in the Am'n
Army'.[3]

As far as the troops were concerned, this declining morale was
bound to be affected by the general neglect of their conditions,
and lack of interest shown by the majority of officers.[4] Sergeant
Lamb pointed out on several occasions how both in peace and
war the general state of a regiment depended on the exertion and
the ability of the commanding officer and his juniors, 'by whom
the men are kept regular, steady, vigilant, and active in all cases'.
He frequently noted the 'indolence or caprice of the officer commanding, who from carelessness, or ill placed confidence, forbore
to inquire and inspect how the men were actually served'. To this,
he ascribed the frequency of desertion.[5] Howe had to order commanding officers at Boston to ensure the messes of their regiments
were visited, to see that the men boiled their pots, since many
were accused of selling their provisions.[6] Charles Stuart noted
after Bunker Hill that wounded soldiers were lying in their tents,
and crying for assistance to remove men who had just died. 'So
little precaution did Gen. Gage take to provide for the wounded
by making hospitals that they remained in this deplorable situation

---

[1] Stuart Wortley, *op. cit.* pp. 139, 153.   [2] Mackenzie, *op. cit.*, II, p. 641.
[3] Quoted in *American Historical Review*, Vol. XXIX, p. 106.
[4] See my chapter on 'The Art of War and the Social Foundations of the
Armed Forces' in the new edition of the Cambridge Modern History, Vol. VII,
and my article on 'The British Soldiers' Life in the mid-eighteenth century',
Army Quarterly.   [5] Lamb, *op. cit.*, pp. 91, 164, 165–6.
[6] E. E. Hale and B. F. Stevens (ed.): *General Sir William Howe's orderly book
at Charlestown, Boston, and Halifax, June 17th, 1775–May 26th 1776*, London,
1890, p. 94. Entry for September 20th.

for three days . . . so careful is the General to save expense, that tho' fresh meat is sold every day at a shilling a pound, he will not see the Hospitals provided with it. We lose more men than ever from wounds, besides their being crowded most inhumanly.'[1]

On June 27th, 1781, Mackenzie recorded the arrival of reinforcements from Ireland, at Charlestown, consisting of three regiments, with only sixty sick, only five men lost by death since embarkation, and wanting only three men to complete their establishment. He believed that before the end of the campaign, not a quarter of those men would be fit for duty, from the unhealthiness of the climate, and the season of the year in which they arrived. Had they done so in November, 'the men would have been by this time better able to bear the heat, . . . and many lives have been saved, which will now fall victims to climate alone'. He thought it 'wonderful' that after so much experience of the impropriety of sending troops from England to America and the West Indies in the spring, when the climate proved most fatal and destructive to them, the practice had not been changed. 'In time of war there may be a necessity for so doing, but there can be none in time of peace, when it was equally practiced. . . . More soldiers are lost to the nation by inattentions of this nature, than by the sword of the enemy.'[2] In every other respect—provisions, wood, quartering—this was typical. For winter quarters in New York in November 1781, several regiments were placed in situations where there were no materials for constructing huts or barracks, and were to camp in tents until they could build huts, or erect other covering for themselves during the winter; this despite the fact that barracks for three thousand, framed and ready to put together, had been on board a ship in New York harbour since the autumn of the previous year. In November 1781, that ship had still not been entirely unloaded, not a stick had been moved to the areas fixed on for their erection, nor had any bricks, of which the chimneys were to be built, been made.[3] The wonder surely is that desertion was not

[1] Stuart Wortley, *op. cit.*, p. 70.
[2] Mackenzie, *op. cit.*, II, pp. 554–5.   [3] *Ibid.*, pp. 687–8.

more frequent, and that mutinies did not break out—on both sides the men gave a striking example of fortitude and obedience.

One of the greatest mistakes made by the British during the war was their consistent under-estimation of their enemy: it was this contempt which caused them to make insufficient preparation, to neglect elementary precautions, to despise the improvisation necessary for American conditions, and to rely upon a complacent superior security, planning from campaign to campaign instead of embarking at once on a decisive overall plan. Despite increasing mention of 'unaccountable mismanagements', it rarely occurred to all ranks of the British to relate their reverses to any part the Americans might have played in them—there was only occasional (and very grudging) admission of their improving qualities. It was this indeed which had a great influence in preventing the British from proceeding in earnest; they continued to believe in the invincibility and sufficiency of the forces sent to suppress the revolution. The declaration by General James Grant in the House of Commons on February 2nd, 1775, that he would undertake to march from one end of America to the other with five thousand men, was characteristic; this common British view of the Americans was also expressed by General Murray, who had fought with them in the Seven Years' War, and was now Governor of Minorca, to Germain on September 6th, 1777: 'the native American is an effeminate thing, very unfit for and very impatient of war'[1]—a view increasingly out of date, as Gage had insisted in 1775.[2]

Before operations had begun, Evelyn was describing his future opponents in such contemptuous terms as 'a set of upstart vagabonds, the dregs and scorn of the human species',[3] while in practice it was this feeling which was responsible for the negligent duty of sentries, of which General Howe complained at Boston in 1775.[4]

The method of attack at Bunker Hill was excellently described by Carrington as 'an armed expression of contempt for the op-

---

[1] *Stopford Sackville MSS., op. cit.,* I, p. 371.   [2] See above p. 85.
[3] Scull, *op. cit.,* p. 51.   [4] Fortescue, *op. cit.,* III, No. 1688.

posing militia'.[1] Lord Rawdon hoped in January 1776 that 'we shall soon have done with these scoundrels, for one only dirties one's fingers by meddling with them',[2] while Mackenzie noted in November that year that the odd figures and appearance of rebel troops frequently excited the laughter of British soldiers.[3] In December, the Hessians made little effort to put Trenton in any state of defence; Rall, their commander, believing the rebels incapable of fighting, contemptuously referred to them as country clowns. Admiral Sir Peter Parker, writing of the capture of Colonel Prescot in Rhode Island, stated that the first acknowledged principle of the military was to be prepared for every possible event, and never to despise the enemy, 'yet we see this maxim frequently disregarded by very able and good officers';[4] which Mackenzie confirmed on June 10th, 1777, reporting a surprise attack on a post in Rhode Island, 'the common precautions of having the whole of the men loaded, and one third of them actually under arms throughout the night, had been neglected'.[5] Describing the dispositions at Elk Ferry on August 31st, 1777, Charles Stuart told his father that 'our usual carelessness prevails'. Had there been an active enemy, the dispositions were such that the army could be destroyed in detail, with no possibility of supporting one another. 'It seems singular, that when we are at some distance from these rebels, we omit taking common military precautions as a mode of showing our contempt, and when near to them our chiefs show an odd kind of care which lets every advantage slip from us'.[6] There were no fortifications at Germantown in 1777, Howe believing that works of that kind were 'apt to induce an opinion of inferiority', whereas he wished always to create 'the impression of superiority'[7]—an interesting comment on the state of morale then prevailing.

Robert Biddulph observed the same contempt, writing on September 4th, 1779, from New York. He thought Great Britain could not maintain this country much longer, and never

[1] Carrington, op. cit., p. 113.   [2] Hastings MSS., op. cit., III, p. 167.
[3] Mackenzie, op. cit., I, pp. 111–12.
[4] Barnes and Owen, op. cit., I, p. 290.   [5] Mackenzie, op. cit., I, p. 138.
[6] Stuart Wortley, op. cit., pp. 115–16.   [7] Narrative, op. cit., p. 27.

conquer it: among the things which prevented any alternative step, 'the contempt every soldier has for an American is not the smallest. They cannot possibly believe that any good quality can exist among them'.[1] In February 1781, General Greene was hopeful that from 'the pressing disposition' of Cornwallis, and 'the contempt he has for our army, we may precipitate him into some capital misfortune'.[2] The feeling was apparent even in the final capitulation at Yorktown, where a French observer noted that 'throughout the whole *triste cérémonie* the English exhibited morgue and not a little insolence. Above everything else they showed contempt for the Americans'.[3] This despite the fact that in retaliation for the British refusal to allow General Lincoln at Charlestown in 1780 the full honours of war, the British, when their world turned upside down, were required to march out with colours cased, their drums beating a British or German march. An American, James Thacher, thus described the scene: the royal troops, while marching through the line formed by the allied army, exhibited a decent and neat appearance, each soldier being furnished with a new uniform complete prior to the capitulation. 'It was in the field, when they came to the last act of the drama, that the spirit and pride of the British soldier was put to the severest test: here their mortification could not be concealed. Some of the platoon officers appeared to be exceedingly chagrined when giving the word "Ground Arms", and I am a witness that they performed this duty in a very unofficerlike manner and that many of the soldiers manifested a sullen temper, throwing their arms on the pile with violence, as if determined to render them useless.'[4] British pride was inconquerable, and a great aid to the Americans: even the Loyalist, Samuel Curwen, rejoiced in England at the news of Yorktown, 'perhaps the first of the kind that ever befell this haughty, America-despising people'.

The nature of the country in the American colonies necessitated

[1] *American Historical Review*, XXIX, p. 90.
[2] Greene, *op. cit.*, III, p. 131.
[3] S. Bonsal, *The Cause of Liberty*, London, 1947, p. 158.
[4] James Thacher, *Military Journal during the American Revolutionary War, from 1775 to 1783*, Hartford, 1854.

a new kind of warfare, the 'service of the woods' as against the
regular forms of European warfare, for which the British were
trained.[1] Surprise, mobility and use of ground can still to this day
achieve success, even against vast numbers and improved weapons,
and the British, largely untrained in New World warfare, and
too proud to learn, were here facing masters at this kind of warfare, against whom, proscribed by their European background,
and seeing no real need to descend to the level of the Americans,
they never improvised sufficiently. Lord Percy realised the advantage the Americans possessed at Lexington: he wrote on
April 20th, 1775, that whoever looked on them as an irregular
mob would make a great mistake. 'They have men amongst them
who know very well what they are about, having been employed
as rangers against the Indians and Canadians, and this country
being much covered with wood, and hilly, is very advantageous
for their method of fighting.'[2] The best description of the effect
of that method of fighting, and of the country, upon the British
Regular was given during the Seven Years' War (in July 1758) by
Robert Napier. He described the British as thrown 'in to some
kind of consternation': 'the fire round them, tho' at some distance,
seem'd to alarm them; in the wood, where nothing can be seen,
but what is near, the men's fancy is worse, or the enemy more
numerous than they are; our own fire they are apt some times to
think is the enemy's; our irregulars yelling is believed by those
who are not engaged, to be the enemy; in short . . . numbers of
our people cannot hear a great deal of firing round them coolly. I
mean when they hear and do not see'.[3] And Burgoyne writes
about Morgan's riflemen at Bemis Heights: 'great numbers of
marksmen, armed with rifle-barrel pieces; these, during an
engagement, hovered upon the flanks in small detachments, and
were very expert in securing themselves and in shifting their
ground. In this action, many placed themselves in high trees in

[1] For an extended treatment of this subject, see my 'British Light Infantry in
the Eighteenth Century: the effect of American Conditions', *Army Quarterly*,
January 1952.
[2] C. K. Bolton (ed.): *Letters of Hugh Earl Percy*, Boston, 1902, p. 53.
[3] S. Pargellis (ed.): *Military Affairs in North America, 1748–1765*. London,
1936, pp. 418–19.

the rear of their own line, and there was seldom a minute's interval of smoke, in any part of our line, without officers being taken off by a single shot'.[1]

Thomas Hughes, who arrived in Canada in June 1776, noted that most of the summer was spent in making boats for transporting troops, and training the men 'to the exercise calculated for the woody country of America, with which they were totally unacquainted'.[2] The difference from European methods of warfare was soon obvious to participants. Sergeant Lamb found that in fighting in the woods, 'the battalion manoeuvring and excelling of exercise' were of little use. 'To prime, load, fire, and charge with the bayonet expeditiously were the chief points worthy of attention'.[3] At his first experience of action, near Ticonderoga in 1777, Lieutenant Thomas Anburey thought all manual exercise 'but an ornament'; the only object of importance in it was that of loading, firing, and charging with bayonets'[4]—individual, rather than mass, action. Lamb attempted to justify Burgoyne's conduct of Saratoga by arguing that he had offered battle to draw out the Americans on the plain, where 'veteran and well appointed forces must always prevail over soldiers, such as the colonial regiments were composed of. To such men wood fighting and skirmishing among intersected and intricate grounds, is peculiarly favourable, as there experienced Generals and old soldiers are left at a loss, and obliged to encounter unforeseen obstacles and accidents which demand new movements, and momentary measures, in the execution whereof every officer ought to be an excellent General and every company ably disposed for whatever the passing minute of time might bring about'.[5]

European manoeuvre dealt in days and hours, rather than minutes. It was surely futile to wait for European conditions before getting down to vigorous action—indeed, it was the firm opinion of Gates that had Burgoyne advanced from Ticonderoga in July 1777 with only his auxiliaries, a few light guns, and the

---

[1] J. Burgoyne, *State of the Expedition from Canada*, London, 1780, p. 163.
[2] E. A. Benarins (ed.): *A Journal by Thomas Hughes, 1778–1789*, Cambridge, 1947, pp. 5–6.   [3] Lamb, *op. cit.*, p. 175.
[4] Anburey, *op. cit.*, I, p. 333.   [5] Lamb, *op. cit.*, p. 200.

best of his regulars—his grenadiers and light infantry particularly—he could have got through to Albany in three weeks.
Simcoe, commander of the Queen's Rangers in this war, one of
the best exponents of new formations, wrote that in the colonial
service, only individuals were of importance.[1] The principles on
which Simcoe based his training reveal the difference between
American and European warfare. To begin with, officers and men
on that service should despise all those conventions without which
it would be thought impracticable for European armies to move.
His men were given no opportunity of being instructed in the
general discipline of the army, nor did he consider that necessary
—the essential duties of vigilance, activity, and endurance of
fatigue were best learnt in the field. There were few manual
exercises, but careful instruction was given in firing, and in the
use of the bayonet. No rotation of duties, except in ordinary
camp routine, was allowed—those officers were selected for a
service who appeared to be the most capable of executing it. No
service was measured by the numbers employed on it, but by its
own importance. Particular stress was laid on interior economy—
since cleanliness in every respect not only preserved the health of
the troops but reflected military efficiency. Written orders were
avoided as far as possible: officers were called together to hear
them, and given an opportunity to question them.

Simcoe argued that a light corps gave opportunities to show
professional merit, made officers and men self-dependent for resources, and required that prompt decision which, in the common
rotation of duty, subordinate officers had very little chance of
exhibiting[2]—probably a further reason why senior officers neglected such improvisation. Light Infantry, dispersed and indi-
vidualistic, did not suit the eighteenth-century European pattern.

European habits died hard in America. Burgoyne's orders of
July 14th, 1777, observed that the injunction given about officers'

---

[1] Yet Anburey commented on German ensigns of forty and fifty, commanding troops not much younger, and questioned if they were suitable for an
active and vigorous campaign in the thick woods of America. II, p. 442.

[2] John Graves Simcoe: *A Journal of the operations of the Queens Rangers from
the end of the year 1777 to the conclusion of the late American War*, Exeter, 1787,
pp. 4–5, and Introduction.

baggage before the army took the field had not been complied with (not even by the General himself). Regiments were incumbered with much more baggage than they could possibly have the means to convey when they left the lakes and rivers; any baggage not 'indispensably necessary' must be sent back to Ticonderoga, 'or upon the first sudden movement, it must inevitably be left on the ground'. Burgoyne reminded those gentlemen who had served in America during the last war that the officers used soldiers' tents, and often confined their baggage to a knapsack for months together—an unwelcome, but a very necessary, rebuke.[1] The ordinary soldier, despite the practical experience of Bunker Hill and elsewhere, was still weighed down with full European equipment. 'In marching through a difficult country', Lamb commented, 'he was obliged to bear a burden which none except the old Roman veteran ever bore. He carried a knapsack, blanket, haversack containing four days provisions, a canteen for water, and a proportion of his tent furniture, which, superadded to his accoutrement, arms and sixty rounds of ammunition, made a great load and large luggage, weighing about sixty pounds.'[2]

There was much comment when the European close season for fighting was not observed. Captain Sir James Murray wrote to his sister from Perth Amboy, February 25th, 1777, 'you would hardly believe that *au moment qu'il est*, and *au tems qu'il fait*, which is I assure much more severe than you can have any idea of even in the remotest regions of Perthshire, we should still be fighting away as if it was the month of July, which is in my humble opinion as great an incongruity as wearing point ruffles or eating hot rolls and butter at the season'.[3]

Tactics were also affected by the same European dead hand—the lack of co-ordinated campaigns, the siege rather than the *coup de main*, which vitiated Howe's victory on Long Island in August 1776, and which was responsible for the failure of the French move against Savannah in 1779. If the French, instead of proceeding by the slow steps of a regular siege, had directly

---

[1] Anburey, *op. cit.*, I, pp. 353–4.
[2] *Ibid.*, I, p. 379. Lamb, *op. cit.*, pp. 178–9.
[3] Robson, *op. cit.*, p. 38. See also Stuart Wortley, pp. 87–90.

assaulted the town on their arrival from the West Indies on September 17th, they would have carried it: as it was, the siege failed, and had to be raised in October. Above all, Howe was obsessed with the idea of taking Philadelphia, 1777, seat of Congress and a national capital, the seizure of which would end the war. Even Washington commented to Robert Morris in March 1777 on Howe's failure to 'miss so favourable an opportunity of striking a capital stroke against a city from whence we derive so many advantages, the carrying of which would give such éclat to his arms, and strike such a damp to ours'.[1]

On the British side, the War of American Independence gives precise proof of Clemenceau's well-known comment that war (and for that matter, peace) was too important and serious a matter to be left to the Generals. Contrary to accepted belief, British commanders in America were given great latitude in both their planning and their actions, with results which came far wide of their hopes and intentions: the frequency with which the predictions of the military failed in any way to correspond with the actual event is a characteristic feature of this war, while the prediction that it would be all over 'this campaign' expressed by succeeding Commanders-in-Chief came to have an ominous ring. The majority of the British Commanders in America lacked drive and character, which Napoleon put as 'the ballast without which the ship will capsize'. Passive, impersonal, and weak command had the inevitable result of weakened morale, want of determination and eventually failure. Most of them made pictures of a situation which existed only in their own imaginations, which Napoleon thought the worst fault in a general, and they all lacked the intangible rated highly by both Frederick the Great and Napoleon, luck—an invaluable attribute. General Murray, writing to Germain in November 1778, described the Commander-in-Chief in England, Amherst, as 'a very great favourite of Fortune, which the Romans, I believe very justly, thought a necessary ingredient in their generals'.[2] Lord Wavell has suggested that what was really meant was, 'was he bold?'[3] A bold

---

[1] Carrington, op. cit., p. 295.   [2] Stopford Sackville MSS., op. cit., I, p. 372.
[3] A. P. Wavell, Soldiers and Soldiering, London, 1953, p. 20.

general may be lucky, but no general can be lucky unless he is bold—and this quality was conspicuous only by its absence. However well-prepared, however well carried out, victory in a battle is finally determined by sheer chance. Generals who allowed themselves to be bound and hampered by regulations and old traditions were unlikely to be successful in America.

As early as December 14th, 1775, Charles Stuart wrote to Bute that 'we have a pack of the most ordinary men to command us, who give themselves trouble about the merest trifles, whilst things of consequence go unregarded . . . I hope to God they will send some generals worthy the command of a British Army from home'[1]—a plea which was never answered. Howe is usually criticised for sloth and inactivity, without any consideration of the circumstances and the physical conditions he faced. The British pursuit of the disorganised Americans across New Jersey in 1776 took nineteen days to cover seventy-four miles, not because of Howe's sloth, as is often alleged, but for the more practical reasons of rain, bad roads and destroyed bridges. But Howe, as Galloway said, always succeeded in every attack he thought proper to make, as far as he chose to succeed; the flank march at Brooklyn, and the conduct of Brandywine, suggest that Howe, as befitted one who had commanded light infantry under Wolfe, could well adapt himself to American conditions —when he saw the need to do so. Allan Maclean gave the best contemporary criticism of him, which is still of value: 'a very honest man, and . . . a very disinterested one. Brave he certainly is, and would make a very good executive officer under another's command, but he is not by any means equal to a C. in C. I do not know any employment that requires so many great qualifications either natural or acquired as the Commander in Chief of an Army. He has, moreover, got none but very silly fellows about him—a great parcel of old women—most of them improper for American service . . it is truly too serious a matter that brave men's lives should be sacrificed to be commanded by such Generals . . . Men of real genius cannot long agree with Howe; he is too dull to encourage great military merit—our great

[1] Stuart Wortley, *op. cit.*, p. 74.

men at home seem to be as little anxious about encouraging true
military abilities as our Commanders here . . . Had we a man of
real capacity at the head of the Army, the rebellion would have
been at an end.'[1]

About Clinton, there is a general consensus of opinion. Charles
Stuart considered him unfit to command a troop of horse, let
alone an army.[2] A newcomer to his Army in 1779 described it as
commanded 'by a person that has no abilities to plan, nor firmness
to execute, the most trivial military operation', and repeated the
plea of Stuart for a man of resolution or ability. 'To have an
ignorant, capricious, irresolute commander is the excess of madness in administration.'[3] Clinton was a man to whom complaint
was second nature—'of all men the most jealous', as Germain
described him in September 1780, 'and when he has not the whole
credit of a measure is apt to dislike the plan, however well concerted'.[4] Robert Biddulph pictured him correctly in August 1781,
as not having a strength and soundness of capacity sufficient to
distinguish and decide great objects, 'and like the hungry ass
between two bundles of hay, for want of preference starves'.[5]
There is a curious similarity between Clinton and Lord North.
Both were prone to morbid introspection, pessimistic, desirous of
shunning responsibility, and indecisive; both showed the same
insincerity of desire to give up the first place, into which they
had been 'forced'. Clinton could have done most to retrieve
Burgoyne's situation at Saratoga. Fully informed of Burgoyne's
position, and of Howe's wishes, knowing there was nothing
between his force moving up the Hudson, and Gates, he took
Forts Montgomery and Clinton, sent Vaughan as far as Kingston,
and then, as though appalled by his energy, returned with the
entire force to New York.

Cornwallis never understood the influence which the use of the
navy and of sea-power could have given him. There is a remarkable contrast between his failure in the conduct of operations in
America, where the Navy could have assisted him, and his later

---

[1] *Ibid.*, pp. 105–7.   [2] *Ibid.*, p. 83.   [3] *Verulam MSS., op. cit.*, p. 127.
[4] Historical Manuscripts Commission, *Various Collections*, VI Knox MSS.,
p. 171.   [5] *American Historical Review*, XXIX, p. 103.

successes in India, where such aid was unnecessary. In moving to the Chesapeake (without any authority whatever), he brought his force both within reach of the main American army under Washington, and within striking distance of the French squadron at Rhode Island; his move made possible combined operations by the enemy, for a defensive post in Virginia was liable to become a prey to an enemy with a temporary superiority at sea. As Cornwallis himself saw, an army on the defensive, which failed to gain an early and decisive victory, would find itself unable to maintain its original momentum, and be forced sooner or later to yield up its gains. Burgoyne's main failing was to attempt to co-relate his liking for amateur dramatics (both as author and producer) with his military career: he was always working up to a climax, and when it eventually came, he completely failed in his stage-management through basic incapacity.[1] As soon as he was caught in a trap, and not before, he began thinking up his excuses, particularly his peremptory instructions—whereas as one of his foes noted, the real reason was his own character, 'sanguine and precipitate and puffed-up with vanity, which failings may lead him into traps that may undo him'.[2]

The need for experience of American conditions, and knowledge of American troops, was confirmed when Benedict Arnold, having joined the British, put his new colleagues to shame. As Frederick Mackenzie commented on his expedition into Virginia in early 1781: 'I am almost sorry, (if I may venture to say so), for the sake of the reputation of the British Generals, that such a man as Arnold should have executed with an inferior force, what a British General (Leslie) did not even attempt with a superior one. This is a strong proof how much the success of an enterprise depends on chusing a proper person to command it. Arnold is bold, daring, and prompt in the execution of what he undertakes. The officer who commanded the last expedition, equally brave, but diffident and indecisive'[3]—a comment which

---

[1] On this, see Jane Clark, 'The Responsibility for the failure of the Burgoyne Campaign', *American Historical Review*, Vol. XXXV.

[2] See Fisher, *op. cit.*, II, p. 58.

[3] Mackenzie, *op. cit.*, II, p. 446; see also pp. 521, 551.

could be passed on too many of the British commanders in this war, who resembled closely Robertson, military governor of New York, 'a mixture of good sense, and inconsistency, and seems inclining to dotage'.[1] Mackenzie summed up the position in June 1781: there were very few generals who could be trusted with the command of a corps of any consequence, or the execution of any enterprise of importance. (He named Arnold as the exception, the only one who 'comprehends any military enterprise of a complicated nature'.) He thought 'our military system is undoubtedly a bad one, when the King has it not in his power to bring forth into action the talents of those generals he has at home, among whom there certainly are several men of genius and capacity. But this is an unpopular war, and men of ability do not chuse to risk their reputation by taking an active part in it'.[2] The usual accusation made is that the commanders in America had no chance to show their talents (real or imaginary) because both strategy and tactics were rigidly dictated from London. But this was a convenient umbrella under which mediocre commanders took shelter, which is not borne out by examination of the circumstances. Carleton complained to Shelburne that the arrangements for the campaign based on Canada in 1777 were made in England, even down to the disposition of the small body of troops which was to stay in Canada, and Anburey, in a well-known passage, wrote of operations planned by those, who, sitting in their closets, with a map before them, ridiculously expected the movements of an army to keep pace with their rapid ideas, not only directing general operations, but particular movements of a campaign, 'carried on through a country in interior deserts, and at a distance of three thousand miles, without allowing the general who is to conduct that army, to be invested with powers for changing the mode of war as circumstances may occur'.[3] Howe, as did Clinton later, put as grounds for his resignation the little attention given to his recommendations since the commencement of his command.

In actual fact, the eighteenth-century system of government

---

[1] *Ibid.*, pp. 675–6. See also p. 537. [2] *Ibid.*, p. 551.
[3] Anburey, *op. cit.*, II, pp. 4–6.

was not suited for centralised direction of war, and did not function in that way, not even under the elder Pitt in the Seven Years' War: more centralised control was precisely what was most required in any British administration faced with war, particularly when dealing with commanders such as Clinton. In this case, because of underestimation of the enemy, no master-plan was ever prepared. As John Robinson pointed out in August 1777, war could not be carried on in departments—something was required 'in all the several parts which set the springs at work', to give 'efficacy and energy to the movements, without which the machine must fail'.[1] For lack of it, as General Harvey had foreseen in 1776, America was likely to become 'an ugly job . . . a damned affair indeed'. Unless a settled plan of operations were agreed upon, he quite rightly believed that the British Army would be destroyed (as it was at the last) 'by damned driblets'. Distance (and therefore time) rendered it necessary to leave much to the local commander-in-chief, and this was done—every one of them submitted for the 'next campaign' his own plans and considerations, and few were seriously altered. Neither the general conception nor the detailed plan of the campaign con-ducted from Canada in 1777 was the work of Germain.

The general conception was suggested by Carleton himself in September 1775, when he begged for an army with which to strike a blow to the south. Such a force was sent out in 1776, despite the superior strategical claims of Boston, but Carleton failed to achieve his own purpose. This was once more the object of the 1777 campaign; the detailed plans were prepared by Bur-goyne himself, who was present at their discussion in London. He wrote to Fraser on May 6th, 1777, that 'being called upon at home for my opinion on the conduct of the war on this side I gave it freely: the material parts of it have been adopted by the Cabinet'.[2] (It is worth recalling that in that plan, 'a co-operation of Howe's army was not expected, but the expedition undertaken as an independent enterprize to be executed by the force alloted

---

[1] Barnes and Owen, *op. cit.,* I, p. 240.

[2] C. T. Atkinson (ed.): 'Some Evidence for Burgoyne's Expedition', *Journal Society for Army Historical Research,* Vol. XXVI, p. 129.

for it'.)[1] The instructions later sent to Burgoyne were not ample, because they 'related to a plan formed by the person to whom they were addressed',[2] and this was normally the case throughout the war.

Howe certainly never embarked on any plan which was not his own in conception and detail: he was sent out under no binding or positive instructions, but with full discretionary power to suppress the rebellion. He could refuse (and did) to carry out a direction if he deemed it unwise, impracticable, or too hazardous; and he was never ordered to help Burgoyne, Germain only trusting that what Howe intended in the South would be completed in time for him to co-operate: 'as you must, from your situation and military skill, be a competent judge of the propriety of every plan, His Majesty does not hesitate to approve'.[3] And, despite the fact that all his subordinate commanders, with the exception of Cornwallis and Grant, stressed the necessity of such co-operation, and reprobated the move to the southward, Howe made no alteration in his plans—which Washington and Hamilton found unaccountable on either grounds of common sense or military propriety.[4] General Robertson testified before the Committee of Inquiry into Howe's conduct that he had urged upon Germain the importance of not crippling Howe's movements by positive instructions, and that Germain had acted on this advice throughout.[5] In Clinton's time, as late as November 1780, Germain was still restricting himself to urging on the Commander-in-Chief that 'vigor and alertness, in following up a blow, are the sure means of subduing rebellion'.[6] The nature of the blows was left to Clinton to decide. He sat in perfect inactivity, with not a single attempt to annoy, believing the enemy must collapse from their own internal disputes. Cornwallis not only complained of direction from London, but from New York, Clinton leaving him without 'the smallest particle of discretionary power'—this from a General who had marched into North Carolina, and then into Virginia, without the slightest authority. This was his final excuse

---

[1] *Stopford Sackville MSS., op. cit.,* II, p. 89.   [2] *Ibid.*

[3] *Ibid.,* p. 67.   [4] Freeman, *op. cit.,* IV, pp. 443, 446–7, 451.

[5] Fisher, *op. cit.,* II, p. 69 n.   [6] C.O. 5: 100, 336.

for failing to attack the French, when landed twelve miles from Yorktown, before they joined with Lafayette. This is a subject which still requires much detailed enquiry.

The intervention of the French in 1778, adding national to civil war, created problems which Great Britain had rarely had to face, particularly in the war at sea, on which all in America depended.[1] For the British, empire was a unique blend of sea power and trade. Sea power meant primarily the control of ocean communications, ability to bar the enemy's access to his overseas possessions. Previously in the eighteenth century, Britain, by cutting off enemy warships and merchant vessels, had not only attained naval supremacy but had forced enemy colonies into submission: indeed, a monopoly of empire and sea power such as the British possessed in 1763 was a source of disquiet to all rivals. The second function of sea power was the protection of trade, as the long series of Navigation Acts shows. The destruction of the naval forces of the enemy in time of war became the accepted means to the British end, the destruction of the instrument that defended and guaranteed the existence of commerce. Once an opponent was reduced in battle, or weakened by blockade, his trade routes as well as his colonies were at the mercy of the victor. With the intervention of the French, the prospect increasingly was that Britain's usual position would be reversed, and that all these advantages would be garnered by her opponents.

Britain might have been spared some of her worst humiliation had it not been for the spectacular recovery of France begun almost immediately after 1763, in comparison with the cutting down and neglect of the Navy in this country.[2] In the long-drawn-out duel for Empire between France and England in the 'Second Hundred Years' War', the French had always seen the strategic points which remain vital to this day—they early perceived for example the possibilities of a great circle of river and

[1] On this, see Graham, *op. cit.*

[2] See H. W. Richmond, *Statesmen and Sea Power*, Oxford, 1947 edn. Ch. IV, Part II.

lake stretching from the Great Lakes to New Orleans, which would shut out the British, and give themselves the whole of the North American Continent. But only constant support from France could have made possible the realisation of this idea.

Without the continued support of a strong navy, French possessions in North America were bound to be hostages to the English fleet, and for geographical reasons, France required what she rarely achieved, a two-ocean navy, Atlantic and Mediterranean. Constantly pulled to and fro between imperial dreams and continental attachments, the periods of maritime ardour never lasted long enough to compensate for the prolonged intervals of indifference and neglect when European interests predominated. In 1778, inspired by the motive of revenge, and untroubled by European distractions, France was able to play a decisive part in the operations in the New World. From the time of her intervention, Britain's only hope of carrying on the campaign in North America depended upon her ability to keep her sea communications intact. Had the French immediately secured American bases, and concentrated on that objective, the British would have had to withdraw from lack of supplies. But, in true eighteenth-century fashion, France first concentrated her forces in the Caribbean, to collect sugar islands; and British transports and victualling ships made their way to New York for the better part of two years with comparatively minor interference. When Washington at last secured the support of a strong French fleet off North America in 1781, independence was sealed.

The French Navy, joined in 1779 by that of Spain, was in a position not only to challenge British superiority, but actually to win command of the sea. As Sandwich, who had done much to make good the neglect of the British Navy, put it: 'it will be asked why, when we have as great, if not a greater force than ever we had, the enemy are superior to us. To this it is to be answered that England till this time was never engaged in a sea war with the House of Bourbon thoroughly united, their naval force unbroken, and having no other war or object to draw off their attention and resources'. At the same time, 'we have no one friend or ally to assist us, on the contrary all those who ought to be our allies except Portugal act against us'.[1] The effect of 1763 now came home to roost—and here is another cause of British defeat—political isolation, a failure of diplomacy. In practical terms, from 1778, Britain simply had not the ships to command the seas, whether off Ushant, in the North Sea, in Chesapeake Bay, or in the Indian Ocean: the role of the Navy, as exercised in previous wars, could not be undertaken.

Faced with so painful a dilemma, a less resolute government might have pocketed its pride, and its losses, and concentrated completely on the struggle with the hereditary enemy. Here again, George III saw to the root of this matter. He had written to North on February 9th, 1778, that the only means of making a war against the French successful would be to withdraw the greater part of the troops from America, and employ them with the Navy against French and Spanish settlements. If Great Britain was to carry on both a land war against the rebels, and also contend with France and Spain, 'it must be feeble in all parts and consequently unsuccessful'.[2] Hence his authorisation of North's conciliatory proposals, which offered everything to the rebels save the independence they wanted. This neither the King nor his ministers nor the majority of the politically conscious were prepared to grant—'to treat with independence can never be possible'. What was strategically necessary was politically impossible, with the results foreseen by the King, who was the chief obstacle to the concession of independence. The question is whether, even if the French had not intervened in the North American theatre, Great Britain could have found the resources and men to subdue a quarter of a continent largely in a position to support its own forces, and more than three thousand miles distant.

As it was, the Navy now had to face superior opponents, threats to supplies and communications, constant uncertainty and risks—the expedition to St. Lucia ordered in March 1778 did not sail from New York until early November because of this uncertainty and the presence of a French fleet. These difficulties were apparent

---

[1] Barnes and Owen, op. cit., III, p. 170. See also IV, p. 300.
[2] Fortescue, op. cit., IV, No. 2190.

to all. An increasingly important factor was the caution imposed by the dead hand of the British Permanent Fighting Instructions, coupled with the sacrosanct doctrine of the maintenance of the line of battle. Gambier pointed out to Sandwich as early as September 1778 that 'chiefship, jockeyship, and superiority of skill in manoeuvring was . . . our reliance for victory in case the fleets should engage';[1] these were the very qualities prevented by those instructions. A commander might break most other commandments with some hope of survival, but if he broke the parallel, conterminous, inviolable line, the odds were that he broke himself. The need for risks to be taken was prevented by the almost inevitable result. George III quite rightly emphasised to Sandwich on March 6th, 1780, that the country which would hazard most would get the advantage, and that by keeping our enemies employed, we should perplex them more than by a cautious, less active line of conduct.[2] He reiterated this on September 3rd, 1781—this country, with such numerous enemies, must be ruined 'unless what we want of strength is made up in activity and resolution. Caution has certainly made this war less brilliant than the former; and if that is alone to direct our operations . . . without much foresight it is easy to foretell that we must be great losers'.[3] This placed great responsibility upon naval commanders. As Sandwich said to Rodney in September 1780, it was impossible to have a superior fleet in every part, and unless 'our commanders in chief will take the great line as you do, and consider the King's whole Dominions as under their care, our enemies must find us unprepared somewhere, and carry their point against us.'[4] But men like Rodney were rare; the average commander was represented more by men like Rear-Admiral Thomas Graves—who, in the course of a few hours on September 5th, 1781, twice held the main western fleet of France, and with it the issue of the war, in the hollow of his hand, and let it slip by rigid adherence to the line, never more fatal than on that occasion.

[1] Barnes and Owen, *op. cit.*, II, p. 311.
[2] *Ibid.*, III, p. 243. See also p. 164.
[3] *Ibid.*, IV, p. 55.   [4] *Ibid.*, III, p. 231.

All operations in America and the West Indies after 1778 really became combined operations, and for these the British were not yet ready. The reasons why there were so few decisive combined operations before the present day emerge clearly from this war—the peculiar difficulties involved in days of sail and poor communications, the shunning of co-operation between service leaders unable to appreciate each other's problems and snags, which also involved subordination of one service to the other. The question is not one of incompetence in army and naval commanders, but of mutual distrust and friction, at their height in this war. Peter Parker, who took part in one of the earliest of such operations against Charleston, South Carolina, in 1776, told Sandwich 'how necessary the most perfect harmony is on such occasions'.[1] It was the absence of such harmony and confidence in some principal commanders which Ambrose Serle deplored in April 1778.[2] Rodney noticed this friction as soon as he arrived in the West Indies to take over command in 1779; by December 1780, the position was such that he advised Germain 'if Administration would consider the difficulty of making different Commanders-in-chief agree they would find it answer their own and the nation's expectations better, if there was, during this very important crisis, but one commander-in-chief, by land or sea, responsible for the war both in America and every part of the West Indies'.[3] Even discounting Rodney's personal ambitions, the overwhelming difficulty here was the absence of sufficient facilities of communication; but the stalemate caused by the friction between Clinton and Arbuthnot, which prevented almost any operations between July 1780 and July 1781 showed the need for a better system of command than yet existed. Private pique too often took the place of national duty.

Ships, not fortresses, or land victories, were the key to supremacy in the New World, and ships not necessarily in American waters, as the Seven Years' War showed. George III put it to Sandwich on June 24th, 1781, that if we could demolish either a

[1] *Ibid.*, I, p. 168.   [2] Tatum, *op. cit.*, p. 282.
[3] *Stopford Sackville MSS.*, *op. cit.*, II, pp. 194-5.

considerable French or Spanish squadron, 'we should then be in a situation to gain our wonted superiority at sea, without which an honourable end to the war is not to be effected'[1]—a thesis later proved by the Battle of the Saints in April 1782. Washington wrote to de Grasse in August that 'whatever efforts are made by the land forces, the Navy must have the casting vote in the present contest'.[2] Loss of the command of the sea—off Brest as much as off the American coast—was the prime cause of the surrender at Yorktown, and that surrender finally convinced the British of the impossibility of recovering the American colonies. The British failed to bring off the customary last victory on their traditional element—the sea (an element whose assets had been largely ignored by her military commanders). As Mackenzie wrote on September 15th, 1781, 'Everything depends on the event of the action which is likely to happen between the fleets. Should our fleet be defeated the loss of the whole army under Lord Cornwallis is much to be dreaded, the consequence of which would be that we could no longer attempt to prosecute the war against the rebels, and must necessarily admit their claim of independence: on the contrary, should our fleet be successful, and gain a decisive victory over that of France, we have a prospect of defeating the united forces opposed to Lord Cornwallis; and thereby putting an end to the rebellion'.[3] The Navy had the casting vote in the contest, and was unable to secure the decision —in Mackenzie's opinion, partly because of caution and of lack of confidence: 'they do not seem to be hearty in the business, or to think that the saving that Army is an object of such material consequence.'[4]

One factor with increasing political force has to be considered— what George III described as 'the load of debt we labour under', the mounting expense of the war and the declining state of British finances. Opposition groups in Parliament were at last able to find an issue on which they could unite, and in which they could enlist more general support—especially that of the

[1] Barnes and Owen, op. cit., IV, p. 162.   [2] Richmond, op. cit., p. 156.
[3] Mackenzie, op. cit., II, p. 633.   [4] Ibid., p. 664.

supremely important body in the eighteenth-century House of Commons, the independent country gentlemen, who were particularly concerned about the growing financial burden of war and, therefore, about economic reform. It was the country gentry and the actual electorate, not the masses, who originated and largely supported the so-called popular movement of 1779-1780; it was a number of Yorkshire freeholders (who considered that the land tax placed an unfair burden on them) who summoned the meeting of the gentry of that county for December 30th, 1779, some of them men who hitherto had actually supported the Government, were totally free from all group influence, and equally unconnected with the leaders of Administration or their opponents. The balance in the House of Commons was held by these independent members, over sixty of whom voted for Dunning's well-known resolution on April 6th, 1780, that 'the influence of the Crown has increased, is increasing, and ought to be diminished', and whose refusal to support his later resolution of April 24th that till grievances were redressed, the existing Parliament should neither be prorogued nor dissolved, was responsible for its defeat. To support a mere general resolution was one thing, to suggest action distasteful to all conscientious politicians quite another. It was the action of this group again which was decisive in the fall of the North Administration in 1782, and in the establishment of the younger Pitt in 1784.

Lord North had foreseen the trouble financial difficulties might cause, when he had advised the King on March 25th, 1778, that the country was totally unequal to a war with Spain, France and America. 'Great Britain will suffer more in the war, than her enemies; he does not mean by defeats, but by an enormous expense, which will ruin her, and will not in any degree be repaid by the most brilliant victories';[1] Savile sensed the same disquiet in July 1779 when he told the Duke of Portland that Englishmen would soon realise 'we were to be taxed and stamped ourselves, instead of inflicting taxes and stamps on others'[2] There was not

---

[1] Fortescue, *op. cit.*, IV, No. 2247.
[2] Manuscripts of William Henry Cavendish-Bentinck, third Duke of Portland, July 19th, 1779, University of Nottingham Library.

only the disruption of trade and loss of markets as the war expanded, but the increasing weight of taxation—in 1776, the Land Tax was increased from three to four shillings, the carriage tax extended to stage coaches, the stamp duty on deeds raised from two shillings and sixpence to three and sixpence, and an additional halfpenny placed on the newspaper tax; in 1777, a tax was imposed on men servants, the stamp duty increased to five shillings, and a tax placed on property sold by auction; in 1778, the wine tax was increased, and a tax placed on inhabited houses; in 1779, there was a general rise in customs and excise of 5%, but 15% on beer, soap, candles, and leather, and the carriage tax was extended. This heavy burden of expenditure and taxation was behind the increasing questioning of the war. The comment by Lord Pembroke to Sir William Hamilton on May 1st, 1781, was representative: 'our expenses, extravagances, and the wonderful ignorance and profusion in the finance line are more than enough to undo us alone'.[1] The same waste was visible in America from an early date—on June 6th, 1777, Serle remarked 'nothing seems quick and urgent but expense',[2] and Mackenzie frequently commented on the same topic.[3]

Expense and final defeat also played their part in the increasingly bitter political struggle between the Administration and the group in opposition, who took every opportunity to discredit the ministry. In it can also be discerned the main constitutional theme of the reign of George III: the distribution of power between Parliament and the King: the practical difficulties of which arose from their uncertain and undefined mutual relations. The Revolution settlement of 1689, which set the framework for constitutional and political development until 1837, left the monarch with a sphere of action defined more negatively than positively. It was clear what he could not, less clear what he could, do. The confusion over George III's position came from this uncertainty, resolved by no enactment or open admission or irreversible course of precedents. He exercised the influence allowed him by the Con-

---

[1] Lord Herbert (ed.): *The Pembroke Papers 1780–1817*, London, 1950, p. 119.
[2] Tatum, *op. cit.,* p. 230.
[3] Mackenzie, *op. cit.,* II, pp. 423, 687–8.

stitution, and was confronted by a different conception of his position which has triumphed since, but was quite alien to eighteenth-century theory and practice alike. In that first trial of strength between the old ideas and the new, George III was the real victor.

The brief 'Whig' success in 1782–3, caused as much by circumstances (a unique national disaster) as by principle, has led many to antedate the continuous development of modern political concepts. In particular, the consecration of party by its development since the nineteenth century deceived posterity into thinking that Burke had the better of the argument in his own generation, whereas few eighteenth-century administrations were composed of members of a single group. Burke constructed a theory of politics from generalisations, many of them false, based on incidents in the career of his patron, Rockingham: it was his, not the national, interest which Burke sought to foster. His much-lauded economic reform was intended more to reduce the political influence of the Crown, incidentally strengthening that of the great leaders, than to increase efficiency or to save money. As a correspondent put it to Shelburne in 1780, Burke's proposals were more specious than useful, more eloquently expressed by him in public than seriously digested in private by men of business. The younger Pitt performed immense labours in fields of which Burke had only talked. By 1782, the Opposition, after years of exclusion in the political wilderness, was out to eliminate from politics the King's personal will, and to take away his undoubted right to make ministerial arrangements: a right which by misreading the events of the first half of the century, when the King had not exercised the influence allowed him by the Constitution, they mistakenly imagined belonged to them. Failure in the American War alone enabled Rockingham to impose terms upon the King in 1782 which the generality of politicians would never have supported in normal times—terms in themselves requiring an amount of legislation initiated and directed by the Government which was novel in what was essentially an age of executive government. In 1783, because no one else would stand forth, Portland, catspaw for Charles Fox, presented even greater claims—a free hand in the composition both of the ministry and its programme, men as well as measures, in which the King must acquiesce. 'The Cabinet once laid before me, he expected that on his coming to the head of the Treasury, I should rely on his making no propositions but such as he thought necessary for my affairs and consequently that I should acquiesce in them.' As the King continued, 'this unexpected idea, I fortunately did not treat with the warmth it deserved, but on finding that the Duke would not see the singularity of the proposition . . . said I must have time to consider of a proposition I thought so novel'.[1] This, the greatest straining of the Constitution as understood in the eighteenth century, was not by the King, but by the 'virtuous' Whigs. Nevertheless, the distorted idea of a King, alone obstructing something that everybody else wanted to do, still passes for history in flagrant contradiction of the facts.

Although Parliament had a right to criticise the King's instruments of government, and to demand their removal, it was not yet competent to take over the right of designating Ministers and of deciding on measures—indeed, the only time it did so in the eighteenth century, the 'infamous Coalition' gave practical proof of its inability. Only the development of organised party gave to the House of Commons this positive power of designating Ministers rather than supporting Ministers chosen by the Crown, a power by no means clearly acknowledged in 1837. As Professor Pares has re-emphasised, party was the power which maintained in motion the irresistible weapons which the House of Commons possessed against the King. Until Parliament grew up, the monarchy could not be de-personalised; until the distribution of power between King and Parliament was resolved, the King had to continue to do for the country what it had not yet the means of doing so well for itself. In fact, before the present political system could come into operation, the conditions of political life had to change—the removal of the King from active politics, the waning of the influence of the Crown, the slow substitution for it of the people as the directing force in politics, genuine economic and political reform, the extension of the

---

[1] Fortescue, *op. cit.*, VI, No. 4268.

authority of Parliament into spheres previously those of the monarch, the coalition of political groups into defined parties containing an ever-higher proportion of the House of Commons, with definite programmes (often embarrassing and inconvenient) in which the wishes and interests of a public now able to watch and criticise had to be considered and requiring detailed legislation by Government—developments not effective until well into the nineteenth century. After the peculiar forcing house of the War of American Independence, the new ideas in politics tentatively originated by the war lapsed when the situation returned to normal under the younger Pitt, and served for nothing but an example for future time. Nevertheless, their influence on the conduct of the war, particularly in its later stages, should not be overlooked: there is some support for the view that the attitude of the opposition groups strengthened the hands of the enemies of this country.

These were the main problems and disadvantages that confronted the British: as Lord North suggested in March 1778, "enough to employ the greatest man of business, and the most consummate statesman that ever existed',[1] and certainly too much for one whose main characteristics were rightly described by the King in 1772 as 'natural good nature and love of indecision'.[2] However the British Empire had been built up, the American colonies were certainly lost through absence of mind. The British shuffled between policies of firmness and appeasement until it was too late effectively to apply either. Even so, in marked contrast to almost every war fought by this country, Great Britain began the War of American Independence favourably placed both in standing and resources. She failed to pursue an energetic policy in the beginning, when the rebellion might have been crushed before France entered the war, believing that appearance of regulars alone would deter the rebels. Next, she refrained from using against kinsfolk the preventive measures that would have been taken at once against any ordinary enemy. She failed throughout to exploit colonial military weakness, and when

[1] Fortescue, op. cit., IV, No. 2239.
[2] Ibid., II, No. 1100; also, Pemberton, Lord North, London, 1938. See my essay in British Prime Ministers, London, 1953.

it was finally decided to resort to force, she failed to apply that force directly on land and sea in overwhelming strength at the vital strategic centre. Ultimately, both standing and resources were insufficient to meet the exceptional difficulties and the extra-ordinary combination of powers which faced the British, and which, to the disgust of George III, made this war 'less brilliant than the former'.

[NOTE. The War of American Independence began with the skirmish at Lexington on April 19th, 1775, and ended at Faunce's Tavern when Washington bade farewell to his officers on December 4th, 1783. The issue of the War was really decided at Yorktown on October 19th, 1781. Preliminaries of Peace were signed by Britain, the United States, France and Spain on January 20th, 1783. The Peace of Versailles was signed on September 3rd, 1783.]

VII

WHY AMERICAN VICTORY?

In April 1782, M. de Brentano, A.D.C. to the Comte de Rochambeau, Commander of the French expeditionary forces in America, reiterated the view that though the people of America might be conquered by well-disciplined European troops, the country of America was unconquerable.[1] In fact, the natural strength of the country was such that without a powerful movement of the colonial people in favour of Britain, it was optimistic to hope to conquer it. Given the ability and the will to build up and maintain a well-disciplined force (which was the overriding American problem in this war), there could be no question that the colonials were best adapted, and best suited, to fighting in their native terrain. There was a point beyond which European discipline and experience were bound to falter in strange conditions against native knowledge and craft, against an enemy, as Lieutenant Hale, 45th Foot, described them in March 1778, 'whose chief qualification is agility in running from fence to fence and thence keeping up an irregular, but galling fire on troops who advance with the same pace as at their exercises'.[2] Charles Lee had remarked on colonial advantages in 1774 that the yeomanry of America were infinitely more suited to war than the peasantry of other countries: they were accustomed from their infancy to firearms, and expert in the use of them, 'whereas the lower and middle people of England are . . . almost as ignorant in the use of a musket as they are of the ancient catapulta'; they were also skilful in the management of the instruments necessary for all military works, such as spades,

[1] *Shelburne, MSS.,* Ann Arbor, Michigan, 34, p. 2. John Trevor to C. J. Fox, April 16th, 1782.
[2] W. H. Wilkin, *Some British Soldiers in America,* London, 1914, p. 245. Hale contrasted this with the slowness of the Hessians, 'the greatest disadvantage in a country almost covered with woods'.

pickaxes, and hatchets.[1] They only required the addition of the essentials necessary to form fixed units of infantry for active service—and these were not as speedily acquired as he then expected them to be. Indeed the success of the militia at Bunker Hill persuaded many that this victory could be repeated, without any need to organise regular forces.

From the beginning, the Americans were eminently suited for improvised bodies of light infantry, but these, valuable as they were in colonial conditions, were not the whole story. R. H. Lee wrote on February 14th, 1775, of riflemen that, for their number, they made the most formidable light infantry in the world. He estimated that the six frontier countries of Virginia alone could produce nearly six thousand of these men, with 'their amazing hardihood, their method of living so long in the woods without provisions with them, the exceeding quickness with which they can march to distant parts, and above all, the dexterity to which they have arrived in the use of the rifle gun. There is not one of these men who wish a distance less than two hundred yards or a larger object than an orange—every shot is fatal'.[2] But how long could such men be kept together as a coherent body? Their indiscipline, he added, was quite as remarkable as their skill with the rifle, while General Schuyler, after reviewing troops at Ticonderoga in July 1775, observed that the officers and men were all good-looking people, decent in their deportment, excellent material for good soldiers, as soon as he could get the better of 'this nonchalance of theirs'.

The building up of a force from nothing was a major colonial achievement in this war—the setting up of an army, military establishment, staff and command, and supplying it with material requisite for a long-drawn-out struggle—but possibly the most difficult part of this task, among what Chatham once described as 'an irritable and umbrageous people' was the achievement of effective discipline, the basis on which all ultimately rested. The major obstacle to this was stated by Washington in January 1777 —a people unused to restraint must be led, 'they will not be drove,

---

[1] *Lee Papers,* Collections New York Historical Society, 4 vols. New York, 1872-5, Vol. I, p. 162.   [2] Montross, *op. cit.,* p. 71.

even those who are ingaged for the war, must be disciplin'd by degrees'—and it particularly concerned the militia, and new engagements: 'we must not expect the same ready obedience therefore from New, as from old Troops accustomed to obey'.[1] As Jefferson explained to Lafayette, mild laws, and a people not used to war and prompt obedience, often rendered orders ineffectual, and obliged the American commanders either to temporise or to attempt to accomplish their object in some other way. The attainment of the object of discipline had to be gradual. Washington began by advising Colonel Woodford of the Virginia militia (who were amongst the best) to be strict in his discipline, to require nothing unreasonable of his officers and men, but to see that whatever was required was punctually complied with. He should reward and punish according to merit, without partiality or prejudice, listen to complaints and redress them if well founded, and if not, discourage them to prevent frivolous ones; above all 'to impress upon the mind of every man the importance of the cause, and what it is they are contending for' (knowledge and morale being an essential support of good discipline). He should avoid too great familiarity to his officers, lest he lost the respect necessary to support effective command,[2] in what was a public rather than a private cause. It was this which militia too often forgot. Every individual had his own particular notion of things, and considered himself capable of conducting and directing operations: the establishment of a distinction between officers and men was a formidable problem when all were supposedly equal. Should a man's advice be neglected, or a course followed contrary to his opinion, he was often prone to think himself slighted, and prepared to leave for his home. Richard Montgomery said of the New England forces in 1776 that every man was a general, not one of them a soldier. It is not surprising that there were occasional disappearances when these men faced the fire of British regulars for the first time, nor that they engaged in settlement of private quarrels whilst about national business—as did the Virginian militia in Norfolk in 1776. As Pendleton described it, this was not uncommon 'in New

[1] Freeman, op. cit., IV, p. 388.   [2] Ibid., III, p. 521.

Troops unaccustomed to the advantages of discipline, and with young officers whose martial ardor has not been tempered by experience in service'.[1]

In the absence of effective discipline, almost everything depended upon success, upon 'the prospects of the day; if favourable, they throng to you; if not, they will not move'.[2] In the dark days of late 1776, this had a potent influence upon the British effort: what was the use of taking the field if the American forces were going to melt away? It was surely better to wait for the end of December, when the term of enlistment of the bulk of the colonial army expired (a term known almost to an exact hour by the men concerned). The danger was clearly seen by Washington, who believed the game 'pretty nearly up' unless every nerve was strained to recruit the new army with the greatest possible expedition. De Rochambeau himself wrote to Vergennes, July 16th, 1780, that the Americans could not be depended upon: 'their means of resistance are only momentary, and called forth when they are attacked in their homes. They then assemble for the moment of immediate danger and defend themselves. Washington commands sometimes fifteen thousand, sometimes three thousand men'.[3]

The individualism of the Americans was a lasting problem, which troubled both sides. John Moore, serving as a captain in the 82nd Foot in Nova Scotia in 1779, noted how frequently he had to sit on general courts martial because the officers of the provincial corps were continually quarrelling among themselves, and misbehaving.[4] After the failure of the American attack on Penobscot Bay in that year, the British were given unexpected assistance when soldiers and sailors, who blamed one another for the failure, settled the troubled relations between the services by coming to blows, and killing each other. This individualism affected all colonial movements and formations. As Washington explained to Lafayette about his plan totally to expel the British

[1] D. J. Mays, *Edmund Pendleton 1721–1803*, 2 vols., Cambridge, Mass., 1952, II, p. 81.
[2] G. M. Wrong, *Washington and his Comrades in Arms*, Yale, 1921, p. 209.
[3] Carrington, *op. cit.*, p. 504.
[4] Carola Oman, *Sir John Moore*, London, 1953, p. 50.

from the Southern colonies, the difficulty did not so much depend upon obtaining a force capable of effecting that purpose, as upon the mode of collecting that force to the proper point.[1] Although Thomas Hughes, as a prisoner in January 1780, had to confess of a regiment of Continentals that they had 'more of the military in their appearance that I ever conceived American troops had yet attain'd', he still noted that they refused to march further because of cold weather, and called their Colonel a damned rebel rascal: 'their officers do not seem capable of obliging them'.[2] He came here to the key to discipline, which was too rarely found in the eighteenth century. It was best explained by a master of training, Sir John Moore, at the beginning of the next century in his camp at Shorncliffe. Moore told his officers in 1803 that the only way of having a regiment in good order was by every individual thoroughly knowing and performing his duty, beginning with the officers first. If they did not fully understand their duty, it could not be expected that men would or could perform theirs as they ought. When officers were perfectly acquainted with the system, they could teach the men, and by their zeal, knowledge, good temper and kind treatment, weld a regiment into a whole. Only then could discipline be carried on without severity, with officers attached to the men, and men to the officers.[3]

The Americans had begun the war impatient of the known forms of discipline, though everyone else still adhered to the belief that savage discipline alone could hold together men inspired by no great or common ideals or purpose. Even so, Washington, who belonged to an older school, considered in 1775 that three things prompted men to a regular discharge of their duty in time of action—natural bravery, hope of reward and fear of punishment. The first two were common to both untutored and disciplined soldiers; it was the third which most obviously distinguished the one from the other. John Adams

---

[1] Paul A. W. Wallace, *The Mühlenbergs of Pennsylvania,* Philadelphia, 1950, p. 227.   [2] Benians, *op. cit.,* pp. 79–80.

[3] Oman, *op. cit.,* p. 404, and *Passages in the early military life of General Sir George Napier, written by himself,* London, 1884, p. 12.

wrote of the American forces which invaded Canada in 1775 that he was anxious for their fate, 'as they are not the best accoutred or disciplined', but he consoled himself that they were filled 'with that spirit and confidence that so universally prevails throughout America, the best substitute for discipline'.[1] When this spirit seemed insufficient and too spasmodic to build up a colonial force, recourse was had to the traditional code of punishment as the basis of discipline. Although colonial leaders affected great indignation at flogging in the British Army, thirty-nine lashes became the ordinary penalty for desertion in the Revolutionary militia, and was embodied as early as June 1775 by Congress in the Articles of War. The Judge Advocate-General's recommendation that the maximum number of lashes be increased to one hundred was embodied in the revised articles of September 1776, whilst Washington's suggestion in February 1781 that Courts Martial be given power to increase to a maximum of five hundred was only narrowly rejected.[2] This basic code, with the addition from 1778 of Von Steuben's uniform system of training (which included officers training recruits), was the scaffolding within which an American regular force was constructed and maintained in being, from the abundant promising material of 1775. At Valley Forge (synonym for misery and indomitable endurance), the American steel was tempered. The colonials had both conviction and purpose—the making of an army; their morale benefited from strict discipline intelligently administered. Already veterans (the ore was tested in the sequence of military events of which Valley Forge was the central phase, from the operations in New Jersey in 1777 to the return to White Plains in July 1778), seasoned to the fatigues and frustrations of war, the hardest part of soldiering, they only needed professional training, a herculean task. A uniform system of drill and manoeuvre had to be imposed upon a collection of regiments trained by a miscellany of methods; steadiness, exactness, accountability had all to be instilled. Valley Forge was the making of an army from a half-starved mob of

[1] C.O. 5: 134. October 4th, 1775.
[2] On this, see Bernhard Knollenberg, *Washington and the Revolution, A reappraisal*, New York, 1941, pp. 216–19.

ragged men: the proof of the forge was Monmouth Court House, where troops unsettled by one man's incapacity (Charles Lee) turned from disorder and retreat to disciplined resistance and moral victory.

The army had also to be maintained in supplies. Here again, the importance of administrative detail was underlined, and a major colonial problem focused—the efficient use and effective co-ordination of colonial resources, which had previously defeated every administration. The Americans here faced the exacting task which had confronted the British in previous colonial wars, and despite all that was done, only external support (as in the past) saw them through—even those materials and supplies in which America was self-sufficient had to be assembled and distributed. The Americans found here the same difficulty as would have frustrated any British attempt after 1763 to create a workable imperial system for so vast a territory as they had to administer —sheer lack of personnel with sufficient administrative experience. The wonder is not that there were occasional fiascos (dreams abound at times like these), nor that corruption and profiteers appeared, but that in the years of need, the colonies were able to build up a solid commissariat able to grapple with the situation —very largely the work of Nathaniel Greene as Quarter-Master General, aided by the Americans now having both scope and encouragement for exertion. Vigorous American operations of every kind were impracticable until supplies were organised and readily available at all key points. Washington's realisation of this, and his refusal to be stampeded by public clamour into what could only end in disaster, are among his major claims to lasting reputation. The key to this part of his career is to be found in his statement to Greene in November 1777: 'our situation is dis-tressing from a variety of irremediable causes, but more especially from the impracticability of answering the expectations of the world without running hazards which no military principles can justify, and which, in case of failure, might prove the ruin of our cause; patience and a steady perseverance in such measures as appear warranted by sound reason and policy must support us under the censure of the one, and dictate a proper line of conduct for the attainment of the other'.[1] As in every other field, so in the commissariat, knowledge had to be gained through practical experience, in which mistakes were quite as valuable as successes to untrained and unprepared personnel.

As Washington pointed out in 1777, the army might have more to dread from disorder in its own Commissary than from anything the enemy might do—a comment to be proved by the later troubles in 1780. In 1775, there were probably no more than two hundred gunsmiths in British North America, chiefly in the middle colonies.[2] The British capture of Forts Washington and Lee in 1776 took 146 pieces of artillery, over 12,000 shot, shell and case, 2,800 small arms, 400,000 musket cartridges—a grievous loss for a country limited in its resources of manufacture of such items, and increased by men taking their arms with them when their enlistments expired. This was only solved by the arrival early in 1777 of 23,000 muskets and 1,000 barrels of powder from France. On clothing and food, on regular and plentiful supplies, the comfort, cleanliness, health and spirit of the men depended: without them, nothing could be expected.

Valley Forge was the nadir:[3] troops were unable to do duty through shortage of clothing and footwear—indeed Washington always believed that Howe would have won the war had he vigorously attacked at that time, in the most testing months of Washington's command. Conditions there were yet another proof of the strong disposition of the colonials to suffer all things rather than submit—to be ill-sheltered, half-clad, cold, hungry and neglected by an ignorant, incapable and jealous Congress. As Washington characteristically understated, 'we are in a dreary kind of place, and uncomfortably provided'. A colleague posed the real question more strongly in January 1778 when he said he had seen soldiers turned out into the frost and snow in such poor condition that it would melt the heart of a savage—to defend the rights of the very people (the profiteers and traders) who were doing everything they knew to add to the distress of the soldiers.

---

[1] Freeman, op. cit., IV, p. 553.   [2] Mays, op. cit., II, p. 44.
[3] See A. H. Bill: Valley Forge, The Making of an Army, New York, 1952.

Conditions gradually improved, but throughout the war, only French provision of clothing, tents, and arms, and French financial aid, relieved the too sudden strain on the scattered colonial resources (and contributed to the adverse feeling always present in days of conscious resurgent nationalism to an indispensable benefactor). In the first clash at Lexington, General Gage was rightly attempting to secure supplies of arms, to hit the colonial effort where it was likely to hurt most. In the eighteenth century, possession of arms was vital to any revolutionary movement: it was the real motive behind the storming of the Bastille July 14th, 1789, an arms depot and a threatening citadel to people hourly expecting the intervention of foreign regiments surrounding Paris.

Throughout this difficult period of building up an army, down to the French entry into the war, the situation forced the Americans to the defensive, giving full scope to their talents in constructing works. Their skill with tools was such that the works were usually too extensive for the numbers available to man them—too large to be either adequately finished or adequately defended. Alexander Hamilton best expressed the American motive during this phase: 'it may be asked, if, to avoid a general engagement, we give up objects of the first importance, what is to hinder the enemy from carrying every important point, and ruining us? My answer is, that our hopes are not placed in any particular city, or spot of ground, but in preserving a good army, furnished with proper necessaries, to take advantage of favorable opportunities, and waste and defeat the enemy by piecemeal'.[1] The result was seen when, at the return to White Plains in July 1778, both armies were brought back to the very point whence they set out, 'and that which was the offending party in the beginning is now reduced to the spade and pickaxe for defense'. The continuing presence of the American force at Valley Forge, as an army in being, nullified the British capture of the capital, and prevented the British from dominating the central colonies. (It took 3,000 men to protect waggon trains between Chester and Philadelphia, a distance of fifteen miles.) Restricted

[1] N.Schachner: *Alexander Hamilton*, London, 1946, p. 64.

to little more than the ground they stood on, the British increasingly found subsistence a matter of considerable difficulty. As early as February 1777, Murray had noted 'a pretty amusement known by the name of foraging or fighting for our daily bread. As the rascals are skulking about the whole country, it is impossible to move with any degree of safety without a pretty large escort, and even then you are exposed to a dirty kind of *tiraillerie*, which is more noisy indeed than dangerous *mais qui ne manque pas quelque fois* to be a little troublesome'.[1] Moreover, continual harassment is worse than occasional large-scale actions to men whose morale is deteriorating. Defensive war of positions and posts was not only suited to the conditions prevailing in North America, it was the natural strategy of a weaker, less well trained force. In leaving the initiative to the enemy, it really risked nothing, as the British conduct of operations showed—indeed Hamilton opposed a plan to kidnap Clinton in 1779 for precisely this reason, that the Americans would rather lose than gain by it. By taking off a general whose character and notions they perfectly understood, they would only make way for another, perhaps more able, officer who would assume the offensive— the prerequisite of victory, which was again obtained by the Americans through external aid.

A continued obstacle to the building up of an army and its supplies (an obstacle which prevailed for longer than the war) was the parochialism and jealousy of each colony. The new Imperial policy, after 1763, even in its confused application, had admittedly created a self-conscious unity in the thirteen colonies. The colonists, though not yet a nation, had become a people in themselves. There was a basic social unity, which only required political passion to turn it into nationalism, but that same political passion stirred the still glowing fires of localism—even in much more developed eighteenth-century England, political issues and power were still personal and local. In the first instance there were few members of Parliament to take a stand on national political questions, whilst the idea of holding a general election on

[1] Robson, *op. cit.*, p. 38.

a given issue was as unknown as the idea of actual representation of the public. Even legislation ostensibly national (in itself, secondary to executive government) had local implications, handled by members as agents of local interests. The vast majority of Americans felt more loyalty to their respective states than to the Union —as Morison and Commager have suggested, it was this which still prevented a real Southern unity after 1861. Local interests and the structure of local society indeed explain the sense in which the War of Independence was a war of sentiment and opinion—by one form of society against another form of society, and why an American Revolution was still necessary after 1783. Washington recognised this obstacle throughout. In 1778, 'the States separately were too much engaged in their local concerns, when the great business of a nation, the momentous concerns of an empire, were at stake'. In 1780, he was certain that 'unless Congress are vested with powers, by the separate States, competent to the great purposes of war, or assume them as a matter of right, and they and the States act with more energy than they have hitherto done, our cause is lost'. He quite rightly discerned that it was impossible to drudge along in the old way any longer. 'By ill-timing in the adoption of measures; by delays in the execution of them, or by unwarrantable jealousies, we incur enormous expenses and derive no benefits from them. One State will comply with a requisition of Congress; another neglects to do it: a third executes it by halves: and all differ in the manner, the matter, or so much in point of time, that we are always working up hill'. He feared that one head would gradually change into thirteen under stress of events, and by return to custom and tradition. As the failure of the Albany Plan only twenty-six years before had shown, the colonial governments were loth to surrender any of their prerogatives to a central authority, not even one of their own choosing and making: and the raising of men and money for campaigns, although grown beyond the action of any single State legislature, was still basically a State matter.

In fact, here again the sudden strain of war, coming immediately on a new and strange national structure, was too much for the level of political intelligence existing in the American colonies in 1775. The greatest danger here was the likely effect of division on external support. After the mutiny of two Connecticut regiments in 1780, Washington emphasised that if the Americans disappointed the intentions of the Court of France 'by our supineness, we must become contemptible in the eyes of all mankind; nor can we after venture to confide that our allies will persist in an attempt to establish what, it will appear, we want inclination or ability to assist them in'. This was certainly the opinion of many French participants in 1782. They regarded the Americans as 'a steady, persevering people', but without activity, or a spirit of union enough long to preserve independency. Compared with the English, they had neither their vices nor their virtues: some of their greatest admirers at a distance were disappointed in their national character upon a nearer view, and were surprised that they had made the exertions they had, and had supported their union and independence even as long as they had.

Neither France nor Spain had intervened to help the Americans make the United States of America, but for realistic reasons of Imperial policy—to put a halt to British expansion which had reached such an alarming position in 1763. There was little belief that the United States would long survive the war— de Brentano believed in April 1782 that they would prefer some kind of honourable loose connection with Great Britain to a precarious independence (an idea which Shelburne at least seems to have considered). Even if it did remain an independent nation, it would be weak, and would eventually break up into its component parts and disappear, or attach itself to a stronger power. The internal divisions and jealousies in America, added to its dependence on European assistance for its survival, and the confident opinion in Europe that a federal republic could only persist in a small geographical area, explain why most Europeans believed that the American experiment would quickly fail, and were prepared to reap the ultimate benefit. As De Voto has put it, the problem of the United States was elementary: to survive the clash of domestic interests and philosophies, the rivalries of states and the resistance of citizens unused to a federal government, the efforts of outsiders to destroy it by breaking it up from within, by making war on it, or by getting it involved in war.[1]

That it did so in the testing time of war and after, was a triumph of spirit, impelled by a common danger and nurtured by hope, the food of morale—as even the British found. John Moore in garrison in Nova Scotia noted that the hope of being attacked was the only thing that rendered garrison life supportable.[2] Although the Americans had to substitute a national for a local patriotism, a general for a particular interest and loyalty, there is no question that colonial morale, whether particular or general (and both served that purpose), far surpassed that of the British. Survival gave an immediate purpose: to establish in being the independence achieved in fact. There was no divided objective behind American action. The low proportion of native-born Americans among deserters, cited by loyalists as proof that revolution was no longer supported, proved rather that most of them were sticking to the colours. No force of military police however efficient, no courts martial however drastic in sentence, could have saved the Army from anarchy and dissolution if this had not been so. In the long months of want at Valley Forge, there was no general disobedience of orders among the troops in the continental service, excepting the refusal of two brigades to march against the enemy unless given supplies for the expedition. De Kalb rightly commented that no European army would have similarly endured such hardships; indeed, the declining spirit of the British under conditions less arduous shows the truth of the comment. Inactivity and reverses on the colonial side were never able to break down morale. There must be either pride or principle to make a soldier. No man will think himself bound to fight the battles of a state that leaves him to perish for want of clothing and supplies, nor can the sentiment of pride inspire a soldier in situations which render him more an object of pity than of envy—situations too common for the American forces.

It was something deeper which kept American forces in the field. Stedman's view that the mutinous spirit which appeared

---

[1] Bernard De Voto, *Westward the course of Empire*, London, 1953, p. 335.
[2] Oman, *op. cit.*, p. 50.

in those forces in 1780–1 arose from distress more than dissatisfaction is surely correct: despite their arrears of pay, want of
clothing and regular supplies (legitimate and long-borne grievances), they refused all suggestions from the British to desert, and
go over. This was in marked contrast to the conduct of the other
side: many of the German mercenaries, knowing and caring
nothing for the cause in which they had been forcibly enlisted,
deserted after encouragement by Congress, which issued a
manifesto in German making liberal offers of land to any foreign
soldier who should leave the British service. Nathaniel Greene
felt in February 1778 that such patience and moderation as the
American soldiers manifested under their sufferings at Valley
Forge did the highest honour to their magnanimity; a view
confirmed by Lafayette in 1781 when he repeated De Kalb's
tribute more strongly: 'Human patience has its limits. No
European army would suffer the tenth part of what the Americans
suffer. It takes citizens to support hunger, nakedness, toil, and the
total want of pay, which constitute the condition of our soldiers,
the hardiest and most patient that are to be found in the world'.
As Edmund Pendleton argued in 1787, it was the greatness of this
spirit of America, already on its way to becoming a state of mind,
that had been found sufficient to oppose the greatest power in the
world.[1]

This spirit, which Gage had noted as 'an uncommon degree of
zeal and enthusiasm' in June 1775, was noted by the more sensible
British observers, and recognised as a formidable obstacle—but
this was discounted by the widely held contemptuous opinion of
the colonials as a despicable rabble. A man who recognised
colonial quality as clearly as Gage, who insisted on the difficulties
the British would have to face, was obviously unsuitable to keep
command whilst this view held sway. 'A ferment throughout the
continent . . . united the whole in one common cause . . . the
country people . . . raised to such a pitch of phrenzy as to be
ready for any mad attempt they are put upon'[2]—what madness
was this? Gage had surely served too long in colonial stations.

---

[1] Mays, *op. cit.*, II, p. 262.
[2] Carter, *op. cit.*, I, p. 380. To Dartmouth, October 30th, 1774.

But the testimony of others, with similar experience, supported him. Sir Francis Bernard, governor of New Jersey 1758–60 and of Massachusetts Bay 1760–9, doubted whether all the troops in North America, though probably enough for a pitched battle with the strength of that province, were enough to subdue it, 'being of great extent, and full of men accustomed to fire arms . . . they have not hitherto been thought brave; but enthusiasm gives vigour of mind and body unknown before'.[1] The practical proof of this spirit is found in Lord Percy's description of Lexington: 'whoever looks upon them as an irregular mob, will find himself much mistaken . . . Nor are several of their men void of a spirit of enthusiasm . . . for many of them concealed themselves in houses, and advanced within ten yards to fire at me and other officers, though they were mortally certain of being put to death in an instant'.[2] Gage remarked again on June 25th, 1775, that it might naturally be supposed that troops of the Rebel army would return home after such a check as they had got at Bunker Hill, but not so: 'in all their wars against the French they never shewed so much conduct attention and perseverance as they do now'.[3] An observer described to a correspondent in England at the end of that month all the provinces arming and training in the same manner, 'for they are all determined to die or to free it is not the low idle fellow that fight only for pay but men of great property are common soldiers who say they are fighting for themselves and posterity'.[4]

In September 1777, Arbuthnot confided to Sandwich that surrounded as the rebels were by distress, they were deaf to every solicitude of taking the oath of allegiance, or subscribing to any Act whereby they may be liberated. 'End this business when it may, it will require the greatest exertion of parts to put the colonies upon a permanent footing of utility to Great Britain. An army will not do it.'[5] It had in fact gone far beyond a military matter. Sir George Collier, writing to the same minister in

---

[1] E. Channing (ed.): *The Barrington–Bernard Correspondence*, Harvard, 1912, Introduction, p. xii. To Dartmouth, December 24th, 1774.

[2] Bolton, *op. cit.*, p. 53.   [3] Carter, *op. cit.*, I, p. 407.

[4] Mays, *op. cit.*, II, p. 23.   [5] Barnes and Owen, *op. cit.*, I, p. 296.

October, believed the inveteracy and rancour of the people in the New England provinces against Government to be so great that 'I hardly believe it will be got the better of during this generation'.[1] Robert Biddulph, writing after the taking of Charleston in 1780, noted the peace of this country was fully established, 'but there is such a fund of hatred and animosity in the hearts of the people, as time only can extinguish. The men being prisoners do not dare to speak out, but the women make full amends for their silence, they amuse themselves by teaching their children the principles of rebellion, and seem to take care that the rising generation should be as troublesome as themselves . . .'[2] This, in the most trying period America had to endure—as Washington put it to de Guichen in September, 'the Government without finances; its paper credit sunk, and no expedients it can adopt capable of retrieving it; the resources of the country much diminished by a five years war, in which it has made efforts beyond its ability; Clinton in possession of one of our capital towns and a large part of the state to which it belongs; the savages desolating the other frontiers; . . . Cornwallis . . . in complete possession of two states, Georgia and South Carolina; a third, North Carolina, by recent misfortunes at his mercy . . .'[3] Yet the British could make nothing of this situation. What could they offer to satisfy the feeling which sustained the Americans?

Beset by the difficulties inherent in first organising, and then maintaining in being, an army, all American commanders were in an even more harassing position than their British counterparts. Washington, as Boudinot said in April 1778, had both his heart and his hands full, but possessed a remarkable ability to concentrate even under the worst pressure. These men were too much encumbered to attend to everything, and could only rarely fully devote themselves undisturbed to the solution of a strategic or tactical problem: the strain on them was heavy and persistent. As Greene put it, the science or art of war required a freedom of thought and leisure to reflect upon the various incidents that daily

---

[1] *Ibid.*, p. 303.   [2] *American Historical Review*, XXIX, p. 94.
[3] Louis Gottschalk: *Lafayette and the close of the American Revolution*, Chicago, 1942, p. 130.

occurred, which could not be had where the whole of one's time was engrossed in clerical employments, which confined his thoughts as well as they filled his time.[1] The modern acceptance of waste in war as a matter of course was not possible for the colonial leaders—accounting for shillings and pence was as normal for them as not receiving the supplies for which to account. At one time or another, every one of them was in the irksome situation described by Washington in February 1776 in a typically restrained comment: 'to have the eyes of the whole continent fixed, with anxious expectation of hearing of some great event, and to be restrained in every military operation for want of the necessary means of carrying it on, is not very pleasing, especially as the means used to conceal my weakness from the enemy conceals it also from our friends and adds to their wonder'.[2] At first, it took more than the Americans could manage to find out what the enemy would do (they mistakenly expected them to do something on a large scale). Charles Lee wrote in April 1776 that he was like a dog in a dancing-school, not knowing where to turn or to fix himself. 'The circumstances of the country intersected by navigable rivers, the uncertainty of the enemy's designs and motions, who can fly in an instant to any spot with their canvas wings, throw me . . . into this inevitable dilemma.'[3] In any case, it would have taken almost a magician to divine what Howe actually did in 1777, contrary to common sense and military propriety. Washington had no doubt that his opponent would have pushed up the North River to co-operate with Burgoyne, and that Burgoyne would proceed no further south than Ticonderoga until he knew that this co-operation had begun. What happened, a complete failure of stage management in what was to have been a dramatic masterpiece, Washington (and many others) could scarcely believe.

The belief expressed by both Jacob Duché and Lafayette was common: that Washington was the Revolution, that cause and commander were synonymous, that the existence of the Army

---

[1] Jared Sparks (ed.): *Correspondence of the American Revolution*, 4 vols., Boston, 1853, I, p. 264.

[2] Freeman, *op. cit.*, IV, p. 21.   [3] See Mays, *op. cit.*, II, p. 99.

and the liberties of America depended on him. Less common was the realisation that he had to resist reckless demands for instant action till all was ready, and merely to harass and inconvenience his enemy until then. Washington clearly realised the danger of losing what had been built up by aiming too high. Apart from this personal embodiment of purpose, possibly his next virtue was the exemplification of the patience and determination necessary for success—his quality appeared in the full hold he took of the only real opportunity given to him, participation in the final scene at Yorktown where Cornwallis, in Guilford Dudley's exquisite description, was 'completely Burgoyned'. De Rochambeau told Lafayette in August 1780 that the surest way of losing the confidence of troops was to expose them to danger through private and personal ambition:[1] the colonial forces were never in danger of this from Washington's deep determination of spirit, his innate refusal to accept defeat, his calm and firm bearing which justifiably inspired confidence. Like John Moore, Washington certainly looked a good general in height, composure, dignity—all important when high commanders shared the actual process of fighting with their men.

There were strong political reasons, of which Washington was well aware, behind his appointment to the chief command— the need to join Virginia, foremost in riches, power and extent, the largest and most populous colony in the general movement. These were well expressed by Eliphalet Dyer of Connecticut when he wrote 'tho I dont believe as to his military and for real service he knows more than some of ours but so it removes all jealousies, more firmly cements the Southern to the Northern, and takes away the fear of the former lest an enterprising eastern New England general proving successful, might with his victorious army give law to the Southern or Western gentry'.[2] But by 1781, there could be few who doubted the real ability of Washington in command. Imperturbable, sober, and steady, he was at his best in adversity—bad news served only to stiffen his resolution. Already he was able to disregard what he could not

---

[1] Louis Gottschalk: *Lafayette and the close of the American Revolution*, Chicago, 1942, p. 118.   [2] Mays, *op. cit.*, II, p. 24.

avert, 'a deliberate refusal to be the *avant-coureur* of calamity'. Skilled in adaptation and improvisation, he had in 1775 a solid reputation for doing well whatever he undertook, unswerving from his purpose; and his ability to extricate himself from difficult situations had been displayed as early as 1754.

His greatest weakness when he took over command, as he himself confessed to Sullivan, was 'the want of experience to move upon a large scale', in which he was typical of nearly every colonial commander—lack of practice in the formulation and subsequent practical testing of strategical plans of any magnitude. He had never in person directed artillery or cavalry; he had never met the varied administrative problems implicit in the organisation of large bodies of men on such a scale. He who had operated a regiment on a frontier was now to direct an Army on a continent: the issues facing him were immense, and he had to make war throughout deficient in men, material, and money. Washington frankly told Congress at the outset that his abilities and experience might not be equal to the extensive and important trust assigned to him. But his relative incapacity and American conditions alike favoured him. He knew he could not hope to match British commanders in regular engagements, but if he could lure them into surroundings to which they were unaccustomed, the advantage would be his. He took the decision, accepting the heavy burden it laid on morale and colonial support, that on his side the war should be defensive, a war of posts: 'We should on all occasions avoid a general action, nor put anything to the risk unless compelled by a necessity into which we ought never to be drawn.' He must harass the British while he trained his army, and the unexpected respite given him by the British was put to good use. When Washington willingly, or of necessity, met the British, he had to employ simple strategic principles, because he knew no other, and did not command officers or men sufficiently trained to execute an elaborate plan, had he been equipped to formulate one.

His first venture in strategy on a scale of any magnitude, Arnold's advance on Quebec 1776, was a failure; his one attempt at a difficult strategic combination, the simultaneous convergence of columns on Germantown in 1777, was not a success. But his conduct and example, 'the balance of his parts', throughout the testing time, were measureless in their value and influence. Like all great commanders, he was aided by sheer good fortune—indeed de Kalb believed in September 1777 that whatever success he might have would be owing to this, and to the blunders of his adversaries, rather than to his own abilities—but this always enters in assessing any command. In Washington's case, good chance is perhaps best seen in the advanced position of the Hessians at Trenton 1776, and the weather which persuaded the duty officer there to cancel the regular patrol two hours before daylight. Weather incidentally is an important factor too often discounted in explaining events of eighteenth-century military operations—the drizzling mist succeeded by heavy rain for two days after the Brooklyn Heights battle on August 27th, 1776, which retarded the approach of the British to the American entrenchments, covered Washington's retreat, and prevented the British fleet approaching New York; the storm on September 16th, 1777, which put arms and ammunition out of use when Howe had turned the American right flank at White House Tavern, and skirmishing between the main forces had begun; the storm which disabled both British and French fleets off Newport, Rhode Island, on August 10th, 1778; the heavy rain which prevented Cornwallis, in his pursuit of Morgan after Cowpens, from crossing the Catawba on January 29th, 1781; and finally the storm of October 16th, 1781, which caused the recall of the vanguard of Cornwallis's army after its crossing York River to Gloucester Point in an attempt to break out, and precipitated the surrender.

Among Washington's colleagues, there were misfits, but considering their background, and the repute of their opponents, remarkably few—and most of them later corrected their errors in the best school, that of experience. Two may be singled out: Charles Lee and Gates. Alexander Hamilton was somewhere near the truth about Lee when he noted his preconceived and preposterous notion of being a very great man; Lee might be, in Washington's opinion, the first in military knowledge and experience, but he knew and believed it too well, and was fickle, violent tempered, jealous, and above all he despised prudence, the most essential colonial quality at this time. His greatest value to the Americans was perceived by Benjamin Rush—his ability to instil basic military fundamentals, and to lessen the superstitious fear felt by colonials of the valour and discipline of British regulars. Gates shared this over-confidence. Relying upon the prestige of Saratoga, thoroughly sure of victory in every engagement he undertook, he nearly matched the British commanders in neglecting elementary precautions and duties, as in his failure to reconnoitre before Camden. American commanders as a whole probably relied too much on Councils of War—the surest way to do nothing, as mad Anthony Wayne most sanely commented —but this was natural to men of their background and experience, and was still frequent practice in the British Army. In any case, the Americans had grasped, and practised, one factor of utmost importance—the freedom requisite in eighteenth-century conditions to subordinate commanders. Washington's orders were rarely explicit or restrictive. 'Your own good sense', he wrote to Schuyler on June 26th, 1775, 'must govern in all matters not particularly pointed out as I do not wish to circumscribe you within narrow limits.'[1] At times, the absence of sufficiently firm instructions to inexperienced subordinate commanders was a reason for reverses, as when Washington gave Putnam, in charge of the Long Island defences on the eve of the engagement at Brooklyn Heights, no specific instructions about the disposition of the troops, merely telling him to prevent the enemy approaching his defences 'at all hazards'.

Robert Jackson, discussing in 1804 the reasons for American victory, estimated the military character of the American people only because they had established themselves in independence against the will, and in spite of the armed force, of a powerful parent state.[2] That result, in his opinion, was due to bad management on the British side rather than to great exertion on the

[1] Freeman, op. cit., III, p. 468.
[2] Robert Jackson: A systematic view of the formation, discipline, and economy of Armies. London, 1804, pp. 130–33.

American. The force employed by Great Britain had been more than sufficient to have made a desert of America, but it could not subjugate a people not confined by a barrier in the rear, who were resolved to forego the connection with this country, and were determined to live free. With this determination, the Americans might have been invincible against even the best efforts of British arms, but their determination was never put to the test in this way. Jackson omits to take into account the invaluable assistance rendered by Great Britain's Imperial rivals: otherwise, he surely comes near the truth of colonial independence, which was sealed when Washington at last secured the support of a strong French fleet. What Washington stated as the two imperative necessities early in 1781, 'a constant naval superiority on these coasts' and a loan of money, could only be provided by France, who by the end of 1781 had advanced twenty million francs to the Americans. As Professor Graham points out,[1] even had there been no Yorktown, it is most unlikely that Great Britain could have quashed the rebellion. As long as British troops could be regularly supplied from home, they might have kept their footholds in New York or Charleston, but the occupation of a few strategic settlements on a long coastline did not and never could mean the subjugation of so vast a territory. Even if the French had not intervened in North America, could Great Britain, bereft of allies, and occupied with powerful enemies elsewhere, have found the resources and the men to subdue a quarter of a continent three thousand miles away? The dominating factor in the break-up of the first British Empire was political isolation: the results of the Peace of Paris came belatedly home to roost.

[1] G. S. Graham: 'Considerations on the War of American Independence', *Bulletin Institute Historical Research*, Vol. XXII, No. 65.

VIII

CHANGES OF PLAN,
DECEMBER 1777—JUNE 1778

After the disaster of Saratoga, October 17th, 1777, the possibility of French intervention in the American War of Independence increased. For Great Britain, colonial rebellion would then become international war, necessitating a change of plan in the whole strategy. On that need alone was there basic agreement. The British, therefore, attempted to conciliate the American colonies, both by approaches to the American ambassadors in Paris, and also by a wider plan, involving a Peace Commission being sent to America, so as to be able to turn their attention solely to the French menace. This attempt failed because the British did not cede enough to satisfy the Americans—they offered everything except independence, but this they were not prepared to grant: 'to treate with Independence can never be possible', George III wrote to Lord North on January 13th, 1777.[1]

This attitude was responsible for the second basic factor in British planning—it implied a continued defensive war in North America, and presented the problem of how best to utilise limited resources, dangerously strained with the entry of France into the war. In the best eighteenth-century tradition, with the announcement in London, March 13th, 1778, of the treaties between France and the rebels, there developed a third factor— the plan of striking a rapid blow against the French in the West Indies. This plan depended for its execution and success on a naval superiority which French entry into the war undermined, immediately and continuously.

These three factors—peace with the colonies, continued defensive war against them, and a major offensive against the French, were never clear and distinct in the minds of ministers,

[1] Fortescue, *op. cit.*, Vol. IV, No. 2161.

though clarity, directness, and decision were the essential requirements. There was instead constant interaction and consequent confusion. With the announcement of the French-
American alliance, Lord Carlisle,[1] head of the 1778 Conciliatory
Mission, doubted whether 'the idea of sending the Commissioners
from England was not, and ought not to be totally abandoned'.
He was shocked at 'the slovenly manner with which an affair so
serious in its nature had been dismissed' by a meeting, March 13th,
1778, between the Commissioners, Lord North, Lord George
Germain, and the Attorney- and Solicitor-Generals;[2] he noted
'the sulkiness of some, the childishness of others, and the haste
with which everything was hurried',[3] qualities the very reverse
of those required for efficient planning. Nevertheless, the project
of conciliating the colonies was not abandoned; but those taking
a leading part in it were never directly informed of the modi-
fications necessarily caused by the adoption of continued war
against the colonies, and a major offensive against the French.
This they learnt from the Commander-in-Chief only after their
arrival in America; they constantly and consistently protested
that it removed any real basis for the success of their Commission.

> Putting the French out of the question, [wrote Carlisle to
> his father-in-law, Lord Gower in September 1778] the
> alteration of the system of the war was in itself sufficient to
> destroy, when known, all hope of success. We endeavoured to
> strike the blow before that change became known . . . the
> only chance we had of benefiting our country by our labours."[4]

The need for a change of plan was universally agreed. Sir William
Howe wrote to Germain on December 11th, 1777, that if the
reports about Burgoyne were correct, 'so heavy a misfortune'

[1] Frederick Howard, fifth Earl of Carlisle.

[2] Edward Thurlow and Alexander Wedderburn.

[3] Historical Manuscripts Commission, Fifteenth Report, Appendix Part VI,
Carlisle MSS. (later referred to as Carlisle MSS.), p. 377.

[4] Ibid., p. 373. See also pp. 336, 341–2, 345–7, 351, 372, 378–81, and William
Eden to Germain, June 19th, Stopford Sackville MSS., Vol. II, pp. 115–16.
Granville Leveson-Gower, second Earl Gower, later Marquess of Stafford
(1721–1803), was Lord President of the Council, 1767–79.

must cause a material alteration in the plan of carrying on the war.[1] Arrival in London of the news of the Convention of Saratoga led to an equal appreciation that in a situation 'very serious but not without remedy',[2] there must be some change of plan.

The King wrote to Lord North on December 4th, 1777, that the wisest step was to act only on the defensive with the Army, and with great activity as to the troops. Canada, Nova Scotia, the Floridas, New York, and Rhode Island must probably be the stations for concentration, but those who had served in those posts, particularly Lord Amherst,[3] must be consulted, and they would be able to point out what would be best.[4] North agreed that some material change of system would be required:

I do not see that as yet the storm is risen to a height that absolutely requires a change of hands at home, but the consequences of this most fatal event both in America and in foreign parts may be very important and serious, and will certainly require some material change of system. No time shall be lost, and no person who can give good information left unconsulted in the present moment, and I hope that the approaching adjournment of Parlt will soon leave us at leisure to give all our time to the executive business of government.[5]

Approaches to the American representatives in Paris began in December. British agents offered to Deane and to Franklin a safe-conduct to London, permanent places in the American nobility which the Government proposed to create in the colonies,

[1] C.O. 5: 94, 749.

[2] Fortescue, *op. cit.*, III, No. 2904. George III to Lord North, December 4th. The news first reached England on December 2nd, by way of Quebec. Burgoyne's dispatch did not arrive until December 15th.

[3] Jeffrey, Baron Amherst, had been Commander-in-Chief in North America, 1758–64. Described as the 'Court Sal Volatile' in 1775. W. S. Taylor (ed.): *The Correspondence of William Pitt, Earl of Chatham*, 4 vols., London, 1840, IV, p. 448.

[4] Fortescue, *op. cit.*, III, No. 2094.

[5] *Ibid.*, No. 2095. See also Germain to Howe, December 11th, *Stopford Sackville MSS.*, II, p. 84. For views amongst other groups in England, see Keppel to Rockingham, January 7th, 1778, T. Keppel, *The Life of Augustus Viscount Keppel*, 2 vols., London, 1842, II, pp. 13-16.

and an immediate armistice in the war.[1] Franklin, who was informed on December 17th that Louis XVI had decided to recognise the independence of the American colonies, and to sign a treaty of commerce and friendship with them, kept such approaches going, since they increased his bargaining powers. The most important of these approaches was that made by William Johnstone Pulteney, Member for Shrewsbury, and elder brother of Commodore George Johnstone, a member of the Conciliatory mission. Pulteney had offered to go to Paris in December 1777 to find from Franklin the lowest terms on which America would lay down arms. He wrote to Germain on December 6th that he had 'always wished the most perfect freedom of America with respect to taxation and charters; but . . . the indissoluble union of Great Britain and America'.[2] In late March, he took over to Paris offers of conciliation.[3] The announcement of the treaty of amity between France and the American colonies made both the King and Lord North consider that peace with America, 'reserving a dependence', was a most desirable object— by ending the war with that country, it would be possible 'with redoubled ardour to avenge the faithless and insolent conduct of France'. Only so was it proper to keep open the channel of intercourse with 'that insidious man', Franklin. In briefing North as to Pulteney's instructions, the King was quite emphatic:

> I will never consent in any treaty that may be concluded a single word be mentioned concerning Canada, Nova Scotia, or the Floridas, which are colonies belonging to this country, and the more they are kept unlike the other colonies the better, for it is by them we are to keep a certain awe over the abandoned colonies, where good garrisons must be constantly kept.[4]

[1] See J. G. Miller, *Triumph of Freedom, 1775–1783*, Boston, 1948, pp. 300–1.

[2] For his approach to Franklin, see Fortescue, *op. cit.*, IV, Nos. 2246, 2250–1, 2253, 2282; C. van Doren, *Autobiographical Writings of Benjamin Franklin*, London, 1946, pp. 437–9, 442–3, and his *Secret History of the American Revolution*, pp. 70–3, 85, 102.

[3] *Stopford Sackville MSS.*, II, pp. 81–2. See also pp. 82–3, 85. For his views in general, his *Thoughts on the Present State of Affairs with America, and the means of conciliation*, London, 1778.

[4] Fortescue, *op. cit.*, IV, No. 2251. To North, March 26th. For North's views, see Nos. 2246–7, 2250.

Pulteney saw Franklin on March 29–30th, and George Johnstone later claimed, when submitting the terms to Lord Carlisle, during the voyage to America,[1] that Franklin had approved the offers of conciliation then made. They were:

(1) The present Governments to remain. But the King to name a Governor out of these.[2]

(2) Judges and all civil officers to be named by them, care being taken of the rights of patent officers. Courts of Admiralty for prizes only.

(3) No negative on acts of Assembly, except such as affect the trade with Great Britain, or the trade of any other colony. But no negative as to acts for prohibition of negroes, or for establishing paper currency, if not made a legal tender in private payments. All acts to be transmitted for due notification. Acts prohibiting luxuries affecting all country as equally to pass without negative.

(4) No appeals to Privy Council except in prize cases from Courts of Admiralty in time of war.

(5) Congress to subsist—its powers to be defined. The King to name a President.

(6) No taxes to be imposed, nor any military force kept up without consent of Assemblys. Officers to have commissions from his Majesty subject to being removed on address of Assembly.

(7) The ungranted lands and quit rents to be given to the Colonies upon an equivalent.

---

[1] 'Heads of Accommodation taken from papers perused May the 6th on board the "Trident", 1778, sumitted by G.J.'—'copy of propositions discussed between Dr Franklin and Mr Pulteney in March and April 1778: and observations upon the Heads of Accommodation'. *Carlisle MSS.*, pp. 337–9, and B. F. Stevens, *Fascimiles of Manuscripts in European Archives relating to America, 1773–1783*, 25 vols., London, 1889–95, I, No. 68.

[2] The first article only of Carlisle's observations is of real importance: 'If they sd. be content with their present Governments little objection occurs to this article, as the constitution of those governments, are essentially different, any union injurious to Great Britain seems to threaten less by leaving them their anterior forms'.

(8) To have a free trade from and to all places but not to interfere with the grants to exclusive companys now subsisting. No officers of customs to subsist.

(9) To have representatives to Parliament.

(10) Mutual amnesty—mutual restitution. Mutual compensation for wanton damage.

(11) Immediate cessation of hostilities by sea and land.

(12) The King is and shall be the only supreme Governor, and to have power of war and peace, and alliances after the present general pacification.

(13) All judicial proceedings and other legal instruments to run as formerly in his name.

(14) Forces to be annually voted for defence of Colonies, and paid by them. Officers to have commissions from the King, and removable as above by address.

(15) A contribution to be settled as to increase with their growth.

(16) All bounties, drawbacks, and prohibitions in their favour to cease.

(17) The expense of their own civil government to be paid by them.

(18) All hostile resolutions of theirs to be annulled.

This scheme allowed equal participation in the benefits of the British Constitution, with the virtual concession of Home Rule, and a new political organisation even on terms laid down by the Americans. There were to be Treaties for the suspension of arms, and for the establishment of peace, friendship, and commerce. Franklin wrote to Pulteney on March 30th[1] that when he first had the honour of conversing with him on the subject of peace, he mentioned it as his opinion, that every proposition, which implied the colonies' involuntarily agreeing to return to a dependence

---

[1] A. H. Smyth, *Writings of Benjamin Franklin*, 10 vols., London, 1916, Vol. VII, pp. 124-6.

on Britain, was now become impossible; that a peace on equal terms undoubtedly might be made; and that, though the American representatives in Paris had no particular powers to treat of peace with England, they had general powers to make treaties of peace, amity, and commerce, with any states of Europe.[1] Franklin had thought they might be authorised under this to treat with Britain, 'who, if sincerely disposed to peace, might save time and much bloodshed by so treating directly'. Franklin had also given Pulteney his opinion that in any treaty to be made, Britain should endeavour, by the fairness and generosity of the terms she offered, to recover the esteem, confidence, and affection of America—without which the peace could neither be beneficial nor lasting—a view which Pulteney had shared. Franklin now found, from these propositions, 'that the ministers cannot yet divest themselves of the idea, that the power of Parliament over us is constitutionally absolute and unlimited; and that the limitations they may be willing now to put to it by treaty are so many favours, or so many benefits, for which we are to make compensation':

As our opinions in America are totally different, a Treaty on the terms proposed appears to me utterly impracticable, either here or there. Here we certainly cannot make it, having not the smallest authority to make even the Declaration specified in the proposed letter, without which, if I understood you right, treating with us cannot be commenced. . . . Such a treaty we might probably now make with the approbation of our friends, but, if you go to war with them on account of their friendship for us, we are bound by ties, stronger than can be formed by any treaty, to fight against you with them.

Franklin did not, therefore, accept these terms, as later suggested by George Johnstone to Lord Carlisle,[2] though he admitted to de Rayneval on April 1st that the propositions 'would

---

[1] On this point, see also Franklin to David Hartley, M.P. for Hull, February 26th, 1778, *ibid.*, p. 115.

[2] See also Franklin to Joseph Reed, March 19th, 1780, *Smyth*, VIII, pp. 43–6.

probably have been accepted, if they had been made two years ago. I have answered that they have come too late.'[1]

The question of a change of hands had already arisen abroad, if not at home, by the intimation of Howe that he wished to resign his command;[2] his replacement was now one of the problems facing the King and Lord North. Germain acquainted the King on January 10th, 1778, that the Cabinet had met that morning, and taken into consideration the general state of the war in America, particularly that part of Howe's letter in which he desired to be recalled. The Lords of the Cabinet had directed Germain to submit to the King's determination their humble opinion upon that subject whenever the King should please to order him to attend.[3] Germain saw the King on January 12th, and it is clear the Cabinet had recommended Amherst as successor to Howe.[4] On the same day, Amherst, 'though with every expression of duty declined in fact, though out of decency on being strongly pressed he took time to consider though gave no room to expect he will accept'.[5] The King wrote to North on January 13th that he had done all he could to effect what the Cabinet 'unanimously thought the most desirable step'. He now proposed that the mode of conducting the American war be deliberated upon without loss of time, and Amherst be examined in the Cabinet on this subject. The King's general view was:

... perhaps the time may come when it will be wise to abandon all North America, but Canada, Nova Scotia and the Floridas, but then the generality of the nation must see it first in that light; but to treat with Independence can never be possible.

From his discussions with Amherst, the King had gathered 'some essential points'.

---

[1] *Smyth*, VII, pp. 128–9. For further approaches to Franklin in April by David Hartley, see Guttridge, *op. cit.*, pp. 280–7.

[2] October 22nd, 1777. To Germain, *Stopford Sackville MSS.*, II, pp. 80, 9–90.

[3] Fortescue, *op. cit.*, IV, No. 2153.

[4] *Ibid.*, No. 2156, North to the King, January 12th, and No. 2162, Germain to the King, January 13th.

[5] *Ibid.*, No. 2161. The King to North, January 13th.

(a) After the disaster of Saratoga, an army of 40,000, additional to what there was at present, was essential to carry on an offensive land war with any practical effect.

(b) A sea war was the only wise plan, to prevent the arrival of military stores, clothing, etc., to the rebels, which must distress them and make them come into what Britain may decently consent to.

(c) 'at this hour they will laugh at any proposition'.

(d) The mode of war should be settled first, then the General who was to command.

It would be difficult to get Howe to remain and not less so to get Germain to act with him. And, in the King's view, what was still more material to be settled was the plan on which Administration was to repel the different attacks of opposition when Parliament met:

as to the calling for Papers, the proposing enquiries, etc. this must be digested by you and I hope is already so nearly ready that you may open the whole to the Cabinet when next it meets, and have a minute taken that when the debate in both Houses, on the state of the nation from want of previous concert the conduct may not be opposite.[1]

The Cabinet met on both January 17th and 18th.[2] Amherst attended the first meeting at Lord North's, his opinion being desired 'upon the most eligible mode of carrying on the war next campaign in America.'[3] At the second, Suffolk communicated a minute of Amherst's opinion concerning the most proper mode, and the necessary force, for carrying on the war, an opinion taken 'yesterday morning' at Lord North's by some of the Lords of the Council.[4] Lord North reported to the King of this meeting

[1] *Ibid.* For North's reply, No. 2163. See also No. 2164.

[2] *Ibid.* No. 2170, 2172; 2171 gives the correct sequence of events.

[3] *Ibid.* No. 2170. Also present, North, Sandwich (First Lord of the Admiralty), and Suffolk (Secretary of State for the Northern Department).

[4] *Ibid.* No. 2172. Also at Lord North's. Present—North, Suffolk, Sandwich, Bathurst (Lord Chancellor), Gower (Lord President), Dartmouth (Lord Privy Seal), and Weymouth (Secretary of State for the Southern Department).

on January 18th that although they had come to a resolution respecting only a part of Amherst's opinion, they talked over the whole of it. The necessity of communicating this plan to the Commander-in-Chief, the manner of doing it, who should be Commander-in-Chief, the method to signify the King's pleasure to Howe if he remained at the head of the Army, the reinforcements to Canada and to East Florida, had all been considered, but postponed for a day or two, that Germain (not present at the meetings) might be acquainted with the business. They had come to a resolution which would not admit of any delay (the Admiralty were to give immediate orders for preparing transports to convey the reinforcements to their destination) and they wished if possible to have an old corps sent to Halifax, Nova Scotia, considering that place too important to be left to new levies.[1]

Lord North, who had announced to the House of Commons shortly after the news of Saratoga had been received that he would present a complete and far-reaching peace plan after the Christmas recess, was much concerned by the end of January about 'a proposition for peace with America', because of

> the necessity he thinks there is, from the situation of affairs, of endeavouring to draw some of the Colonies from their claim and plan of independency upon Great Britain.

This would be difficult, but the proposition most likely to succeed would be an exemption for the future from Parliamentary taxation for any colony renouncing its claim to independency:

> To give up the levying of positive taxes here is to give up in effect nothing, as it is pretty certain that none will for the future be ever levi'd by the British Parliament.

He went on to make further suggestions, approved by the

---

[1] *Ibid.* No. 2171. Approved by the King on January 19th, No. 2174. The King had meanwhile been in touch with Barrington (Secretary-at-War), who had seen the minute of January 17th. See No. 2173 and No. 2175, Barrington to the King, January 19th and 20th.

Solicitor-General, and consented to by the Attorney-General, which would meet with much contradiction:

> To repeal the tea duty, to repeal the Massachusetts Charter bill, and to give, by act of Parliament, ample promises to Comissioners to settle every other point.[1]

Replying to this on January 31st, it was the view of George III that any such proposition was of little use—

> not from any absurd ideas of unconditional submission my mind never harboured; but from foreseeing that whatever can be proposed, will be liable, not to bring America back to a sense of attachment to the mother country, yet to dis-satisfy this country, which has in the most handsome manner cheerfully carried on the contest, and therefore has a right to have the struggle continued until convinced that it is in vain.[2]

North should not be in a hurry to produce any plan of this kind, with every letter from France adding to the appearance of a speedy declaration of war. In such an eventuality, we might find it wise to strengthen forces in Canada, the Floridas, and Nova Scotia, withdraw the rest from North America, and 'without loss of time' employ them in attacking New Orleans and the French and Spanish West Indian possessions. Success there would repay the great expense incurred. At the same time we should continue to destroy the trade and ports of the rebellious colonies, and thus soon bring both contests to a conclusion:

[1] *Ibid.* No. 2179. The correct sequence here is No. 2160, 2179 (from internal evidence, January 30th and not 29th as placed by Fortescue) and 2182. No. 2181 refers to, and should precede, No. 2168 of January 16th. No. 2179 is docketed on the original in pencil '30th January 1778 rel. to several plans to bring about a peace with America'. No. 2158 dated by Fortescue ? January and placed at January 12th is also January 30th: it is the answer to points raised in No. 2179.

[2] *Ibid.* No. 2182. Walpole had written to Mann on September 1st, 1777, that 'in one thing alone all that come from America agree, that the alienation from this country is incredible and universal; so that, instead of obtaining a revenue thence, the pretence of the war, the conquest would only entail boundless expense to preserve it. The New World will at last be revenged on the old'. P. Toynbee (ed.): *The Letters of Horace Walpole*, 16 vols., Oxford, 1903–5, X, p. 103.

. . . this country having its attention diverted to a fresh object, would be in a better temper to subscribe to such terms as Administration might think advisable to offer America, who on her part will at such a time be more ready to treat than at the present hour.

The King did not mean by this to reject all ideas of laying a proposition before Parliament, if a foreign war should not begin that session:

. . . I trust you will first fully state to the Cabinet your ideas, where I am persuaded you will find every member willing with candour to examine them, after which you will lay the result before me; and when the whole is thoroughly digested shew it to the principal men of business of the House of Commons, both in office, and those of weight with the country members, that the House may not as, on a former occasion, from want of previous notice, be staggered and persons oppose from not understanding the subject before them.[1]

On February 2nd, the King considered that Chatham's disavowing the unjustifiable lengths the Rockinghams would go in favour of America[2] would assist the introduction into Parliament of the proposal North intended to make of new arranging the Commission,[3] increasing the powers of the commissioners, and getting rid of some acts of Parliament that were in the present state of affairs a bar to forming any solid reconciliation with the American colonies. The King now looked on the recall of General Howe as settled, and expected that his brother, Lord Howe, the naval commander, would also wish to return.[4] Howe's resignation was

[1] Fortescue, op. cit., IV, No. 2182. For Germain's opinion, see No. 2188.

[2] Information contained in North's letter to the King of February 1st, 1778, and not 1768, as dated by Fortescue, op. cit., II, No. 588.

[3] The Commission taken out by Admiral Lord Howe in 1776, naming him and his brother, General Howe, as being authorised to receive the submission of such individuals or communities as might throw themselves on the King's mercy. Published by circular declaration to the late Royal Governors in North America on July 14th, Tatum, op. cit., p. 32.

[4] Fortescue, op. cit., IV, No. 2184. Richard, fourth Viscount and later first Earl Howe, naval Commander-in-Chief in North American waters, 1776–78.

approved by Germain, permission being given him to return to England, in a letter written on February 4th;[1] Clinton was written to on the same day that he was to relieve Howe, and would shortly receive his orders for the operations on the next campaign. Meanwhile, he was to act as opportunity offered.[2]

On February 9th, the King made an acute analysis of the strategic situation which, if fully acted on, had great possibilities; but which his own views on the position of the American colonies prevented from being put into execution. He wrote to North that should a French war now be our fate, the only means of making such a war successful would be the withdrawal of the greatest part of the troops from America, and employing them against the French and Spanish settlements, for if we were to carry on both a land war against the rebels, and also contend with France and Spain, 'it must be feeble in all parts and consequently unsuccessful'. North should not delay in bringing his American propositions into the House of Commons, after proper communication to the leading persons.[3] North introduced his motions on February 17th—to renounce all claim to taxation, and to empower Commissioners to treat with any persons or bodies of men in America for peace.[4] On that day, the King wrote to North, referring to the permission given General Howe

---

[1] *Stopford Sackville MSS.*, II, pp. 92–3. The packet carrying the letter sailed on February 16th (Fortescue, *op. cit.*, IV, No. 2331); the letter was received at Philadelphia on March 27th, not 'in April' as stated, J. W. Fortescue, *A History of the British Army*, III, p. 253. See *Stopford Sackville MSS.*, II, pp. 92–3.

[2] C.O. 5: 95, 56. Clinton was in New York, not in England (as stated by G. O. Trevelyan, *The American Revolution*, 4 vols., London, 1899–1907, III, p. 308); he moved to Philadelphia from there, arriving on May 7th (Tatum., *op. cit.*, pp. 286, 290). [3] Fortescue, *op. cit.*, IV, No. 2190.

[4] Walpole believed them caused by the 'urgency of the moment . . . to prevent the pretended spirit of pacification from being anticipated by France's notification of her alliance with the American states to all Europe'. Toynbee, *op. cit.*, X, p. 190. To Mason February 19. See also p. 194. The treaties of amity and commerce, and of mutual defence between France and the rebels, the latter a conditional alliance to go into effect only in the case of war between France and Great Britain, were signed on February 6th; the formal announcement of them by the French Ambassador in London was not made until March 13th.

to return home by Germain, who had written 'coldly'. Germain should write again to Howe by the vessel taking out North's propositions, communicating to Howe the idea of changing the plan of the war, which Germain might very properly attribute 'to the opinion I have of the General and his having intimated that on the present mode, and with his present force, he could only the next campaign maintain what he has now in his possession'. Howe should be given latitude to do what might seem to him most eligible until the arrival of Clinton, or some other successor.[1] North should see Germain on February 18th, settle the transmitting to America of a proper account of the conciliatory propositions, and a suitable letter to Howe that 'may encourage him to act with spirit until the arrival of his successor'.[2] Drafts of the bills required by the conciliatory proposals were sent to America by the frigate *Andromeda* on February 20th, before Parliament had acted on them. They arrived on April 20th. Lafayette, writing to Henry Laurens, President of Congress, on April 21st, thought 'there must be under hand some very black scheme—he [Lord North] can't fight us out but hopes to negotiate us out of our rights'.[3]

It now remained to select the Commissioners. At the head was Lord Carlisle, Treasurer of the Household, who accepted on February 22nd, on condition 'that I might be joined by men whose characters, rank in life and abilities might restore that importance and weight to the commission that it might lose by my youth and inexperience', and that 'no powers should be denied to us to bring the business to a quick termination, stop the effusion of human blood, and hinder the other nations from rising on our

[1] Fortescue, *op. cit.*, IV, No. 2195. From internal evidence, this should be dated February 17th not 18th, and precede No. 2194. The second letter received by the King from Lord North (mentioned in No. 2195) is placed by Fortescue as No. 2632. It should be dated February 11th, 1778, and follow No. 2193, which in the original is dated 15th altered to February 16th. The correct order is 2193, 2632, 2195, 2194. It is of note that the historian of the British Army should imagine Howe still commanding in America in May 1779, as suggested by the placing of No. 2632.

[2] *Ibid.*, No. 2194. For Germain's letter to Howe, February 18th, see C.O. 5: 95, 63–4, and *Stopford Sackville MSS.*, II, p. 143.

[3] *South Carolina Historical and Genealogical Magazine*, VIII, p. 63.

mutual destruction'.[1] Carlisle was joined by William Eden, M.P. for Woodstock, Under Secretary in the Northern Department, and a member of the Board of Trade and Plantations, who offered to go if certain persons whom he named could not be induced to go, and if the commission were filled up by those whom he should like. He saw Carlisle on February 25th, and accepted on March 5th.[2] He also brought forward Richard Jackson,[3] M.P. for New Romney, and Counsel to the Board of Trade. 'I bent to the persuasion that his accurate knowledge of the country . . . and his long and familiar acquaintance with her interests', wrote Carlisle, 'would outbalance the insignificance of his situation and the obscurity of his name'.[4]

These three met at Lord North's on March 13th to receive the outlines of instructions, and compare the different ideas of the business in which the commission was to be employed, and again on March 29th, when Jackson produced 'many adverse arguments'. On March 30th, Jackson refused to go with the commission; he thought it 'idle and ruinous to go to war with France', 'we should proceed immediately to give independence to the colonies', the commission was 'of no consequence except to satisfy the people of this country'.[5] He was replaced on April 1st by Commodore George Johnstone[6]—'this union of men of different political ideas upon former proceedings relative to America we flattered ourselves would at least convey a strong proof of the rectitude of our intentions, and the fairness of proposals we had to tender'. The Commissioners, to whom were

[1] *Carlisle MSS.*, p. 377.

[2] *Carlisle MSS.*, p. 322. See Knox's comment on Eden's appointment, Historical Manuscripts Commission, Various Reports VI, *Knox MSS.*, p. 266.

[3] 1721–87. Agent for Connecticut 1760–70, for Pennsylvania 1763–70, for Massachusetts Bay 1765–70.

[4] *Carlisle MSS.*, p. 377. Shelburne had described Jackson in November 1767, with Amherst and Franklin, 'three gentlemen that were allowed to be the best authorities for anything that related to America'. C. van Doren (ed.): *Letters and Papers of Benjamin Franklin and Richard Jackson, 1753–1785*, Philadelphia, 1947, p. 2. [5] *Ibid.*, pp. 28–9.

[6] See above, p. 5. His personality is well shown in the constant quarrels and disagreements between the civil and military power in West Florida during his period as Governor of West Florida, 1763–7.

[7] *Carlisle MSS.*, p. 378.

added the Commander-in-Chief in North America, were best summed up by Lafayette, writing to Henry Laurens on June 12th, after their arrival in Philadelphia on June 6th: Lord Howe, 'a very brave man, a good seaman, . . . who in the civil way is no body, and who will not shine in his political commission';[1] Sir Henry Clinton, 'a military pedant, somewhat blunderer and nothing more'; Johnstone, 'a sensible man, but a dangerous one— his being in the opposition till this moment has made him popular—but his being chosen for a commission where many ministerial blunders are to be brought to the light, is a certain mark that he has been corrupted . . .'; Eden, 'unknown to me, and unknown to the world'; and Lord Carlisle, 'a fine gentleman, very well powdered, and a man of *bon goût*—he began by ruining his own fortune, and wanted to get the reputation of a man belov'd by the ladies . . . however he is a good poet'.[2]

While the Commission was forming, much else of importance had been decided.

On March 3rd, the King was convinced that France would inevitably go to war.[3] If she did 'take off the mask', it ought to be considered 'whether the season is too far advanced for an attack on the West India settlements of France, or whether to be delayed untill the autumn in either case the troops for that service must be taken from North America'. He then went on to detail further arrangements both for forces at home and in America, and for the navy, but thought it 'wisest not to be in a hurry'.[4] And on March 10th he wrote:

the old lion will be roused and must shew that resolution and activity that alone can keep his wonted station, and deserve the respect of other nations.[5]

[1] Lord Howe did not actually serve on the Conciliatory mission.

[2] *South Carolina Historical and Genealogical Magazine*, VIII, pp. 4-5. See also the views of Horace Walpole; Toynbee, *op. cit.*, X, pp. 197, 216, and Doran, *op. cit.*, II, p. 213.

[3] The correct order of the letters on March 3rd in Fortescue is No. 2203, 2202, 2201, 2204. No. 2386 placed by Fortescue at the end of June 1778, North to the King, undated, from internal evidence is March 3rd, 1778, and should precede No. 2203.   [4] *Ibid.*, No. 2204.

[5] *Ibid.*, No. 2212, both to North.

The theme that the war must be prosecuted upon a different plan was taken up by Germain, in his most secret instructions for the next campaign written to Clinton on March 8th.[1] The most essential interests of the British Empire were now deeply engaged. The power, reputation, and future welfare of this nation depended in a great degree on the successful employment of the forces under Clinton's command. However desirous the King might be of putting an end to this unhappy contest by the way of negotiation, he did not think fit to slacken any preparation which had been judged necessary for the carrying on of the war—

> it being His Majesty's firm purpose to prosecute it with the utmost vigor in case the colonies shall obstinately persist in their refusal to return to their allegiance, and pay obedience to the constitutional authority of Government.

In the summer, we might send out 10 or 12,000 British soldiers and a regiment or two of Germans, but 'considerable as such a reinforcement, if we can effect it, must be allowed to be in our present circumstances', the war must be prosecuted upon a different plan from that upon which it had hitherto been carried on. The main features of the new plan were that, by October, Clinton was to provide for:

(a) the security of all our American possessions, with some additional force from Great Britain to Canada, both to secure that province, and to act as a base for operations against the rebellious colonies.

(b) A strengthening of Nova Scotia and Newfoundland.

(c) The Floridas must not be left exposed.

(d) Should he find it impracticable to bring Washington to a general and decisive action early in the campaign, he was to relinquish the idea of carrying on offensive operations against the rebels on land. As soon as the season permitted, he was to institute a raiding policy on posts on the coast from New York and Nova Scotia, to seize or destroy every

[1] They were communicated to the Commissioners, see *Stopford Sackville MSS.*, II, p. 115.

ship or vessel in the different creeks or harbours, wherever it was found practicable to penetrate; also to destroy all wharfs and stores and materials for ship building, so as to incapacitate the rebels from raising a marine, or continuing their depredations upon the trade of England, already so much annoyed by their ships of war and privateers.

(e) If it was necessary to carry out this policy, the main body of troops should be withdrawn from Philadelphia, leaving only a "sufficient strong post" there.

(f) After this, an attack was to be made on the southern colonies, with a view to the conquest and possession of Georgia and South Carolina. There was a strong belief that the South would return to allegiance, the North thus being left to their own feelings and distress to bring them back to their duty. Operations against the Northern colonies would be confined to cutting off their supplies and blockading their ports.

Despite these long and detailed instructions, all was left to Clinton's discretion, the King committing to him the planning, as well as the execution, of all the operations appearing to him to be the most likely means of crushing the rebellion and restoring the constitutional authority of Government in the colonies.[1] There was no mention of operations against the French West Indian islands.

News of the alliance between France and the rebels, announced in London on March 13th, completely altered the situation. The Cabinet met that day, coming to no final decision.[2] On March 14th, at Weymouth's house, it agreed to submit to the King, amongst other matters, that three or four ships of the line and three other two-decked ships be sent from America for the defence of the Leeward Islands, also that four thousand men be ordered to embark with the line of battle ships for those islands.[3] St. Lucia

---

[1] C.O. 5: 95, 69–94. *Stopford Sackville MSS.*, II, pp. 94–9.

[2] Fortescue, *op. cit.,* IV, No. 2216. Weymouth to the King.

[3] G. R. Barnes and J. H. Owen (ed.): *The Private Papers of John, Earl of Sandwich, 1771–1782* (Navy Records Society, Vols. LXIX, LXXI, LXXV, LXXVIII), 4 vols., London, 1932–8 (later referred to as *Barnes and Owen*), I,

was already being considered as a possible point of attack—a proposal from Captain Lord Mulgrave[1] described its fine harbour, effectively commanding Martinique, and Sandwich noted that if troops were to be sent, care must be taken to victual them from home.[2] At this grave moment, Amherst was again called upon to give advice both to the King and the Cabinet[3]—he was to see both on March 17th 'for we have not an hour to lose'.[4] He expressed the following views to the King:

(a) If the fleet were to be collected at Halifax, leaving the American coast open, the rebels would fit out a fleet and attack the islands. Therefore, New York should become the base for both Army and Navy, with the troops withdrawn from Philadelphia, but sending such a detachment to the Floridas as the General thought sufficient to secure them from attack.

(b) The two regiments of Light Dragoons should be sent home, but their horses retained in North America for the service of the Army as baggage horses or for drawing cannon.

(c) Such part of the frigates as were thought absolutely necessary should be brought home.

(d) New York should be the port of rendezvous and the fleet should be employed in destroying all the vessels in the American harbours.

(e) Newfoundland, Nova Scotia, and Canada ought to be reinforced by some of the newly raised corps.

(f) If the Peace Commission found America resolved to join France, then New York and Rhode Island were to be

---

p. 361. Minute of Cabinet. Present: Lord President (Gower), Lord Privy Seal (Dartmouth), Suffolk, Sandwich, Germain, North, Weymouth. For the strategical implications of the French entry into the war, see W. B. Willcox, 'British Strategy in America 1778', *Journal of Modern History*, XIX.

[1] Constantine John Phipps, second Baron Mulgrave, had joined the Board of Admiralty on December 15th, 1777.

[2] Barnes and Owen, I, pp. 325-6, 357-8, 360.

[3] Fortescue, *op. cit.*, IV, Nos. 2219, 2225, 2227.

[4] *Ibid.* No. 2227, the King to North, March 16th.

evacuated, the troops to be employed in attacking the West Indian islands.

The King then sent to Weymouth directions to summon Amherst to the meeting of the Cabinet arranged for that forenoon, March 17th.[1] Amherst was also present at a Cabinet meeting on March 18th which submitted to the King that if there was no certain intelligence of a French fleet, Lord Howe was to be directed to send four ships of the line, three 50-gun ships, two 32-gun ships, two 20-gun ships, and two bomb vessels to the Leeward Islands. This fleet was to convey 5,000 men in transports from Philadelphia for the protection of those islands, and to act offensively against the French settlements. Eight months' provisions should be taken, and thereafter the expedition would depend on being supplied from England.[2]

On March 21st, the intention of making an immediate attack upon the island of St. Lucia in the West Indies, as a result of the 'most offensive proceeding of the Court of France', was developed.[3] Germain informed Clinton that the King,

in consequence of the advice of his most confidential servants, has taken the resolution to avenge the insulted honour of his crown and vindicate the injured rights of his people by an immediate attack upon the French possessions in the West Indies.

It was essential that the object of the expedition should be unsuspected, and in order to divert public attention and conceal the purpose, it had been given out that the troops in America were to return to Great Britain forthwith. Should that opinion be entertained by the French officers in the West Indies, it would

[1] *Ibid.,* IV, No. 2229. See also Barnes and Owen, I, p. 365.

[2] Also present: Lord President, Lord Privy Seal, Sandwich, Germain, North and Weymouth. Barnes and Owen, I, pp. 363–5. Minute of Cabinet. There was another meeting on the same day. Fortescue, *op. cit.,* IV, No. 2223.

[3] By new most secret instructions to Clinton, C.O. 5: 95, 179–185, 193–206. See also Germain to Sandwich (with extracts from the instructions), Barnes and Owen, I, pp. 366–7, 368–70, Germain to the Admiralty, *ibid.,* p. 368, the King to Sandwich, *ibid.,* p. 370.

serve to confirm them in it if Clinton gave the same reason for the embarkation of the troops. If any regiments were too reduced to take the field, the men were to be incorporated into other corps, and the commissioned and non-commissioned officers sent home to recruit. The instructions laid down that the expedition was to attack, and if practicable, to reduce and take possession of St. Lucia. In the event of success, a sufficient force was to be retained for the defence of that island, and the remainder of the troops were to be distributed among our other islands in such a manner and in such proportions as, from the information available, should be judged most proper for their protection and security against any attack of the enemy. The need for secrecy, dispatch, immediate execution and the utmost diligence, was stressed. Clinton was to select an officer of such rank and experience as he thought most fit to carry out the purpose, and the expedition was to arrive before the hurricane season.[1] As a corollary, offensive operations on the continent of North America were to be abandoned save for raids in conjunction with the navy 'to keep up an alarm on the coast of the rebellious provinces'; a force of 3,000 was to be detached for the defence of Florida; Philadelphia was to be evacuated[2] and the troops there were to proceed to New York, 'the possession of which will be so necessary to give dignity and effect to the commissioners' negotiations'.[3] Should these negotiations fail, and Clinton be in danger at New York, he was to move to Rhode Island, and if that could not be held, to Halifax. The planning and preparation of the St. Lucia expedition were thus left to the Commanders-in-Chief in America.

Meanwhile, George III was taking a general view of affairs.

I am resolved to shew the world that neither zeal, activity, nor resolution are wanting in me, when the times require it, to

[1] August to November.

[2] Germain was directed to communicate this to no person whatever except his own under secretary, William Knox, who was to draft the dispatch. See Spector, op. cit., p. 125. Philadephia was finally evacuated on June 18th. Tatum, op. cit., p. 311.

[3] None of these new instructions was divulged to the Peace Commissioners, who received their instructions in March 1778. This was later the source of many complaints from them.

forward with the greatest expedition every measure that can
be necessary for the security or honour of my Dominions.[1]

The keynote in every department was to be 'vigour and
activity'.[2] Preparations for the dispatch of the Commissioners to
America continued, but the King trusted that the expense was
not to fall on his civil list—'it is as much a part of the American
contest as the victualling ships or any other of the expenses this
unfortunate affair has made necessary'.[3] The Conciliation Acts
had been sent to America on March 16th:[4] the Royal instructions
and the Enabling Act of the Commission (18 Geo. III, c. 13)
were published on April 12th; the Commission, under the Great
Seal, on April 13th. The Commission[5] set up Commissioners
'appointed to treat, consult and agree upon the means of quieting
the disorders now subsisting in certain of our Colonies, plantations,
and provinces in North America'. The instructions[6] were prepared
by Wedderburn, the Solicitor-General, who according to Knox
'was very desirous his friend (Eden) should succeed in the
negotiation, and the instructions were most liberally framed for
that purpose, so diametrically against his former conduct'; in
Knox's opinion, 'if the colonies had accepted the offers the Commissioners were impowered to make, the people then would have
had all the advantages of British subjects without any share of the
burdens of Empire . . .'[7]

The instructions authorised the granting of pardons; the
arrangement of a suspension of arms, the suspension to June 1st,
1779, of the operation of any act passed since February 10th, 1763,
in so far as it related to America, the making of temporary
arrangements for colonial governments, and the conclusion of
a treaty in accordance with the instructions—such a treaty being

[1] Fortescue, op. cit., IV, No. 2245. To North. March 24th.
[2] Ibid., No. 2256, March 29th.
[3] Ibid., No. 2270. To North, April 3rd.
[4] 18 Geo. III, c. 11, repealing the Massachusetts Bay Act of 1774; 18 Geo. III,
c. 12, for removing all doubts and apprehensions concerning taxation and the
tea duty.
[5] For this, see Carlisle MSS., p. 323; Annual Register, 1778, pp. 315–20.
[6] For them, see Carlisle MSS., pp. 322–33.
[7] Knox MSS., op. cit., pp. 266, 277–8.

subject to confirmation by Parliament. Several general lines of discussion were examined:

The claim to independence should be admitted during the time of treaty, and for the purpose of the treaty.

There should be no standing army in America in time of peace without their consent, provided that provincial forces were organised.

No alteration in Governments and charters but by their own consent; some of the first offices should be given to Americans.

Governors might ultimately be elected, but the King must approve the election, and issue the commissions, as also for political and civil magistrates, and officers of the provincial forces.

A general assembly or Congress might be allowed, but the sovereignty of the mother country should not be infringed— and this should be referred home before becoming a concluded article of any Treaty, as should also any proposal made by the Americans for representation in the British Parliament.[1]

Arrears of quit rents should be given up: burdensome offices suppressed.

A contribution should be made by the colonies to the public charge.

There should be an examination of trade regulations, but any articles agreed should be subject to Acts of Parliament, 'and to avoid the revival of any question upon right and authority, a representation from our colonies may precede the Act'.

Admiralty Courts should be restrained in their operation.

If a repeal of the Declaratory Act were proposed, a declaration should be framed upon the close of the whole treaty of the respective rights of Great Britain and America.

[1] In view of the offer made by the Commissioners on June 9th, it is of note that neither the Enabling Act nor the Instructions authorised them to put forward the question of seats in Parliament. See Germain to Knox, July 23rd, *Stopford Sackville MSS.*, II, pp. 144–5.

The basis of any treaty should be the condition in 1763: if a treaty with Congress failed, the Commissioners should apply to bodies of men, or individuals: and if failure was complete, a final Declaration should be issued, setting out the earnest wishes of Great Britain for composing the differences.

The Commissioners were not to consider these instructions as precluding them from entering into an examination and decision of any matters not mentioned: they were at liberty to proceed upon every matter within the compass of their commission, 'and to give all possible satisfaction to the minds of our subjects in America, consistent with that degree of correction which is essentially necessary for preserving the relation between us and our subjects there'. Nor were they to break off the treaty on the other party's insisting on some points which they were directed not to give up,[1] but were to wait for further orders on such points.

Carlisle saw Germain before embarking on April 16th:

> Finding that New York was particularly marked out for the place of our destination, I wished to know the reasons why that place was preferred to Philadelphia; the only answer I obtained was, perhaps that city may not by your arrival be in our hands. Sensible that a variety of active military operations might render it impossible to leave so large a garrison as to ensure the possession of it while the army acted at any distance . . . it never occurring to me that a very different system was to be this year adopted . . . I did not conceive anything further could be hid under these expressions, but that it was not insisted upon that city should be retained at all events, but that it should be relinquished, if other pursuits made the measure justifiable.[2]

The Commissioners sailed on April 24th, and landed at Philadelphia on June 6th, where they met both Lord Howe and General Clinton:

> We were greatly astonished to find they were both under the irresistible influence of positive and repeated orders; which

[1] These were contained in Secret Instructions for the Commissioners. See *ibid.*, pp. 105–6.   [2] *Carlisle MSS.*, pp. 378–9.

orders had industriously been kept a secret from us, though sent out long before our departure . . . calculated to render the Commission both ineffective and ridiculous.[1]

Carlisle thus summed up the position in which they were placed by the conflicting plans of the British ministry:

. . . the order was founded neither in wisdom nor expediency; . . . it was in itself ruinous to the Commission . . . it was adopted to fulfil no other purpose whatever, but of making an attack upon an insignificant West India island at the most unfit season of the year . . . and of reducing the Army by sending a number of men to the Southern Continent; expeditions that admitted of no delay, for which the prospect of attacking the rebel army to great advantage, and for which the peace and reconciliation that might flow from such advantage was no longer to be placed in competition.[2]

The confusion in purpose shown by the changes in plan was reflected in their results: the Conciliatory Mission failed completely; the preparations for the St. Lucia expedition were seriously hampered by the need for continued defensive warfare on the mainland; success at St. Lucia (December 1778) remained isolated, and brought no lasting gain to the British cause.

[1] *Ibid.*, p. 380.   [2] *Ibid.*, p. 383.

IX

THE CONCILIATORY MISSION, AND THE EXPEDITION TO ST. LUCIA, JUNE—DECEMBER 1778

Lord Carlisle, the head of the Conciliatory Mission, arrived in Philadephia on June 6th, 1778; and soon declared himself:

> The only method of putting an end to this disastrous war was by liberal, specific, and intelligible offers to America of reconciliation, supported at the same time by the most active and spirited military operations . . . that were on no pretence to be relaxed or suspended until America had given unequivocal proof of her sincere desire to meet G. Britain, and unite in the endeavour of not only restoring the public tranquillity, but of fixing it upon that basis that neither ambition abroad nor faction at home should be able to destroy.[1]

He was astounded to find Lord Howe and General Clinton, the Commanders-in-Chief, preparing to evacuate Philadelphia, to detach 5,000 men for an attack on St. Lucia, and 3,000 for the defence of Florida; and to abandon the offensive on the continent of North America.[2]

> That which we had always looked upon as the great instrument which was to secure us success, the active and offensive course of military operation, was no longer to support our proceedings . . . our offers of peace were too much the appearance of supplications for mercy from a vanquished and exhausted state.[3]

Carlisle later explained that this situation 'permitted none of the protracting arts of negotiation; it was too nice and critical to

---

[1] *Carlisle MSS.*, pp. 376–7; see also p. 361.
[2] In accordance with the instructions of March 21st.
[3] *Carlisle MSS.*, p. 381. See also p. 345.

attempt any experiment, and we were all convinced that we had no other part to take but at once to display every concession and every inducement which our country had empowered us with'.[1] There followed, June 9th, 1778, the letter of the Commissioners to Henry Laurens, President of Congress—'offers to the Congress as we should not have thought prudent to display in any other circumstances'.[2] The Commissioners, more effectually to demonstrate their good intentions, declared that they were disposed to concur in every satisfactory and just arrangement towards the following:

To consent to a cessation of hostilities both by sea and land.

To restore free intercourse, to revive mutual affection, and renew the common benefits of naturalisation, through the several parts of this Empire.

To extend every freedom to trade that our respective interests can require.

To agree that no military forces shall be kept in the different states of North America without the consent of the General Congress, or particular assemblies.

To concur in measures calculated to discharge the debts of America, and to raise the credit and value of the paper circulation.

To perpetuate our union, by a reciprocal deputation of an agent, or agents, from the different states, who shall have the privilege of a seat and voice in the Parliament of Great Britain, or, if sent from Britain, in that case to have a seat and voice in the Assemblies of the different states to which they may be deputed respectively, in order to attend to the several interests of those by whom they are deputed.

In short, to establish the power of the respective legislatures in each particular State, to settle its revenue, its civil and military establishment, and to exercise a perfect freedom of

[1] *Ibid.*, pp. 281–2.
[2] *Ibid.*, p. 342. See also p. 354, 'the making offers without adhering to negotiations by keeping some back'.

legislation and internal government, so that the British States throughout North America, acting with us in peace and war, under one common Sovereign, may have the irrevocable enjoyment of every privilege, that is short of a total separation of interest, or consistent with that union of force, on which the safety of our common religion and liberty depends.[1]

This was a programme of full self-government, except in matters of trade—and for the adjustment of that, the British were to have agents in Congress or in the several states, while the Americans should equally be represented in Parliament.

Congress replied to this on June 17th, asking for an explicit acknowledgment of independence, or the withdrawal of fleets and armies; an answer which, in Lafayette's opinion, was 'a fine piece'.[2] The position was thus summed up by Simeon Perkins in Nova Scotia:

> The news is the Commissioners from Great Britain have made propositions to the Congress of a settlement on as good terms as can be expected, except a separation, but the Congress refuse even to treat with them until they withdraw their fleet and Army or explicitly acknowledge their independence, which does not seem to be included in their Commission.[3]

W. H. Drayton of South Carolina stated the American objections to the proposals in his letter of June 17th to the Commissioners. The Americans were too well acquainted with the insignificancy of the Scotch representatives in Parliament to expect that American representatives could possess any importance, or that America could derive any advantage from such representation. Moreover, agents sent by Britain to colonial assemblies would be 'spies', and 'agents to purchase our voices'. As Parliament had to confirm any treaty, Parliament would know what Congress had offered to do, but Congress would not know what Parliament would confirm; such unequal conditions must stop any accom-

---

[1] Robert Beatson, *Naval and Military Memoirs of Great Britain from 1727 to 1783*, 6 vols., London, 1804, VI, pp. 429–31.

[2] *South Carolina Historical and Genealogical Magazine*, IX, p. 7.

[3] H. A. Innis (ed.): *The Dairy of Simeon Perkins 1766–80*, Champlain Society, Toronto, 1948, p. 208. Entry July 17th.

modation. Drayton questioned the value to either side of such offers. England gave everything short of independence. America, 'formed for empire, must naturally arrive at it':

> Having tasted of it, she will ever be anxious to possess it again; having by arms acquired a power, but short of independence, she will increase in reputation and ability to become independent, and this will increase her desire to be so; her former success will possess her with confidence and hope; experience will make her ever suspicious of the intentions of Britain . . .[1]

Governor Johnstone was meanwhile making a much more practical but independent approach to the problem of conciliation. Having written to the President of Congress on June 10th,[2] he next made offers of honours and high rewards to those who would bring about a compromise which would restore America to England.[3] These approaches were finally concluded by Congress refusing on August 11th to have any further correspondence or intercourse with him.[4]

The Commissioners' proposals of June 9th went beyond their instructions, which, in particular, gave them no authority to offer seats in Parliament. Lord Carlisle evidently feared reprimand from England on this point. In a letter to Lord Gower, written in early July, he pleaded 'the situation of things, the circumstances of the times' as his defence in infringing legal form.[5] The proposals certainly aroused comment in London. Germain wrote to Knox on July 23rd that this was 'a melancholy beginning' to negotiations:

> The delegates to Parliament from the States of America is a new idea, and by no means any part of the Instructions, as I can recollect, and I think the whole of the proposal is rather

---

[1] Beatson, *op. cit.*, VI, pp. 435–6.   [2] *Carlisle MSS.*, pp. 343–4.

[3] *Annual Register*, 1779, pp. 20–1. See also W. B. Reed, *Life and Correspondence of Joseph Reed*, Philadelphia, 1847, I, p. 379.

[4] See also *Carlisle MSS.*, p. 361. Johnstone left America in September, and arrived in England on October 26th.

[5] *Carlisle MSS.*, p. 350. See also his minute on the conduct of the Commissioners, p. 351.

premature, but as the Congress will not treat with them unless
Independence is acknowledg'd, we shall have nothing to trust
to but the sense of the people at large, should they be tired of
their connection with France, and I still believe if we have any
success in the opening of the war that it will have a great effect
upon the minds of the Americans.[1]

At the same time, North was clear that great care should be taken
in everything spoken and written not 'to give our enemies in
America the least pretence to say that we do not mean sincerely,
and that, when we have brought the colonies to treat, conjointly,
or distinctly, we mean to disavow our Commissioners'.[2] He reiterated this in a further letter to Knox on August 15th:

. . . The letters from hence (though it is impossible to deny
that the Commissioners have exceeded their instructions)
should not give the least ground to suspect that we will not
confirm any agreements they may make . . . As the Commissioners will probably come away, *re infecta*, it is right that the
colonists should suppose that the whole extent of the Commissioners' offer would have been granted, which, indeed,
would be supposing no more than the truth, for as little
pleased as many people are with the terms, I do not think the
nation would refuse them, if they should produce an immediate
peace.[3]

On July 11th, the Commissioners reopened their struggle
with Congress, asking by what authority Congress made treaties
with foreign powers. As they did not recognise the independence
of America requested in the last communication from Congress,
that body decided on July 18th to give no reply.[4] The Commissioners also wrote home on July 11th asking for permission to
return, 'rather than subject the Commission to fresh insult, and
ourselves to the accusation of receiving the public wages, when
we were convinced no benefit could be the consequence of our
remaining any longer.[5] The Peace Commission had by now

[1] *Stopford Sackville MSS.*, II, pp. 144–5.
[2] To Knox, August 8th, *ibid.*, pp. 145–6.   [3] *Ibid.*, pp. 146–7.
[4] *Carlisle MSS.*, pp. 384–5.   [5] *Ibid.*, p. 384.

clearly failed. On August 12th, George III believed that accounts from America seemed to put a final stop to all negotiations—

> further concession is a joke, all that can now be done is steadily to pursue the plan very wisely adopted in the spring the providing Nova Scotia, the Floridas and Canada with troops, and should that not leave enough for New York which may in the end be the case we must then abandon that place, then we must content ourselves with destressing the rebels, and not think of any other conduct till the end of the French [war] which if successful will oblige the rebels to submit to more reasonable [terms] than can at this hour be obtained.[1]

While the farce of the Peace Commission was being played out, what happened to the expedition to St. Lucia, ordered in the most secret instructions of March 21st? On May 3rd, the Admiralty issued further secret instructions to Rear-Admiral Samuel Barrington, appointed Commander-in-Chief of the Leeward Isles Station, January 30th, 1778.[2] These instructions were complementary to those sent to Lord Howe, ordering the detachment to the West Indies under Commodore Hotham,[3] and differed in no important detail from the instructions of March 21st. Barrington was to give the general commanding the troops 'such assistance as he may stand in need of towards carrying that part of his instructions into execution.'[4] Clinton arrived at Phila-

---

[1] Fortescue, op. cit., IV, No. 2405. To North. The Commissioners issued a Declaration August 26th, offering 'not only everything that can be proposed by the French connection, but also many very valuable blessings to this Continent which can never by any possibility be derived from that preposterous connection' (Carlisle MSS., p. 361). See also final Manifesto and Proclamation of October 3rd (ibid., p. 388, and Annual Register, 1778, pp. 320–4).

[2] Samuel Barrington (1729–1800), brother of the Secretary at War, had been promoted Rear-Admiral in January 1778. He arrived at Barbados in June 1778. Vice-Admiral in March 1779, he left for England in July 1779.

[3] William Hotham, first Lord Hotham (1736–1813), was at this time a Commodore, junior to many of the captains on the St. Lucia station, and not an Admiral, as stated by J. W. Fortescue, A History of the British Army, III, p. 264. See D. Bonner-Smith (ed.): The Barrington Papers, 2 vols., London, 1937–41 (Navy Records Society, Vols. LXXVII, LXXXI), II, Intro., XX.

[4] Ibid., II, pp. 15–18. 'That part' referred to the distribution of troops after success at St. Lucia.

delphia on May 7th, and wrote to Germain on May 10th that he hoped in the next week the Admiral could tell him when the fleet for the expedition could be assembled which 'is at present much dispersed upon different services'.[1] The stage was set, the actors in the wings, yet the play did not begin until November 3rd,[2] despite repeated protests of diligence and activity. What obstacles did the service commanders meet in mounting this expedition, unhampered as they were by the departmental 'red tape' at home?[3]

Clinton reported to Germain on May 23rd that uncertainty still prevailed as to when a sufficient convoy could be collected for the expeditions for St. Lucia and the Floridas. He had also found it inexpedient to move from Philadelphia with only part of his Army, so had decided to evacuate the whole to New York, (he arrived there early in July), from where he could dispatch troops sooner, and better provided. He had chosen Grant to command the expedition to St. Lucia, 'as he has to be upon the spot, and his services, in this country much approved of by Sir William Howe'.[4] Grant himself wrote to Germain from Philadelphia on May 24th that he had been honoured with the command of a corps of troops which was to be sent, he believed, from New York to the West Indies, but had not received full instructions from Clinton, and was, therefore, not at liberty to write a public letter. This was merely a private one. He had to take possession of 'the place of our destination': 'the most sickly island in the West Indies, the harbour good, the

[1] C.O. 5: 96, 11.

[2] The fleet sailed from New York on November 3rd not 4th, as stated by J. W. Fortescue, A History of the British Army, III, p. 258. See Grant's report to the Secretary of State on December 31st, Barrington Papers, II, pp. 166–9, Mackenzie, op. cit., II, p. 416, and Carlisle MSS., p. 390.

[3] The Deputy Quartermaster-General in North America hired transports for the expedition to St. Vincent in 1772, fitted them out with every necessary, and prepared all that was required for two regiments to take the field in 15 days. Carter, op. cit., II, p. 611. To Barrington, July 1st, 1772. See also to Hillsborough same date, I, p. 327.

[4] C.O. 5: 96, 41–2. See also Carlisle MSS., p. 380. James Grant of Ballindalloch (1720–1806) had been Governor of East Florida 1763–1775. M.P. Wick Burghs 1773–1780. See p. 127.

water remarkably bad. I should therefore be sorry to remain there with troops which are equal to anything if they are not got the better of by sickness'.[1] He thought the number intended for the expedition small, 'as more than half is not to be counted upon as fit for service after they have been a little time in the West Indies'. This was from experience, but he did not despond: everything he pointed out would be attempted, and he hoped for success, though wishing he was not 'confined to a particular spot'. He went on to make suggestions on money, provisions and ammunition, and asked that, 'in point of powers' the King would put him on the same footing with other officers who had had the honour to command in America and the West Indies. He was sure the service would not suffer by such a trust being reposed on him.[2] On June 5th, Clinton wrote to Germain that the Admiral had told him troops could not be taken on board nearer than Newcastle, on the Delaware, forty miles from Philadelphia;[3] he was therefore going to march through New Jersey, and hoped to be in New York by the middle of the month, 'by which time the Admiral will probably be able to inform me when the ships, destined to convoy the different expeditions will be assembled'.[4] Worse news was to come—on July 11th, Clinton had been told by the Admiral that in view of the arrival of D'Estaing and the French fleet off the coast, he did not think it advisable to send off any expeditions at present. The troops would remain ready to proceed whenever Lord Howe should judge it proper for them to embark and was pleased to order convoys for them.[5] Clinton was still very uncertain on July 27th as to when the troops would depart, 'as I take it for granted that the Admiral will not despatch them till he can ascertain the movements of the French fleet'.[6]

[1] See also Howe's opinion, Fortescue, *op. cit.*, IV, No. 2387, July 3rd.

[2] C.O. 318: 5, 1–2. Barnes and Owen, II, pp. 337–8. Charles Middleton in October 1787 thought 3,000 men sufficient for St. Lucia, with a proper naval force. J. K. Laughton (ed.): *Letters and Papers of Charles, Lord Barham, 1758–1813* (Navy Records Society, Vols. XXXII, XXXVIII–IX), 3 vols, London, 1907–11, II, p. 269. Grant had previously written to Barrington on April 20th for leave at the end of the campaign. W.O. 4: 274, 107, 124, 125.

[3] Described by Serle, Tatum, *op. cit.*, pp. 257–8.   [4] C.O. 5: 96, 45–7.

[5] *Ibid.*, 69. D'Estaing sailed from Toulon in March; there was no formal declaration of war by France until July 10th.   [6] *Ibid.*, 123.

Germain replied to Grant on July 29th, in a secret letter, notifying the King's approval of his appointment. The King, 'as an encouragement to the troops serving under you to distinguish themselves in the execution of your orders', would allow Grant to post all vacancies that might occur in the corps under him, and would give 'the greatest attention' to Grant's recommendations when finally filling such vacancies. After success at St. Lucia, Grant was now given discretion to undertake further operations against other French islands in conjunction with the Naval Commander-in-Chief, as 'is proper to be undertaken and that there is sufficient ground to expect will be attended with success'. Supplies were to be sent from Cork in armed victuallers—the first had sailed on June 24th—and this mode of supply would continue. Grant was to ensure their speedy return. Money for the payment of the troops would be sent out by the Treasury, 'whenever a ship of war can be spared for that service'. The Ordnance Board would be ordered to provide and send out 'a proper supply of ammunition as soon as a return is received of the ordnance you take with you'. Germain held out no hopes of an augmentation of the force, 'unless peace is made with the colonies'.[1] Such a reply did not suggest vigour in at least one department. On the same day, Lord Howe wrote to Rear-Admiral Barrington: he postponed the arrangement for the appointed aid to a future opportunity,[2] deeming it inexpedient to send off the armament for the 'secret service' until the destination of the Toulon squadron could be more prefectly ascertained.[3] Germain, who had not yet received Clinton's letter of July 11th, wrote to him on August 6th deprecating the delay in the West Indies expedition: 'the season will be so far advanced before it may be expected the troops can sail from New York that I fear they will be exposed to the danger of a hurricane on their voyage, and to that of the autumnal diseases upon their arrival'. However,

[1] C.O. 318: 5, 5–12. Barnes and Owen, II, pp. 338–41. Martinique and Guadeloupe were both 'pointed out' to him. Barrington was sent similar orders dated August 14th, received October 18th, *Barrington Papers*, II, pp. 80–2.

[2] *Ibid.*, II, p. 53. Received September 18th.

[3] *Ibid.*, pp. 93–4. Admiralty to Barrington, August 29th. Received November 18th.

he considered Grant's appointment as 'taking the most likely means to insure success'.[1] On September 2nd, Germain approved the measures outlined by Clinton on July 11th,[2] but hoped the French fleet would soon be dealt with; opportunity would then offer for carrying out the secret instructions of March 21st.[3] On September 15th, Clinton was ready to detach the expedition under Grant, as well as the 3,000 men for the Floridas, and one battalion to the Bermuda and Bahama Islands, but with the old snag, 'as soon as shipping was ready'. He continued that 'without this army is greatly reinforced, it must remain on a most strict defensive next year'.[4] Charles Stuart, writing to Bute on September 16th, had the West Indies expedition starting 'next week',[5] but then it was to be the first week in October. His regiment, the 26th, was to have accompanied it, 'but a friend of mine found means to have another appointment without my knowledge'.[6] The difficulty was still with the naval preparations,[7] and Clinton was able to use some of the troops in a move forward on September 22nd, to procure forage, 'have a look at the rebels', and favour the expedition to Egg Harbour.[8] As the naval convoy was now ready, he had directed the troops to fall back in order that such of the regiments as were destined for the expedition might proceed upon it without delay.[9] On October 7th, Stuart ascribed continuing delay to the non-arrival of the August packet.[10] Clinton informed Germain on October 8th that the Admiral having at length been able to appoint a convoy, he would 'in a

---

[1] C.O. 5: 96, 49–50. Germain, writing on July 1st, had imagined the troops as already dispatched. *Ibid.*, 27. [2] See above, pp. 00–00.

[3] C.O. 5: 96, 91–2. [4] *Ibid.*, 217–18.

[5] Stuart Wortley, *op. cit.*, p. 133. [6] *Ibid.*, p. 135.

[7] Gambier to Sandwich, September 22nd, Barnes and Owen, II, p. 315; October 11th, *ibid.*, pp. 319, 321. James Gambier (1723–1789), Rear-Admiral in 1778, had succeeded Lord Howe as naval commander.

[8] For the raid on Egg Harbour, October 5th, commanded by Patrick Ferguson, see C.O. 5: 96, 347–9, 351–8.

[9] C.O. 5: 96, 325–7. To Germain, October 8th. The move forward is described by Cornwallis to Clinton, September 28th, 329–30. Clinton was also prepared to use the force in a combined expedition with the fleet against Boston, mooted in late September. W. B. Willcox, 'British Strategy in America 1778', *Journal of Modern History*, XX, No. 2, p. 118.

[10] Wortley, *op. cit.*, p. 139.

few days' have it in his power to detach to the West Indies 5,000 British effective rank and file, 'a dismemberment which is severe indeed'. For Florida, he proposed sending foreign troops and provincials, whose loss to his army would not be so much felt, but the treaties with the former and the 'understood stipulation' of the latter had precluded his sending them to the West Indies. The whole was 'a wound fatal to the hopes of any future vigour in this Army', and Clinton did not wish to retain its 'mortifying command'. He feared it was not in the power of Great Britain to restore to him the ten British regiments he had lost; 'the very nerves of this army'. The British who remained were in quality equal to them but in number too small 'to animate the over-proportion of foreigners etc who tho' they may be faithful, cannot be supposed equally zealous', and were not equally inured to service. Were all the troops remaining 'of the first stamp, their scanty numbers would stifle any hope that might arise from the consideration of their valour'. Clinton was sure Germain would not wish him to remain 'a mournful witness of the debility of the Army at whose head, had I been unshackled by instructions, I might have indulged expectations of rendering serious service to my country'. He was no longer in a situation to promote the King's interest and wished to resign.[1]

The 'few days' dragged on. Gambier, writing to Rear-Admiral Barrington on October 21st, had stated that Hotham was under orders to join him, and 'will be within a week ready',[2] whilst Stuart on October 24th predicted a departure 'next week'.[3] On that day, the troops came under Grant's orders,[4] and the instructions given to Hotham bear the same date. He was to proceed to

---

[1] C.O. 5: 96, 321–2.

[2] *Barrington Papers*, II, p. 104. Received December 1st, 1778.

[3] Wortley, *op. cit.*, p. 139.

[4] *Barrington Papers*, II, pp. 166–9. The dates and accounts of the expedition are fully covered in this work. There is a valuable eye-witness account by the Hon. Colin Lindsay of the 46th Regt. in Lord Lindsay (ed.): *The Lives of the Lindsays*, London, 1849, III, pp. 331–56 (later referred to as *Lindsay*); see also Barnes and Owen, II, pp. 343–62; *Annual Register*, 1779; 'History of Europe', Chapter 3, and *Gentleman's Magazine*, 1779, April, with a plate facing page 115. The accounts by Fortescue, *A History of the British Army*, III, and *The British Army 1783–1802*, London, 1905, are incorrect in some details.

sea with the utmost expedition to execute these instructions 'according to their utmost sense and spirit'. The fleet consisted of sixty-two vessels. There were forty-two troop transports; one vessel for the Commanding General (the *Charming Nelly*), one for staff officers (the *Roman Emperor*), one for other general officers, three hospital ships, four ordnance ships, six horse ships, one for engineers, one for the transport agent,[1] two forage vessels, and one schooner. Convoying this were two 64-gun vessels, three 50-gun vessels, one 36-gun vessel, and one bomb vessel—seven in all. When the ordnance stores were embarked, such a number of flat-bottomed boats were to be added as Gambier thought proper to send with them. The regiments embarked were the 4th, 5th, 15th, 27th, 28th, 35th, 40th, 46th, 49th, and 55th, all showing a suspicious embarkation strength of 640 men.[2] All the sick of the regiments, less about fifty, were embarked, their complaints being so slight as to render but few of them unfit for actual service.[3] Grant received his final instructions from Clinton on October 29th, and the expedition sailed from Sandy Hook on November 3rd.[4]

The two services had done little better than the departments at home in mounting an 'immediate' expedition, and rumour had given Washington the idea they were going to the West Indies by October 18th, with an almost correct estimate of the strength of the expedition.[5] As the King wrote to Sandwich on October 25th, the expedition could not take effect whilst D'Estaing was in

[1] For his duties, see Curtis, *The Organisation of the British Army in the American Revolution*, New Haven, 1920, p. 125.

[2] *Barrington Papers*, II, pp. 95–8. Giving full embarkation returns, name and tonnage of all vessels, and the manner of distinguishing them whilst at sea.

[3] Clinton to Germain, October 25th, giving the strengths and state of the Expedition as at that date. C.O. 5: 96, 417.

[4] Clinton to Germain of November 8th, *ibid.*, 389. Embarkation was complete on October 29th. The instructions dated October 27th are in C.O. 318: 5, 33–4.

[5] Writing in Rhode Island, Mackenzie noted in his diary on November 5th, 1778, the destination of the expedition, and an almost accurate account of its intentions, II, p. 416. Grant had also wished to take Simcoe's Queens Rangers; see Sir John Graves Simcoe, *A Journal of the Operations of the Queens Rangers from the end of the year 1777 to the conclusion of the late American War*, Exeter, 1787, p. 57.

North America,[1] and shortage of naval vessels had done the rest:

> inadequate, my honoured Lord, [wrote Gambier to Sandwich on 11 October] to the variegated numberless stations, duties and requisitions; what a number lost, burnt and destroyed; how few remaining, and what a terrible state and condition![2]

Germain, writing a most secret and confidential letter to Clinton on November 4th, had no doubt that Grant had now gone,[3] but there were still some in England with doubts. Sandwich wrote to Gambier on November 13th that as a friend he could not help giving a hint:

> the postponing, and much more the putting a stop to the expedition to the West Indies seems to me an ill-judged measure, as it subjects you (and very justly in my opinion) to the blame and clamour that will be the consequence of the loss of our islands. You will observe that though I make use of the word you, I do not mean that the naval commander alone can be found fault with upon this occasion.

It was obvious: 'there is an unwillingness in every department in America to the making this detachment, which I conclude arises from your considering only your own immediate wants, and not thinking of our distresses at home'. If the whole force pointed out in the original orders could not be sent, Sandwich continued, 'any force possible should be spared: . . . this is an object that all sorts of people here have set their hearts upon, and upon which they are much in earnest'.[4] Having received letters from Gambier dated November 11th and 23rd,[5] Sandwich was very happy at the sailing of the expedition to the West Indies.

You cannot conceive the sudden alteration that the news

---

[1] Barnes and Owen, II, p. 325.   [2] *Ibid.*, p. 321.

[3] C.O. 5: 96, 262. He reported him under sail on October 27th to the King. Fortescue, *op. cit.*, IV, No. 2459, November 27th. See also Walpole to Mann on November 27th, Paget Toynbee (ed.): *The Letters of Horace Walpole,* X, p. 348, notes Clinton embarking a body of troops for the West Indies but then disembarking them again. The reasons for this final delay have not been traced.   [4] Barnes and Owen, II, p. 328.

[5] *Ibid.*, pp. 317–24 and pp. 324–5.

occasioned among us, as the West India merchants had had a meeting and agreed to make a very hostile representation to the throne, stating that the defence of their property had been neglected, and requesting that immediate reinforcements might be sent from hence without which the loss of our West India islands would shortly be added to our other calamities. Whatever representation now is made will be in a different style.[1]

Germain returned to this feeling of unwillingness, and also of being slighted, in replying to Clinton's wish of resignation on December 3rd. Refusing to accept that resignation, Germain insisted that Clinton could rely on every means being employed to augment his force so as to enable him to act offensively. Even if with the utmost exertions the Army could not be increased to its former number, the King had such reliance upon Clinton's zeal and ability, and on the valour and discipline of the troops, that he felt sure there would be good results the next campaign. The disposition and employment of the troops would be left to Clinton's judgment, as it was always intended they should be. Every measure that Germain might have suggested was submitted to Clinton to execute or not as he thought most fit, and it was by no means intended to 'shackle' him. As for the rulings to evacuate Philadelphia, and send an expedition to the West Indies, it was with much regret, said Germain, that these measures were adopted by the King and all his confidential servants:

the chagrin which it was foreseen those orders would occasion to the General, and the Army, made no inconsiderable ingredient in our concern, but the intelligence we had received of the intentions of France, which the events that have since happened prove to have been well founded, and the necessity of providing for the immediate security of our West India possessions, would not allow of an alternative.

Germain was persuaded Clinton would now join in opinion that those two measures were unavoidable.[2]

[1] Ibid., pp. 328–9.
[2] C.O. 5: 96, 377–83. See also Clinton to Germain December 15th, 1778, C.O. 5: 97, 57–8. 'All can scrutinise the parade of my command, but very few can or ought to suspect its embarrassments'.

From the expedition now at sea, Hotham, on November 6th, detached a swift frigate, the *Venus*, to acquaint Barrington he was on the way, 'judging it essential for the King's service that you should early be made acquainted with the time when I may be reasonably expected to join you'. He sent a copy of the instructions he had been given by Gambier, which was received by Barrington at Barbados on November 23rd.[1] The fleet arrived at Carlisle Bay, Barbados, on December 10th, the military forces being composed as follows:[2]

Officers Present

| | Commission | | | | | | Staff | | | | |
	Cols.	Lt.-Cols.	Maj-ors	Capts.	Lieuts.	En-signs	Chap-lain	Adju-tant	Q.M.	Sur-geon	Mate
R.A.				3	1	6			1	1	1	1
4th	1	1		5	10	6		1	1	1	1
5th	1	1		6	11	5		1	1	1	1
15th	1			6	10	4		1	1	1	1
27th	1	1		8	10	3		1			1
28th				8	11	3		1	1	1	1
35th	1	1		8	11	3		1	1	1	1
40th		1		7	9	3		1	1	1	1
46th	1	1		5	9	3		1	1	1	1
49th	1	1		8	11	3		1	1	1	1
55th	1	1		6	11	2	1	1	1	1	1
Total	8	8		70	104	41	1	10	11	10	11

Effective Sergeants, Drummers, Rank and File

| | Present and fit for duty | | | Absent on Command and Recruiting | | | Sick | | |
	Ser-geants	Drum-mers	Rank and File	Ser-geants	Drum-mers	Rank and File	Ser-geants	Drum-mers	Rank and File
R.A.	5	6	169						
4th	29	22	489	1		3			12
5th	27	14	465		1	1	3	2	32
15th	28	16	392	2	2	5			10
27th	30	22	462			6			42
28th	29	22	504	1					13

[1] *Barrington Papers*, II, pp. 94-5.
[2] Army State, December 10th, C.O. 318: 5, 13.

35th	30	20	507						11
40th	30	22	485			6			9
46th	25	21	454	5	1	11			16
49th	29	20	501	1	2	3			20
55th	30	22	517			7			10
Total	292	207	4,945	10	6	42	3	2	175

	Total Effectives			To Compleat		
	Sergeants	Drummers	Rank and File	Sergeants	Drummers	Rank and File
R.A. ..	5	6	169			
4th ..	30	22	504			56
5th ..	30	17	498		5	62
15th ..	30	18	407		4	153
27th ..	30	22	510			50
28th ..	30	22	517			43
30th ..	30	20	518		2	42
40th ..	30	22	500			60
46th ..	30	22	481			79
49th ..	30	22	524			36
55th ..	30	22	534			26
	305	215	5,162		11	607

The fleet sailed from Barbados under command of Barrington
on December 12th, fifty-nine transports and sixteen ships of the
fleet,[1] and arrived off St. Lucia on December 13th, disembarka-
tion of the light troops commencing that same afternoon by use
of the flat boats, and continuing on the morning of December
14th,[2] 'ten regiments of the finest fellows that ever drew a
trigger'.[3] According to prisoners taken on December 14th, the
whole enemy force upon the island consisted of 180 men of the
regiment of Martinique and some 50 or 60 of the inhabitants in
arms. The prisoners observed that 'with so small a force, they
never could have thought of opposition, but that a few shots

[1] Not 'within twenty four hours' as stated by Fortescue, *A History of the
British Army*, III, p. 264, and *The British Army*, p. 121.

[2] Not on December 12th and 13th, as given by Fortescue, *A History of the
British Army*, III, p. 264. Correct dates are given in *The British Army*, pp. 122–3.

[3] Barnes and Owen, II, pp. 344–5.

from their twenty-four pounders were necessary for the honour of France'.[1] This opposition was, however, strongly augmented by the arrival of a French fleet and transports under D'Estaing on December 14th. Full-scale operations commenced on December 15th and continued until the re-embarkation of the French on December 28th.[2] Grant's forces were divided into three brigades:

(a) 4th, 15th, 28th, 46th and 55th Regts. under Prescott.[3]

(b) 27th, 35th, 40th and 49th Regts. under Calder.[4]

(c) The reserve of the 5th, the Light Infantry and the Grenadiers under Medows.[5]

and there was much closer co-operation between the Army and Navy than had been the case at Charleston in 1776.[6] The fiercest action was fought by the Reserve on December 18th. 'The fire of our troops was concentrated upon them like the focus of a burning glass', wrote Lindsay;[7] 'a fire so hot that no drum could equal its perpetual noise'. Noted another observer, 'this body of heroes of ours . . . determined to defend themselves, naked as they was (not having time to entrench themselves)'.[8] Medows acted with considerable bravery—but from his Brigade Orders of December 13th, he had hoped for much from the 'active gallantry' of the Light Infantry, the 'determined bravery' of the Grenadiers, and the 'confirmed discipline' of the 5th Regiment of Foot.[9] (The art of writing communiqués is longstanding in the British Army.)

---

[1] *Lindsay*, p. 333.   [2] The French fleet sailed on December 29th.
[3] Robert Prescott (1725–1816). Mackenzie noted of him in Rhode Island in 1778 as 'much chagrined with every body', II, p. 394—a man who easily took offence and felt slighted, II, pp. 388, 392, 400–3. He became a Major-General in 1781. Not to be confused with Richard Prescot, captured at Rhode Island in 1777, and exchanged for Charles Lee.
[4] Sir Henry Calder was made a Major-General on November 26th, 1782.
[5] William Medows (1738–1813).
[6] *Barrington Papers*, II, pp. 130, 132, 162, 164, 169. Barnes and Owen, II, p. 354.
[7] *Lindsay*, p. 351.
[8] Barnes and Owen, II, pp. 350–2. 'The Almighty struck with us and we conquered', he concluded. *Ibid.*, p. 356.
[9] *Lindsay*, pp. 334–5. For Medows' conduct, pp. 343, 346.

After the evacuation of the French forces to Martinique, articles of capitulation were agreed with the inhabitants of St. Lucia on December 30th.[1] Meanwhile, the correspondents were busy. Lindsay wrote of 'rank and luxuriant vegetation choking up the woods', 'myriads of disgusting reptiles', 'noxious exhalations', the island totally uncultivated and 'nearly in a state of nature'.[2] Until December 23rd, everyone had been without tents, and 'wet both day and night incessantly'.[3] The officers had only salt provisions left,[4] 'though we were without the means to dress our pork, this was not the first time we had eaten it raw, or sliced and broiled upon the end of a bayonet, with yams and plantains ... affording to a hungry man no despicable meal'.[5] Lindsay particularly commented upon the polite behaviour of the French, 'a very different style of war from that which we had been used to in America'.[6] Grant gave a brief account of operations, writing to Germain on December 26th from Morné Fortune what was to be considered 'as a card', as a more particular account would follow by an Aide-de-Camp on the first safe conveyance.[7] This fuller account was written on December 31st,[8] from 'the most difficult country war was ever made in'.

With St. Lucia successfully occupied, the British commanders turned their attention to the further objects pointed out in the instructions of 1778. Those of March 21st had stipulated that, after providing a force sufficient for the defence of St. Lucia, the remainder of the troops were to be distributed among the other British possessions in the Leeward Islands, so securing them

---

[1] They are reproduced in *Barrington Papers*, II, pp. 141–47.

[2] *Lindsay*, pp. 333–4. See also p. 351.   [3] *Ibid.*, p. 341.

[4] *Ibid.*, pp. 336, 349.   [5] *Ibid.*, p. 339.   [6] *Ibid.*, p. 350.

[7] C.O. 318: 5, 15–17. This 'card' was sent to Barbados, the Governor of which was unable to get a proper vessel to send to England and the letters were still there in February. Grant to Germain, February 5th, 1779. *Ibid.*, 95–97.

[8] *Ibid.*, 25–29. It was sent off in the care of Grant's A.D.C. by the sloop *Weazel* on January 10th, 1779, but the ship was taken by a French frigate off St. Eustatia three days later. Grant was sure his A.D.C. would throw the dispatches overboard (To Germain, February 5th, C.O. 318: 5). The sloop *Pearl* sailed on February 7th, and the dispatches carried by it were delivered in London on March 23rd, the official news of the capture of St. Lucia being published as a *London Gazette Extraordinary* the next day.

from enemy attack. On July 29th, Germain had ordered Grant to attack other French possessions, indicating both Martinique and Guadeloupe as suitable objectives;[1] similar instructions, dated August 14th, had been sent to Barrington.[2] The Commanders on the spot soon realised that concentration was essential; this ruled out the possibility of further offensive action. For the forces under their command, this meant inactivity, consequent boredom, increasing sickness, and a serious decline in morale. Instructions from England at first repeated the policy of dispersion. Faced with the problem of military and naval resources, the 'change of plan' was then modified—the British troops in St. Lucia were to be replaced by troops more seasoned to tropical conditions, and were to be returned to the mainland to assist operations there. This plan was frustrated by French naval superiority. Ministers at home then decided to reinforce both military and naval forces in the Leeward Islands: grandiose projects, revealing the continued over-facile optimism of the ministers, which failed to develop because of the grim realities on the spot.

The announcement of the Franco-American Treaty of Amity (March 13th, 1778) meant that colonial rebellion had become national war; it necessitated a change of plan in the whole of British strategy.[3] This was contained in the instructions sent to Clinton March 21st, 1778, whereby, in the best tradition of eighteenth-century warfare, France was to be attacked in the West Indies, by troops taken from the main theatre of war, whilst merely defensive operations in the shape of a naval war, with troops used to guard naval bases and to help in coastal raids, were to continue on the American mainland. The expedition against St. Lucia, envisaged in those instructions, sailed from New

[1] See above, p. 208.

[2] See above, p. 208. Barrington was superseded in the naval command on January 6th, 1779, by the arrival of Vice-Admiral John Byron (1723–1786). Byron was replaced by Rear-Admiral Hyde Parker (1714–1782) in August 1779, and had no further active employment.

[3] For this change of plan, see W. B. Willcox: 'British Strategy in America 1778', *Journal of Modern History*, XIX, No. 2.

York on November 3rd, and captured its objective on December 28th, whilst by the autumn, the war on the mainland appeared to be in its usual condition of stalemate. The Franco-American alliance had produced no tangible results: British defence in America had brought them no nearer to victory.

X

THE RESULTS OF THE AMERICAN
REVOLUTION

With the American Revolution, the problem of inter-state organisation crossed the Atlantic. The colonies themselves, in their making of a federal constitution, had then to decide the allocation of power between central and local authorities. They began in 1781[1] by attempting to avoid too great a central power—at first denying Congress power either to tax or to regulate commerce—which were precisely those rights of the British Government the colonists had questioned and challenged; but this ended in chaos, and had to be revised in 1787. The colonists then admitted in part the pre-revolutionary constitutional contentions of the British, and the value of the old colonial system. That system could not have been as bad as the colonists had painted it, else they would not have drawn so much from it. They adopted the old colonial representative system—Connecticut retained its old charter until 1818, Rhode Island until 1843. Every state but Vermont placed control of the government firmly in the hands of persons possessing property.

The political nation, as in England, was formed of those with a stake in society: there were property qualifications of varying degrees for voting, and proportionately higher ones for office. In many cases, the colonial qualifications remained unaltered, thus perpetuating the control of the older established eastern tidewater sections, as well as the struggle between west and east arising from disproportionate representation. The attitude of the leaders in the colonies was summed up by Hamilton's words at the 1787 Federal Convention: the mass of the people 'seldom judge or

---

[1] The Articles of Confederation became effective on March 2nd, 1781, over four years after their first adoption by Congress, and their submission to the States for acceptance.

determine right'. It was the well-born and rich, the colonial 'aristocracy', who should have a distinct and permanent share in government. In all coasting trade regulations the Navigation Acts were followed. The control exercised over western lands since 1763 was even more rigidly applied. The submission of colonial legislation to Privy Council review was imitated by the establishment of courts to decide upon the constitutionality of acts of both State and Federal legislatures. Here was yet another revolution which brought back much of the familiar surroundings which in 1775 seemed to have been given up for ever.

The Republican and Federalist parties which developed after 1787 (of which the present Democratic and Republican parties are the descendants) merely continued in a new form the divisions present in colonial America which we have seen at work in this period, and just as in England, so in America national politics were partly local, based on local standing, local affairs, and local feuds. These divisions were the planting-slaveholding interest against the mercantile, shipping, financial interest, South against North, East against West, new rising against old-established classes and regions. Add to these divisions, the prevailing opinion in Europe that a federal republic could persist only in small areas, and the reason why most Europeans believed that the American venture would quickly fail is apparent: dependence on European aid, instability, and dissolution were confidently predicted. As late as 1803, Napoleon was clear that in selling the Louisiana territory to the United States, and thereby doubling its size, he was preparing her eventual break-up. Such a large, divided, and unwieldy republic must split apart, and European powers might then share in the spoils.

Whoever would study the eighteenth-century British constitution and its practice should consider both the American Constitution of 1787 and its practice to this day, for it is there preserved as if kept in a refrigerator. The President is the chief and only executive: so, too, was the King in eighteenth-century Britain. Leadership in policy was expected to be one of the functions of the President: so too was the choice of the various heads of departments. The Secretaries of State and of War were made responsible to the President, who could remove officials without the consent of the Senate. A Cabinet officer in the United States may still almost emulate the words of Burke in his 'Thoughts on the Present Discontents': keep himself totally estranged from his colleagues, differ in council, privately traverse, publicly oppose, and yet continue in favour. He may retain office even when disagreeing with policy, because his primary duty is to carry out the orders of the chief executive: this was Cabinet practice in Great Britain in this period. Government must be carried on: here is the key to the British attitude before, and the American after, the American Revolution. This copying of the British pattern was the main fear of those who formed the first opposition in the new American political scene: they believed that the ultimate object of the Federal Constitution was to convert the existing republican form of government into monarchy, taking the English constitution as the model.

The eventual demarcation of the boundary with Canada, the opening up of the West, and all the internal development that those steps implied, were the real cause of the turning away from Europe, of that isolationism which only ended in the present generation (the same reason also explains a similar tendency in all nineteenth-century settlement Dominions). Washington wrote in his Farewell Address in 1796 that it was the true policy of the United States to steer clear of permanent alliances with any part of the world, and trust to temporary alliances for extraordinary emergencies. In 1798, Congress revoked, and declared null and void the treaty of permanent alliance with France, concluded twenty years before by Benjamin Franklin, the first, and until the present time the last, treaty of alliance the United States has ever contracted with any European nation. In his Inaugural Address of 1801, Thomas Jefferson used the phrase 'entangling alliances', thinking specifically of alliances with European nations, and this became sacrosanct in American political thinking, the first commandment, as it has been described, in American foreign relations.

The most important result of the cleavage in the Anglo-Saxon, English-speaking world, which the American Revolution effected, occurred in the sphere of foreign relations, for to that cleavage can be traced many of the calamities of the twentieth century—the two world wars, and the recurrent economic crises. Moreover, the remarkable retention of the memory of the 'misdeeds' of George III and British Imperialism (constantly expressed significantly enough in Mid-West papers and journals) was an important factor in dividing the British and American front to the Russians at Yalta, as Chester Wilmot has argued.[1] The continued belief of the Americans that the British were inveterate Empire-builders and land grabbers, and that neither the Americans nor Russians had any tradition of Empire building by force, not only bedevilled Anglo-American strategy, preventing the exploitation of the Balkans from the Mediterranean, but also handed over control in post-war central Europe to the Russians. This same suspicion still mars Anglo-American co-operation, and is in part responsible for the considerable measure of disunity which prevails between the two great Anglo-Saxon peoples, a disunity which gives constant opportunity to any skilful and determined opponent to drive wedges between them. The present day has seen the fulfilment of the prediction made in 1780 by Thomas Pownall, a late governor of Massachusetts Bay. He then saw America as having taken its equal station with the nations upon earth, far removed by nature from the old world and all its enthralling interests and wrangling politics, and without an enemy or rival. He questioned whether that most enterprising spirit, which had inspired the achievement of a new system, would be content to remain as limited by nature. He foresaw that commerce all over the world would open the door to emigration, and that by constant inter-communication, America in time would approach nearer to Europe. 'North America has become a new primary planet, which, while it takes it own course in its own orbit, must shift the common centre of gravity'.

In 1790, the boundaries of the Republic included 800,000 square miles; by 1860, 3 million. The population in 1790 was around 4 million people; by 1950, 149 million. The lure of the frontier, as later events confirmed, was not to be withstood; west-

[1] Chester Wilmot: *The Struggle for Europe*, London, 1952, Chapter XXXII.

ward the course of empire took its way, until the limit was reached. The most characteristic figure of American society, as Mr. Douglas Reed once insisted, was the person arrived from, or anxious to be, somewhere else. Restlessness has been a constant factor in American development; though no open spaces remain to conquer, America is still full of people moving around, to try something new somewhere else. This restlessness was a cause of a further by-product of the American Revolution in North America, the Dominion of Canada. This was essentially a consolidation of the scattered colonies which had remained within the British Empire, and which, alongside of the American Republic, had inevitably to become united in order to survive and develop at a pace in any degree comparable to that of their progressive neighbour.[1]

As far as Great Britain was concerned, the American Revolution gave considerable impetus to the movements for both parliamentary and economic reform. The radical measure for more equal representation and more frequent Parliaments arose from the questions posed by the American Revolution: what were the powers of the English Parliament, and on what basis did they rest? The financial expense of the war, which added £160 million to the National Debt, likewise gave a great urge to the cutting down of useless offices, sinecures and pensions, and formed the basis of the financial policy of the younger Pitt.

Lord North's ministry collapsed in 1782 because of disaster in the war, and the brief Whig success in 1782-3 was caused as much by that circumstance, a unique national disaster, as by new constitutional principles. The new ideas in politics, originated by the war, lapsed when the situation returned to normal under the younger Pitt.[2] Their premature appearance had led many to antedate the continuous development of modern political concepts, in particular those of modern responsible government and the development of party. The consecration of party by its

[1] Alexander Brady: *Democracy in the Dominions,* second edition, London, 1952, p. 39.

[2] On this point, see D. G. Barnes: *George III and William Pitt, 1783-1806,* London, 1939. See also R. Pares: *King George III and the Politicians,* Oxford, 1953.

development in the nineteenth century and after has deceived posterity into thinking that Burke had the better of the argument in his own day, whereas in fact few eighteenth-century administrations were composed of members of a single group. Those who accept accounts of this period and the claims made by contemporary writers have been tempted to over-emphasise the political importance, the conscious purposefulness and the growth of these constitutional movements. The tentative beginnings of economic and parliamentary reform, and new Cabinet practice, served for nothing but to educate the people, and to be an example for future times.

But, although the monarch continued to do for the nation what it had not yet the means of doing adequately for itself, Parliament, when it learnt to exercise power, possessed it irresistibly. It was in the logic of the settlement of 1688–9 that ultimately Parliament must prevail, and take over from the monarch powers as yet his. The ultimate direction of policy still centred in the Crown as supreme magistrate and head of the Executive. He was expected to frame policy, and to choose the men who would carry it out, and secure parliamentary approval for it. Although Parliament had the right to criticise the King's instruments of government, and to demand their removal, it was only the growth of firmly organised and disciplined party which enabled it to acquire the right of designating ministers and of deciding on measures. Until the nineteenth century the Crown exercised its powers and remained the directing factor in political life. So long as the monarch furnished support in Parliament by the use of the influence of the Crown, and decided on men and measures, he was bound to remain active in political life. The Constitution, although free as Pitt said in 1805, was yet monarchical.

Nevertheless, by 1837 the transition from royal to parliamentary government was approaching, both in principle and practice: the country was nearly ready to accept Fox's prematurely enunciated thesis of 1784 that Kings should reign but not rule. Besides the old age and madness of one king, and the unmanliness and weakness of his successors, deeper factors had been at work since the American Revolution. Problems were larger and more complex, the conditions of political life were changing. Genuine political and economic reform had lost the Crown the control it previously exercised over the composition of the Lower House. (The younger Pitt performed immense labours in fields of which Burke had only talked.[1]) There was a growing tendency towards a two-party system, with proprietary groups disappearing, and the two parties containing between them an ever greater proportion of the House of Commons, and supporting definite programmes: a development which reduced the scope for the exercise of royal choice. There was growing cohesion in the Cabinet, now taking the initiative independent of the King's referring questions to it, to whose opinion, if ministers insisted, the King in the last resort would have to yield. Something recognisably like a modern Prime Minister had emerged—an avowed and real Minister, as Pitt described it in 1803, possessing the chief weight in the Council, and the principal place in the King's confidence.

Parliament was gradually extending its authority into spheres previously those of the monarch. Public opinion was replacing the Crown as the directing force in British politics. For most of the eighteenth century, 'public opinion' was only visible at times of crisis, but after the ferment caused by the American Revolution, it gradually developed during the movement for parliamentary reform and in the rising wave of humanitarianism, and was fostered by better, more independent, newspapers, and by parliamentary reporting. Governing empirically gave way to pledges and programmes, often embarrassing and inconvenient, in which the wishes and interests of a public now more able to watch and criticise had to be considered. Thus, between 1783 and 1837, the personality of the monarch ceased to be the pivot of politics but gradually became the rallying point for the emotions and thoughts of those who had taken its place as the directing political force. If the political authority offered to Victoria was likely to be limited, the opportunity for personal conduct,

[1] A. S. Foord: 'The Waning of the Influence of the Crown', *English Historical Review*, Vol. LXII, pp. 484–507.

character and example was not: there was scope for an entirely different kind of personal monarchy, in which the symbolism of the office was to develop freely.

Too much has also been made of the results of the American Revolution on the ideas about colonisation prevailing in 1783. It never occurred to George III to doubt that Great Britain's prosperity in the future, as in the past, was inextricably bound up with the possession of territories and interests overseas. He told Shelburne during the peace negotiations in 1782 that it was from the East and West Indies we must now alone expect any chance of putting this country into a flourishing state once more. If, at the peace, we were not very cautious as to what concessions we made in those parts, nothing but ruin would ensue. In fact, of the acquisitions which had been made in these areas in 1763, only Tobago was relinquished. Moreover, as Adam Smith had remarked to a young friend who lamented the ruin of the nation in the American War, there was a great deal in a nation: ruin would only come if what was left was neglected. The revulsion against actual settlement colonies, naturally accentuated by the quarrel with the Americans, strengthened the emphasis visible since 1763 on the creation of a network of commercial exchange through the Pacific and Indian Oceans—informal rather than formal expansion, a chain of trading posts, protected at strategic points by naval bases. By 1815, with naval superiority confirmed, even these bases came to be considered unnecessary. In 1782–3, Shelburne placed emphasis on trade rather than dominion (which later became the keynote of the Free Traders, in whose view the building of colonies stood condemned as the most troublesome and least profitable of all methods of doing business overseas). All the themes brought to fruition by the Free Traders in the next century were opened in the years immediately after the American Revolution.

The hope and intention was to find markets for the widening range and quantity of British manufactures, which a limited Empire was increasingly unable to consume. The opening up of new markets would enable a diversity of commodities, earned by home production, to flow to this country, both raising the standard of living and fostering industry and trade, while any surplus could be sold to European countries on advantageous terms. This raises a vital issue for further study: to what extent was the 'Industrial Revolution' responsible for the Second British Empire? By the terms of the peace settlement, Shelburne hoped to extend this form of commercial expansion in the west as well as in the east, by establishing the basis for a new Anglo-American partnership, in which the United States would become the colonising power, building new communities and opening up the wilderness, while Britain would supply the needed manufactures. He regretted the separation of countries united by blood, principles, habits, and every tie short of territorial proximity, and wished to see a new connection better adapted to the present temper and interests of both countries.[1] This wish was shared by many: it had been well described by David Hartley as early as 1777. He thought the friendship of America, 'which is now the rising world, and which will in a few years be multiplied an hundred fold, would be an infinite recompense, in exchange for an irksome dominion, onerous to them and barren to us'. In 1778, he suggested cementing the two countries together by a mutual nationalisation in all rights and franchises to the fullest extent. 'We are derived from the same stock; we have the same religion, the same manners, the same language, the same temper, the same love of liberty and of independence, and if we must be seemingly divided, let there be at least an union in that partition'.[2]

But such hopes and ideas as these challenged the ark of the economic covenant of Empire, as independence did the political, and were opposed by many interests. The essence of what change took place in the Empire after 1783 was the slow development of this new economic policy, which in turn made possible a new kind of colonialism. To what extent, if at all, should a canalised system of imperial trade, based on the principle of metropolitan monopoly, be relaxed in order to secure the benefits of reciprocity with the inheritors of a continent? Was it possible, or desirable, to modify a system of economic nationalism by establishing a bi-

---

[1] See, *e.g.*, his letter to Richard Oswald, July 27th, 1782. Add. MSS., 42, 363, f. 255.   [2] Guttridge, *op. cit.*, pp. 258–60.

national partnership? From the purely mercantile point of view, the loss of the colonies was believed to be small, since an independent America gave no increase of resources, wealth, or power to Britain's Bourbon rivals. Britain herself would not greatly suffer if the Americans were prevented, as the Navigation Acts prevented them, from enjoying as foreigners the same access to British colonial ports and markets which they had enjoyed as colonists. But the British West Indies would: their development and prosperity had depended upon the Old Colonial System. A great part of their trade had been with the North American mainland, carried in American ships, and they still required provisions from there to maintain their production of sugar and its by-products. Adam Smith argued that any restraint of trade there would hurt loyal subjects much more than revolted ones. Pitt brought forward a bill in 1783 to enable the American states to continue to enjoy their previous privileges in British ports and markets. He believed British commerce would gain more than it would lose by such a concession, and was prepared to face the risk of American competition in the carrying trade. Vested interests and established prejudice, though strongly challenged, eventually carried the day. William Knox, who framed the regulations for trade between the United States and the British West Indian islands, firmly re-established the Navigation Acts 'so as utterly to exclude American shipping'. Was it not more important than ever, it was argued, to underpin the whole network of ocean trade by preserving the deep-sea fisheries, and the carrying trade with the remnants of the Western Empire, as nurseries for British seamen?

Even so, the notions of Adam Smith and his disciples gained considerable influence after 1783. The United States were accorded a more favoured position in trade than had been enjoyed by any other foreign power in relation to the British Imperial economy. The bonds of economic dependence were broken, yet Anglo-American trade increased: by 1790, British exports to the United States were back to their pre-war figures, and the excess balance of trade in favour of this country was greater than it had been in 1772. The Americans were obliged by sheer necessity to continue trade, because only Great Britain was in a position adequately to supply her wants. The Navigation Acts were maintained to the very end for purposes of naval security, but as economic defences were found to be economic barriers, exclusion gave way to an extension of the Free Port system, and then to the reciprocal lowering of barriers connected with Huskisson, and to the gradual breakdown of the Old Colonial System.

A desire to recompense those who had remained loyal was also seen in a further aspect of policy after 1783. An attempt was made to construct a new self-contained Western Empire in which British North America—Canada, Nova Scotia, New Brunswick in particular, the home of the United Empire Loyalists and of many Highland emigrants[1]—should take the place of the revolted colonies, and supply the raw materials and foodstuffs required by the British West Indies. This attempt to fly in the face of geographic realities was foredoomed to failure. With the loss of the American colonies, the nice adjustment of food-producing units to units of tropical products, and of both to the industrial fabric of the mother country, was broken. The remaining British North American colonies were too poor in resources, too under-developed, too isolated, and too unfavourably situated, to take the place of those which had gone. The years between 1783 and 1820 proved to politicians and business men alike that the task of reconstructing the profitable self-contained world of the eighteenth century was impossible, even if any longer desirable. By 1820, the West Indian 'interest' had also declined, and Great Britain herself had outgrown the limited colonial system.

Such commercial expansion as there was after 1783 brought problems of its own, unseen by the promoters and supporters—renewed collisions with the French and Dutch required the strengthening of the British position in the East Indies and the Caribbean. Moreover, having sought commercial relations with seemingly stable and independent countries in the Pacific and the Far East, the British found themselves drawn, willy-nilly, into the administration of the large territories inhabited by non-Europeans. The seizure for strategic reasons of the Cape of Good

[1] See C. W. Dunn: *Highland Settler*, London, 1953.

Hope, the Gibraltar of the Indian Ocean—the half-way house to India—in the French Revolutionary War led the British step by step to the Zambesi and beyond, into strange and difficult race relationships. Internal anarchy and French rivalry, events—rather than intention—created the British Raj in India. Even strong supporters of mercantilism, who usually preferred chartered companies to royal colonies, acquiesced in interference and reform in India and elsewhere, because bad and insecure governments meant bad trade. This period thus saw the first attempt to deal with the problems of an alien and coloured Empire.

Parliament, by the Quebec Act, 1774, for the first time directly constituted a colony: in setting up government by Governor and Council only, this Act, as important in the history of the dependent Empire as the Durham report in Dominion history, became the precedent and model for Crown Colony government in non-British dependencies during the nineteenth century. In 1783-4, during the debates over the future of India, which led to Pitt's India Bill, the modern principle of trusteeship was first enunciated. Burke argued that all political power set over men ought to be exercised some way or other ultimately for their benefit: the idea implicit in the Proclamation of 1763, the protection of Red Indians against colonial pioneers, now became explicit. The rights and privileges involved in the government of India were 'all in the strictest sense a trust': Empire, as well as advancing the power and wealth of the ruling authority, should also civilise and develop the ruled. The humanitarian theme in colonial development was here begun: it went further with the Committee for the abolition of the Slave Trade in 1787, and with the impeachment of Warren Hastings, about which surely the most significant thing is that it happened, when a decade earlier it would not have.

Then, contrary to official expectation or desire, the place of the American colonies was taken by new settlements. Botany Bay, in the newly discovered continent of Australia, was founded by 1788, at first primarily as a penal settlement since MacCarthy Island (then known as Lemain Island) in the Gambia, which had been used since 1776, had proved impracticable. A Committee of the House of Commons rejected any further use of the

Gambia on the grounds that the outcasts of an old society could not form the basis of a new one. This underlines another point: the convict was more picturesque than important. It was the free settlers, encouraged from the first, who really created New South Wales, and later colonies in Australia—which indicates there may not have been the pessimism about settlement colonisation described by so many writers. These free settlers took with them social and political ideas developing at home, which later conflicted with the supposed lessons drawn from the American Revolution.

These lessons were that democratic institutions in a colony were a menace, and must be avoided wherever possible—in only one of the colonies acquired between 1793 and 1815 was the old representative system introduced, and Tobago received it since it had been British between 1763 and 1783, and had a vested right to an assembly. Canada was granted the old system in 1791, a concession due to the influx of the Loyalists, while the surviving remnants of the western Empire in the West Indies continued their old system with its fundamental constitutional dilemma—the result of annulling the charter of Massachusetts Bay Colony in 1774 had convinced home authority that a colonial representative legislature should not normally be suppressed without its own consent. But all other acquisitions after 1783 were given the Crown Colony government of Governor and Council. This lesson was reinforced after 1793 by the external pressure of war, which required centralised control over colonial economic and strategic resources, by the determination to enforce what was at first in the colonies a detested humanitarianism, and by the fact that native subjects were neither used nor suited to representative government. Hence, between 1783 and 1815, while the new conception of commercial Empire was developing, there continued to be an Empire of dependencies, each with a definite value, controlled by officials of home appointment, containing as small an independent white population as possible—the old Empire shorn of its greatest anomaly. The political power of the Imperial government was here supreme, and Parliament recognised few (and these self-imposed) limits on its right to legislate for the whole Empire.

The next lesson drawn from the American Revolution was that this right to legislate ought only to be used in cases of absolute necessity, and in particular that colonies must never again be taxed for imperial purposes by the Imperial Parliament. Where assemblies still existed, grants in aid were given from British funds—to Canada until 1818—to prevent further under-mining of colonial officials by local representative bodies. Imperial rule was not relaxed but was tightened after 1783. The belief that the American Revolution showed the ruling groups in this country how to govern colonies wisely is yet another legend of this period, clearly disproved by events in Canada between 1818 and 1837. The essence of what change took place was the slow development of a new economic policy, which made possible a new kind of colonialism. There was in fact, as there always is, a constant interaction between imperial affairs and the social, economic and political background in Great Britain. The eighteenth-century House of Commons, reflection of stabilised complacency, and the American Continental Congress, reflection of frontier vitality, represented social structures already too far apart to be reconciled. But this interaction is shown in the Canada Act of 1791, the first important attempt after the Ameri-can Revolution to establish a workable constitutional relationship between mother country and colony. The declared basis here was assimilation and approximation to the balance of social elements in the British Constitution, and as events showed, that basis did not exist, either in Canada, or in Ireland, where Pitt applied assimilation in its most extreme form by absorbing the Irish legislature into the Parliament of the United Kingdom. Only after 1832, when the British Constitution itself began to broaden out in response to the social and political changes effected by industrialisation, did this interaction become fruitful. The Reform Act of 1832 made possible Lord Durham's Report on Canada in 1839, while the humanitarian campaign against slavery in the Empire contributed to the betterment of labour conditions at home. It was social divergence especially which gave rise to political difference both before 1775 and after 1783, and which fundamentally caused the need to devise constitutional machinery which would satisfy the aspirations of colonial nationalism. Once modern responsible government was introduced in Great Britain, progress in the settlement colonies became possible, and after 1832, the parent society began to approximate to the colonial in terms of middle-class democracy. In fact, in the history of British colonial development, the period between 1774 and 1839 is noteworthy as one in which old and new objectives strain and jostle each other at every point, a conflict of interests in an exceptionally formative period.[1]

Probably the result of the American Revolution most felt in Great Britain immediately, consciously and subconsciously, was the loss of supremacy at sea. Although invasion schemes were the constant exercise of the French authorities in the eighteenth century, there is little doubt that in 1779 this country had been nearer invasion than at any time since 1588, while the number of merchant ships captured between 1779 and 1783, averaging over 600 yearly, led to grave shortages of supplies, and financial trouble. The War of American Independence underlined the dependence of the British on sea power, which in the eighteenth century meant primarily the control of ocean communications, *i.e.,* ability to bar enemy access to his own overseas possessions. Usually, Great Britain, by cutting off enemy warships and merchant vessels, was able to force enemy colonies into submission. This policy was again possible after 1793, and was followed: indeed, it has been argued that the British Empire in 1815 was as much the casual product of naval supremacy as the consequence of any deliberate policy.[2] It is certain that at that time, when Great Britain was the world's largest colonial power, hers was a sea and not a land Empire—composed of trading posts, islands, ports of call and settlements on sea coasts or within easy reach of the sea. The greater part of the land masses in America, Australia, Africa and the Far East, were still closed to European pene-

---

[1] These are well illustrated by the select documents edited by V. T. Harlow and F. Madder, *British Colonial Developments, 1774–1834*, London, 1953.
[2] G. S. Graham: *Empire of the North Atlantic*, London, 1951.

tration, and remained so while overland transport was difficult and slow. It was a nineteenth-century achievement to add land masses to the framework of a sea Empire, and it was eventually the steam locomotive which made that achievement practicable.

The second function of sea power was the protection of trade, as the long series of Navigation Acts shows. The destruction of the naval forces of the enemy in time of war became the accepted means to the British end, which was the destruction of the instrument that defended, and was intended to guarantee, the existence of commerce. Once an opponent was weakened by blockade, or reduced in battle, his trade routes as well as his colonies were at the mercy of the victor. For the British, Empire was a unique blend of sea power and trade, well described by Bolingbroke in 1738: 'the sea is our barrier, ships are our fortresses, and the mariners that trade and commerce alone can furnish are the garrisons to defend them'. As we have seen,[1] a combination of empire and sea power such as the British possessed after 1763 was a source of disquiet and jealousy to all competitors. However the British Empire had been built up before 1775, the American colonies were certainly lost through absence of mind. Successive British administrations shuffled between policies of firmness and appeasement until it was too late effectively to apply either. They failed to pursue an energetic policy at the beginning of operations, when rebellion might have been crushed before France entered the war. They refrained from using against kinsfolk the preventive measures that would have been taken at once against any ordinary enemy. They failed to exploit colonial military weakness; they failed, when they finally decided to resort to force, to apply that force directly on land and at sea in overwhelming strength at the centre of the strategic theatre. Even so, Britain might have been spared some of her worst humiliation had it nor been for the spectacular recovery of France begun almost immediately after 1763. The French Navy, joined in 1779 by that of Spain, was in a position not only to challenge British superiority, but actually to win command of the seas at a vital period. This was the reason why, when Great Britain had as great if not a greater force than

[1] See above, p. 9.

ever she had, the enemy was superior to her. As Sandwich put it, 'England till this time was never engaged in a sea war with the House of Bourbon thoroughly united, their naval force unbroken, and having no other war or object to draw off their attention and resources . . . We have no one friend or ally to assist us, on the contrary all those who ought to be our allies except Portugal act against us'. A main cause of political defeat was political isolation, a result of the jealousy caused by the settlement of 1763, which diplomacy failed to dispel. It was this which prevented Great Britain following her usual naval policy outlined above: she simply had not the ships to command the seas off Ushant, off Chesapeake Bay, in the North Sea, the Mediterranean, or in the Indian Ocean.

During the wars precipitated by the outbreak of the French Revolution, British possessions in North America and elsewhere were in no real danger as long as Britain retained command of the sea, and while the United States remained neutral. Successive naval victories extinguished any fresh claims the French might have made in the New World, in the Mediterranean, and in the East, and guaranteed the integrity not only of British possessions, but of the United States as well. In 1812, that country declared war on Great Britain. The element which influenced the course of hostilities ashore, and decided the outcome, was the British blockade at sea: by 1814, the United States was fighting for her existing boundaries. The absence of external naval assistance is the significant difference between this situation and that which existed between 1778 and 1782. The Napoleonic Wars finally transformed an organisation whose main centre had been the North Atlantic into one that now extended from Canada to the Pacific Islands, a world-wide business concern whose guarantee of security for almost another century was the British Navy. Without undue financial strain, Britain maintained that supremacy at sea—here is the key to her policy at the Congress of Vienna, and throughout the nineteenth century. Behind that shield, the settlement colonies became self-governing, and developed their resources without fear of interference. For most of that century, Great Britain was defensively self-sufficient in coal,-

iron, and other basic materials vital for war production, whilst her man power was sufficient to exploit them. Only the present century has seen the increasing dependence of this country on Middle East and East Indies oil and supplies, American machine tools and steel, and food from a variety of sources, essential now to a British war effort. The eighteenth-century position is now reversed. An enemy attempts to force Great Britain into submission by cutting her off from overseas food and raw materials. As Sir Winston Churchill pointed out during the Second World War, all our plans depended on victory in the Battle of the Atlantic. Without ships Great Britain can neither live nor conquer.

The wheel has turned full circle. The survival of the Mother Country depends upon the maintenance of communications with former colonies, now become self-governing Dominions. Sea power remains a vital link of security, and though control of ocean communications and protection of trade involves new and varied instruments, constantly changing tactics, scientific awareness and inventiveness, there is as yet no adequate substitute for ships as carriers of the bulk of resources from the place of their origin to the place of their destination. The fundamentals remain, and the only method of safeguarding such transport is still by controlling the routes, however much the weapons appropriate for their seizure and maintenance may alter. The role of the Royal Navy is constant—to ensure the freedom of the seas to itself (and those who depend upon it), and deny it to an enemy.

Finally, the American Revolution caused a mental ferment which had far-reaching results. The break-up of the Spanish Empire in Central and South America was foreseen as early as 1781,[1] for nothing succeeds like success, particularly when existing conditions appear to be similar. The considerable French influence in the American Revolution, from the circulation of the Declaration of Independence to that of the Constitutions of the Union and of the separate states, had an important influence on intellectual opinion in pre-revolutionary France. The popular

[1] R. A. Humphreys: 'The Fall of the Spanish Empire', *History*, Vol. XXXVII, October 1952.

effect of the American Revolution on France as a whole is rather more doubtful. How many peasants could read? How many French soldiers served in America after 1778? How many were killed? How many settled in that land? How many returned? And, even of those who did return, were transport facilities such that the news and ideas they brought with them, could spread rapidly and with force throughout the community? Here is another important subject which requires investigation. It seems probable that revolution in France followed the pattern of revolution in non-industrial societies: in the first stage, the movement begins with small groups of intellectuals, with little mass support, who discuss means of applying to their country the ideas which they have originated or imported. For this to become effective, mass support has to be found, which needs practical motives to overcome traditional and religious loyalties. It is certain that one practical grievance in France, the burden of debt and taxation, was caused more by the loans with which French intervention in the War of American Independence and the grants to America were financed, than by the over-worn excuses of Court extravagance.

Everywhere those who followed the American example found that revolution and the acquisition of independence or self-government was not the end, but merely the beginning, of their troubles. There was greater need than ever not solely for dis-cussion of the principles of society, of individual rights, or national policy, but for practical solutions of these difficult questions. It is a lesson which has point for colonies emerging now to control their own government, involving not least a readiness to take the odium for unpalatable decisions which under a colonial régime could conveniently be (and usually are) blamed on the metropolitan power.

ERIC ROBSON

(born 22 April 1918, died 14 May 1954)

Letters from America, 1773–1780. The letters of a Scots officer, Sir James Murray; to his home during the War of American Independence. (Manchester University Press, 1951.)

Lord North, in the symposium 'British Prime Ministers'. (Wingate, 1953.)

Seven Years War in Europe; Social Structure of the Armed Forces and *Art of War in 18th Century.* Cambridge Modern History, Vol. VII, New Series (Cambridge, 1955).

Articles

'The expedition to the Southern Colonies, 1775–1776,' *English Historical Review,* October 1951.

'The raising of a regiment in the War of American Independence.' The 80th Foot, the Edinburgh Regiment. *Journal of the Society for Army Historical Research,* September, 1949.

'British Light Infantry in the eighteenth century: the effect of American conditions.' *Army Quarterly,* January 1952.

'Purchase and Promotion in the British Army in the mid-eighteenth century.' *History,* February–June 1951.

'The American Revolution reconsidered.' *History Today,* February 1952.

'The War of American Independence reconsidered.' *History Today,* May 1952.

'Lord George Germain.' *History Today,* February 1953.

'British colonisation in the seventeenth century.' *History Today,* April 1953.

'The American colonies in the first half of the eighteenth century.' *History Today,* February 1954.

'British Monarchy, 1688–1837.' *Manchester Guardian* Coronation Supplement, May 1953.

'Peninsular Private: a private soldier's account of the retreat to Corunna.' *Journal of the Society for Army Historical Research,* Spring 1954.

Reviews

Contributed regularly to a number of papers and journals, including *The Listener, Manchester Guardian,* and occasionally for the English and American Historical Reviews, and *History Today.*

BIBLIOGRAPHY

This is not a complete bibliography, but is one prepared from notes left by the author of works that he had consulted.

Manuscript Sources

British Museum: Add. MSS. 37833, 37834, 37835 (George III to John Robinson), 42,363.

Carlisle Papers: Historical Manuscripts Commission, 15th Report, Appendix IX, Part IV (1897).

Colonial Office MSS.: C.O. 5 and 318.

Dartmouth Papers: Historical Manuscripts Commission, 14th Report, Appendices, Part X, Vol. II.

Hastings Papers: Historical Manuscripts Commission, Vol. III.

Knox Manuscripts: Historical Manuscripts Commission, Various, Vol. 6 (1909).

Portland Papers (3rd Duke): Nottingham University.

Public Records Office: Pitt MSS., Chatham Papers.

Shelburne Papers: Ann Arbor, Michigan.

Stopford Sackville Papers: Historical Manuscripts Commission, Vol. I, II.

Verulam Papers: Historical Manuscripts Commission.

Wedderburn Papers: Ann Arbor, Michigan, Vol. II, i.

Windsor Castle: George III, Private 1.

Printed Sources

Adams, R. G.: *Political Ideas of the American Revolution.* (Durham, N.C., 1922, re-issued 1939.)

Allen, G. W.: *A Naval History of the American Revolution,* 2 vols. (New York, 1913.)

Anburey, T.: *Travels through the interior parts of America,* 2 vols. (London, 1789.)

Annual Register, 1779.

Armytage, Frances: *The Free Port System in the British West Indies, 1766–1822.* (London, 1953.)

Atkinson, C. T. (ed.): 'Some Evidence for Burgoyne's Expedition', *Journal of the Society for Army Historical Research,* Vol. XXIV.

Baldwin, S. E.: *The American Jurisdiction of the Bishop of London in colonial times.* (Worcester, Mass., 1900.)

Barham Papers: ed. J. K. Laughton, Vols. I and II. (Navy Records Society, London, 1906, 1912.)

Barnes, D. G.: *George III and William Pitt, 1783–1806.* (London, 1939.)

Barrington-Bernard Correspondence, ed. E. C. Channing and A. C. Coolidge. (Harvard, 1912.)

Barrington Papers: (Navy Records Society), 2 vols., ed. C. K. Bonner. (London, 1937–41.)

Basye, A. H.: 'The Secretary of State for the Colonies', *American Historical Review*, Vol. XXVIII.

Beatson, Robert: *Naval and Military Memoirs of Great Britain from 1727 to 1783.* 6 vols. (London, 1804.)

Bell, Major Thomas: *A Short Essay on Military First Principles.* (London, 1770.)

Bellot, H. Hale: *American History and American Historians.* (London, 1952.)

Biddulph, Robert, Letters of: *American Historical Review*, Vol. XXIX.

Bill, A. H.: *Valley Forge, the Making of an Army.* (New York, 1952.)

Bland, Richard: *An Enquiry into the Rights of the British Colonies.* (1766.)

Bonsal, S.: *The Cause of Liberty.* (London, 1947.)

Boyd, J. P.: *Anglo-American Union, Joseph Galloway's plans to preserve the British Empire, 1774–1788.* (Philadelphia, 1941.)

Brady, Alexander: *Democracy in the Dominions.* (Second edition, London, 1952.)

Brinton, Crane: *The Anatomy of Revolution.* (London, 1953.)

Brogan, D. W.: *The Price of Revolution.* (London, 1951.)

Brougham, Lord: *Historical Sketches of Statesmen who flourished in the time of George III,* 3 vols. (London, 1839.)

Burgoyne, J.: *State of the Expedition from Canada.* (London, 1780.)

Carrington, H. B.: *Battles of the American Revolution, 1775–1781.* (New York, 1876.)

Carter, C. E.: 'The significance of the Military office in America'. *American Historical Review*, Vol. XXVIII.

Cartwright, John: *American Independence, the Interest and Glory of Britain.* (1775.)

Clark, D. M.: 'The American Board of Customs, 1767–1783'. *American Historical Review.*

Clark, Jane: 'The Responsibility for the failure of the Burgoyne Campaign'. *American Historical Review*, Vol. XXXV.

Curtis: *The Organisation of the British Army in the American Revolution.* (New Haven, 1920.)

Dickinson, John: *Letters of a Pennsylvanian Farmer.* (1768.)

Dickinson, O. M.: *The Navigation Acts and the American Revolution.* (Philadelphia, 1951.)

Doren, C. van (ed.): *Letters and Papers of Benjamin Franklin and Richard Jackson, 1753–1785.* (Philadelphia, 1941.)

Doren, C. van: *Secret History of the American Revolution.*

Dunn, C. W.: *Highland Settler.* (London, 1953.)

Evelyn, William Glanville, 4th Foot, *Memoirs and Letters of, from North America, 1774–1776,* ed. G. D. Scull. (Oxford, 1879.)

Fisher, S. G.: *The Struggle for American Independence,* 2 vols. (Philadelphia, 1908.)

Flick, A. C. (ed.): *History of the State of New York,* 10 vols. (New York, 1933.)

Foord, A. S.: 'The Waning of the Influence of the Crown'. *English Historical Review*, Vol. LXII.

Fortescue, J. W.: *A History of the British Army.*

Franklin, Benjamin, *Autobiographical Writings,* ed. C. van Doren. (London, 1946.)

Freeman, D. S.: *George Washington, A Biography*. Vol. III, Planter and Patriot. Vol. IV, Leader of the Revolution. (London, 1951.)

Gage, Correspondence of General Thomas, 2 vols., ed. C. E. Carter. (New Haven, 1931–3.)

Galloway, Joseph: *A Candid Examination of the Mutual Claims of Great Britain and the Colonies*. (Philadelphia, 1775.)

Gentleman's Magazine, 1779.

George III, Letters to Lord Bute, 1756–1766, ed. R. Sedgwick. (London, 1939.)

George III, The Correspondence of, 1760–1783, 6 vols., ed. Sir J. W. Fortescue. (London, 1927–8.)

Gipson, L. H.: *Jared Ingersoll*. (New Haven, 1920.)

Gottschalk, Louis: *Lafayette and the close of the American Revolution*. (Chicago, 1942.)

Graham, G. S.: 'Considerations on the War of American Independence', *Bulletin Institute Historical Research*, Vol. XXII. (May, 1949.)

Graham, G. S.: *Empire of the North Atlantic*. (London, 1951.)

Graydon, Alexander: *Memoirs of a Life chiefly passed in Pennsylvania*. (Edinburgh, 1822.)

Greene, A. W.: *The Life of Nathaniel Greene*, 3 vols. (New York, 1867–71.)

Greene, E. B.: 'New York and the Old Empire', in A. C. Flick (ed.): *History of the State of New York*, 10 vols. (New York, 1933.)

Guttridge, G. H.: *David Hartley, M.P. An Advocate of Conciliation*, 1774–1783. (Berkeley, California, 1926.) And *American Historical Review*, 1927.

Hacker, L. M.: *The Shaping of the American Tradition*. (New York, 1947.)

Harlow, V. T., and Madder, F.: *British Colonial Development*, 1774–1834. (London, 1953.)

Harlow, V. T.: *The Founding of the Second British Empire*, 1763–1793. (London, 1952.)

Harper, L. A.: 'The effects of the Navigation Acts on the Thirteen Colonies' in R. B. Morris (ed.): *The Era of the American Revolution*. (New York, 1939.)

Harper, L. A.: *The English Navigation Laws*. (New York, 1939.)

Harper, L. A.: 'Mercantilism and the American Revolution'. *Canadian Historical Review*, Vol. XXIII.

Hartley, David: *Letters on the American War*. (London, 1778.)

Howe, Lt.-General Sir William: *Narrative* (Second edition.) (London, 1780.)

Howe, General Sir William, orderly book at Charleston, Boston and Halifax, June 17th, 1775–May 26th, 1776, ed. E. E. Hale and B. F. Stevens. (London, 1890.)

Hughes, Thomas, The Journal of, 1778–1789, ed. E. A. Benians. (Cambridge, 1947.)

Humphreys, R. A.: 'The Fall of the Spanish Empire'. *History*, Vol. XXXVII. (October, 1952.)

Jackson, Robert: *A Systematic View of the formation, discipline and economy of armies*. (London, 1804.)

Jameson, J. F.: *The American Revolution considered as a Social Movement*. (Princeton, 1926.)

Keith Papers, Vol. 1: ed. W. G. Perrin. (Navy Records Society, 1927.)

Knollenberg, Bernhard: *Washington and the Revolution, A reappraisal.* (New York, 1941.)

Lamb, R.: *Memoir of his own life.* (Dublin, 1811.)

Lee Papers: Collections of the New York Historical Society, 4 vols. (New York, 1872-5.)

Lindsay, Lord (ed.): *The Lives of the Lindsays.* (London, 1849.)

McGuffie, T. H. (ed.): *Peninsular Cavalry General, 1811-1813.* (London, 1951.)

Mackenzie, Frederick, The Diary of, 1775-1781, 2 vols. (Cambridge, Mass., 1930.)

Malone, Dumas: *Jefferson the Virginian.* (London, 1948.)

Mays, D. J.: *Edmund Pendleton, 1721-1803,* 2 vols. (Cambridge, Mass., 1952.)

Miller, J. G.: *Triumph of Freedom, 1775-1783.* (Boston, 1948.)

Montross, Lynn: *The Reluctant Rebels.* (New York, 1950.)

Morison, S. E. and Commager, H. S.: *The Growth of the American Republic,* 2 vols. Fourth edition. (Oxford, 1950.)

Mullett, C. F.: 'English Imperial Thinking, 1764-1783'. *Political Science Quarterly,* Vol. XLV.

Mundy, G. B.: *Life and Correspondence of Admiral Rodney,* 2 vols. (London, 1830.)

Namier, Sir Lewis B.: *England in the Age of the American Revolution.* (London, 1930.)

Namier, Sir Lewis B.: 'King George III. A study in personality'. *History Today.* Vol. III. (September, 1953.)

Nettels, C. P.: *George Washington and American Independence.* (Boston, 1951.)

Oliver, F. S.: *Alexander Hamilton: an Essay on American Union.* (London, 1931.)

Oman, Carola: *Sir John Moore.* (London, 1953.)

Oswald, Richard, Memorandum, 1781, ed. W. Still Robinson, Jr. (Charlottesville, Virginia, 1953.)

Paine, Thomas: *Common Sense.* (London, 1776.)

Pares, R.: *King George III and the Politicians.* (Oxford, 1953.)

Pargellis, S. (ed.): *Military Affairs in North America, 1748-1765.* (London, 1936.)

Pemberton, W. Baring: *Lord North.* (London, 1938.)

Pembroke Papers, 1780-1817, ed. Lord Herbert. (London, 1950.)

Percy, Hugh Earl, Letters of, ed. C. K. Bolton. (Boston, 1902.)

Perkins, Simeon, The Diary of, 1766-80, ed. H. A. Innis. (Champlain Society, Toronto, 1948.)

Pitt, William, Earl of Chatham, The Correspondence of, ed. W. S. Taylor, 4 vols. (London, 1840.)

Price, Richard: *Observations on the Nature of Civil Liberty.* (1776.)

Pulteney, William Johnstone: *Thoughts on the Present State of Affairs with America, and the means of conciliation.* (London, 1778.)

Reed, W. B.: *Life and Correspondence of Joseph Reed.* (Philadelphia, 1847.)

Reid, O. S.: 'An Analysis of British Parliamentary Opinion on American Affairs at the close of the War of Independence'. *Journal of Modern History.*

Richmond, Sir H. W.: *Statesmen and Sea Power.* (Oxford, 1947.)

Robson, E.: 'British Light Infantry in the eighteenth century: the effect of American conditions'. *Army Quarterly.* (Jan., 1952.)

Robson, E.: 'The Art of War and the Social Foundations of the Armed Forces'· *Cambridge Modern History*. Vol. VII, New Series. (Cambridge, 1955.)

Sandwich, John, Earl of, *Private Papers, 1771–1782*, ed. G. R. Barnes and J. H. Owen. (Navy Records Society, 4 vols.) (London, 1932–8.)

Serle, Ambrose: *The American Journal of, 1776–1778*, ed. E. H. Tatum, Jr. (San Marino, 1940.)

Schachner, N.: *Alexander Hamilton*. (London, 1946.)

Schlesinger, H. M.: *Colonial Merchants and the American Revolution*. (New York, 1918.)

Sellman, R. R., M.A., *A Student's Atlas of Modern History*. (London, Edward Arnold, 1952.)

Sharpe, Granville: *A Declaration of the Peoples' natural right to a share in the Legislature*. (1774.)

Sheppard, E. W.: *The Study of Military History*. (Aldershot, 1952.)

Simcoe, Sir John Graves: *A Journal of the operations of the Queens Rangers from the end of the year 1777 to the conclusion of the late American War*. (Exeter, 1787.)

Smith, Justin, H.: *Our Struggle for the Fourteenth Colony*, 2 vols. (New York, 1907.)

Smyth, A. H.: *Writings of Benjamin Franklin*, 10 vols. (London, 1916.)

South Carolina Historical and Genealogical Magazine, VIII.

Sparks, Jared (ed.): *Correspondence of the American Revolution*, 4 vols. (Boston, 1853.)

Spector, M. M.: *The American Department of the British Government, 1768–1782*. (New York, 1940.)

Stark, J. H.: *The Loyalists of Massachusetts*. (Boston, 1910.)

Stevens, B. F.: *Fascimiles of Manuscripts in European Archives relating to America, 1773–1783*, 25 vols. (London, 1889–95.)

Thacher, James: *Military Journal during the American Revolutionary War, from 1775 to 1783*. (Hartford, 1854.)

Thacher, Oxenbridge: *Sentiments of a British American*. (Boston, 1764.)

Trevelyan, G. O.: *The American Revolution*, 4 vols. (London, 1928 edition.)

Trevelyan, Sir George Otto: *Letters on the American War*. (London, 1878.)

Tucker, Josiah: *The True Interest of Great Britain set Fourth*. (London, 1774.)

Tyler, M. C.: *The Literary History of the American Revolution, 1763–1783*, 2 vols. (London, 1905.)

Tyne, G. H. Van: *England and America*. (Cambridge, 1927.)

Voto, Bernard de: *Westward the course of Empire*. (London, 1953.)

Wallace, Paul A. W.: *The Mühlenbergs of Pennsylvania*. (Philadelphia, 1950.)

Walpole, Horace: *Journal of the Reign of King George the Third, 1771–1783*, ed. J. Doran. (London, 1859.)

Walpole, Horace, Letters of, ed. Paget Toynbee. (Oxford, 1903–5.)

Wilkin, W. H.: *Some British Soldiers in America*. (London, 1914.)

Willco.., W. B.: 'British Strategy in America, 1778'. *Journal of Modern History*, XX, No. 2.

Wilson, James: *Considerations of the legislative authority of the British Parliament*. (1774.)

Wortley, E. Stuart: *A Prime Minister and his son*. (London, 1925.)

Wrong, G. M.: *Washington and his Comrades in Arms*. (Yale, 1921.)

INDEX

Adams, John (1735–1826): 1, 7, 39, 55, 56, 64, 66, 117
——— Samuel (1722–1803): 7, 17, 36
Admiralty Courts: 31, 51, 64, 198
Albany (Congress): 13, 36, 47, 91, 163
American Dept.: *see* Colonies
Amherst, 1st Lord, General (1717–97): 48, 85, 134, 177, 183, 193
Anburey, Thomas, Lieut.: 94, 100, 106, 138
Andromeda: 188
Arbuthnot, Marriot, Admiral (*c.* 1711–94): 101, 145, 167
Army, American: 94 *et seq.*, 123, 127, 129–30, 134, 137, 142, 146, 153 *et seq.*
———, British: 48–50, 64, 93 *et seq.*, 123 *et seq.*, 153 *et seq.*, 180, 191–9, 200 *et seq.*, 211 *et seq.*
Arnold, Benedict (1741–1801): 137, 138, 171
Ashburton, Lord: *see* John Dunning
Assemblies, Elected: 10, 11, 12, 38, 69, 91, 163, 202
Assistance, writs of (General Warrants): 64
Auckland, Lord: *see* William Eden

Bacon, Francis (1561–1626): 4
Barbados: 215
Barrington, Samuel, Admiral (1729–1820): 205, 208, 210
———, William, 2nd Viscount (1717–93): 26, 33, 34, 86, 87, 115
Bath, Marquess of: *see* Weymouth
Bathurst, 2nd Earl (1714–94): 183
Belasyse, Lord, later 2nd Earl of Fauconberg (1699–1774): 67
Bell, Thomas: 99
Bellot, H. Hale: 8
Bemis Heights: 94, 130
Bennington: 106
Bernard, Sir Francis (*c.* 1711–79): 26, 33, 167
Biddulph, Robert: 95, 125, 128, 168
Bland, Richard: 78

Bolingbroke, 1st Viscount (1678–1751): 235
Boston: 104, 139
———, 'Massacre': 66, 67, 68, 88
———, Merchants: 77
———, Port Bill: 69, 115
———, 'Tea Party': 17, 23, 44, 68
Botetourt, Lord: 61
Boudinot: 168
Bramley, Robert, Rev.: 16
Brandywine: 97, 98, 105, 135
Brinton, Crane: 41
Brogan, D. W.: 58, 91
Brooklyn Heights: 94, 98, 109, 116, 121, 135, 172, 173
Brougham and Vaux, 1st Lord (1778–1868): 36, 62
Brunswick: 120
Bunker Hill: 97, 100, 125, 127, 167
Burgoyne, John, General (1723–92): 94, 105, 109, 130, 132, 137, 139, 169, 176
Burke, Edmund (1729–97): 22, 36, 45, 59, 61, 149, 226
Bute, 3rd Earl of (1713–92): 135, 209
Byron, John, Admiral (1723–86): 9, 102

Calder, Sir Henry, General (d. 1792): 216
Camden: 173
———, 1st Earl (1713–94): 63, 78
Canada: 94, 105, 112, 138, 158, 182, 185, 232; (Act, 1791) 233
———, French in: 1, 10, 13, 43, 47, 48, 87
Canning, George (1770–1827): 12
Carleton, Sir Guy, 1st Lord Dorchester, (1724–1808): 118, 138, 139
Caribbean: 3, 9, 103, 142
Carlisle, 5th Earl of (1748–1825): 176, 179 n., 181, 188, 198–9, 200, 203
Carter, William: 100
Carteret, Philip, Admiral (d. 1796): 9
Carolina, North: 7, 8, 11, 12, 58, 140, 168
———, South: 6, 8, 12, 68, 71, 95, 111, 168

Catawba, R.: 172
Cartwright, John: 80
Champlain, Lake: 118
Charleston: 95, 126, 129, 145, 168
Charming Nelly: 211
Chatham, Earl of: *see* William Pitt
Chesapeake: 107, 137
Chester: 161
Chesterfield, 4th Earl of (1694–1773): 65
Church, Episcopacy: 1, 33, 56
Churchill, Sir Winston: 237
Clarendon, 1st Earl of (1608–74): 58
Clinton, Gen. Sir Henry (*c.* 1738–95): 95, 96, 98, 99, 114, 136, 140, 145, 168, 187, 191, 200, 205, 209, 213, 218
——, George, Governor (1739–1812): 11
Coinage, Currencies: 7
Collier, Sir George, Admiral: (1738–95) 167
Colonial system (mercantilism): 2–7, 10; (royal) 12, 64; (corporate) 12; (proprietary) 12; 14, 32, 43, 50, 79 *et seq.*, 90, 220, 229
Colonies, Secretary for (1768): 18, 21, 96
Commager, H. S.: 14, 163
Conciliatory Mission, 1778: 73, 176, 179–80, 196, 199, 200, 204
Congress, First Continental, 1774: 41, 43, 69–70, 73; (Second) 71, 198, 202, 204, 221
——, Stamp Act, 1765: 58–9, 220
Constitution, American, 1787: 77, 221
——, British: 17, 18, 23, 30, 37, 77–9, 80, 148
Conway, Harry S., F.-M. (1721–95): 21, 63
Cook, James, Captain (1728–79): 9
Cooke, Governor: 112
Continental association: 72
Cornwallis, 2nd Earl (1738–1805): 100, 105, 114, 129, 136, 146, 168, 172
Council, legislative: 11
Cowpens: 100, 172
Crown Point: 118
Curwen, Samuel: 129
Customs, Board of: 51, 62; (Boston) 64; 180, 185

Dalrymple, Alexander (1737–1808): 9

Dalrymple, Sir John, 4th Bart. (1726–1810): 10
Dartmouth, 2nd Earl of (1731–1801): 21, 22, 73, 90, 104, 183n
Deane, Silas: 177
de Brentano: 153, 164
de Chastellux, Marquis, General: 94
Declaration of Independence, 1776: 28, 74
—— of Rights, 1774: 35, 54, 72
Declaratory Act, 1766: 10, 60, 68, 197
de Grasse, Admiral: 146
de Guichen, Admiral: 168
de Kalb, Baron: 165
Delaware: 12, 107
De Rayneval: 181
de Rochambeau, Comte, General: 95, 153, 156, 170
D'Estaing, Admiral: 207, 211, 216
Dickinson, John: 64
Dorchester, Lord : *see* Carleton
Downshire, Marquess of: *see* Hillsborough
Drayton, W. H.: 202
Duché, Jacob: 169
Dudley, Guilford: 170
Dunning, John, 1st Lord Ashburton (1731–83): 147
Durham, 1st Earl of (1792–1840): 11, 231, 233
Dyer, Eliphalet: 170

Eden, William, 1st Lord Auckland (1744–1814): 83, 198, 196
Egg Harbour: 209
Elizabethtown: 120
Elk Ferry: 128
Enabling Act, 1773: 196
Evelyn, W. G., Capt.: 27, 115, 127

Fauconberg, 1st Earl of: 67
Federatism: 80 *et seq.*, 164, 220, 222
Florida: 207, 210
Fort Clinton: 136
Fort Edward: 105
Fort Lee: 160
Fort Montgomery: 136 (renamed Vaughan in his honour)
Fort Washington: 99, 160
Fox, Charles James (1749–1806): 24, 36, 85, 149, 225

France: 13, 62, 73, 103, 120, 133, 141, 142, 143, 153, 164, 167, 174, 175, 185, 187, 190, 192, 207; (Franco-American Treaty) 218, 222; 235

Franklin, Benjamin (1706–90): 13, 28, 30, 35, 36, 44, 55, 75, 78, 83, 91, 177, 179, 222

Fraser, Colonel: 139

Frederick II of Prussia (1712–86): 60, 134

Freeman's Farm: 94

Free Port Act, 1766: 46, 61–2, 230

'Friends of America': 88

Gage, Thomas, General (1721–87): 22, 23, 27, 34, 83, 85, 87–90, 104, 105, 114, 125, 161, 166

Galloway, Joseph: 12, 70, 71, 135

Gambier, James, Admiral (1723–89): 111, 144, 212

Gates, Horatio, General (1728–1806): 172, 173

George III (1738–1820): 16 et seq., 28, 33, 75, 78, 82–5, 116, 120, 143, 144, 145, 146, 148–52, 175, 177, 182, 185 et seq., 205, 208, 210 et seq., 223, 225, 227

Georgia: 6, 7, 11, 12, 58, 168

Germaine, Lord George: see Sackville

Germantown: 128, 172

Gibbon, Edward (1737–94): 75

Gloucester Point: 172

Gower, 2nd Earl, 1st Marquess of Stafford (1721–1803): 176, 183n

Grafton, 3rd Duke of (1735–1811): 23, 45, 63, 82

Graham, G. S.: 174

Grant, James, General, of Ballindalloch (1720–1806): 102, 127, 206, 208–11, 217–18,

Graves, Thomas (later Lord Graves) (1725–1801): 144

Graydon, Alexander: 31, 38, 40, 41, 91

Greene, Nathaniel, General: 123, 129, 159, 166, 168

Grenville, George (1712–70): 2, 33, 44, 45, 50, 55, 58

Grey, Charles, General: 95, 116

Guadeloupe: 8, 218

Guilford, Earl of: see Lord North

Guilford Court House: 96

Hale, Lieut.: 153

Haldimand, Sir F., General (1718–91): 83

Hamilton, Alexander (1757–1804): 29, 140, 161, 172, 220

——, Sir William (1730–1803): 148

Hancock, John (1737–93): 113

Harcourt, Col.: 116, 120

Harlem Heights: 98

Harlow, V. T.: 8, 62

Harper, L. A.: 76n, 77

Hartley, David (1732–1813): 16, 30, 53, 75, 81, 104, 228

Harvey, Edward, General: 139

Hastings, Marquess of: see Rawdon

Hawley, Joseph: 78

Head of Elk: 105, 107

Henry, Patrick; 58, 70

Hessians: 115, 128

Hillsborough, 1st Earl of, and Marquess of Downshire (1718–93): 18, 65, 86

Hotham, 1st Lord, Admiral (1726–99): 205, 210

Howe, 3rd Viscount, General (1724–58): killed at Ticonderoga

——, 4th Viscount, 1st Earl, Admiral (1726–99): 27, 107, 116, 119, 186, 194

——, Sir William, General (1729–1814): 95, 96, 98, 99, 104, 105, 107, 109, 110, 113, 114, 116, 119, 121, 127, 128, 133, 135, 138, 140, 176, 182, 186, 200, 205

Hughes, Thomas: 94, 131, 157

Huntingdon, 10th Earl of (1729–89): 110

Imperial defence: 49, 175 et seq., 234–7

Independence, Declaration of (4 July, 1776): 28, 74

Indian Affairs, Supt. of: 47–8

Indians: 13, 47–8, 87, 231

Iron manufacturer: 5, 6

Irvine, William, Colonel: 94

Irving, Charles: 73

Jackson, Richard (1721–87): 26, 30, 189

——, Robert: 173–4

Jay, John (1745–1829): 44

Jefferson, Thomas (1743–1826): 35, 45, 123, 155

Johnston, Samuel (1709–82): 104

Johnstone, George, Governor: 181, 189, 203

Kalm, Peter: 12
Keppel, 1st Viscount, Admiral (1725–86): 177n
Kingston: 136
Knox, William: 12, 196, 203, 229

Land banks: 7
Langdon, Samuel: 16
Lafayette, Marquis de (1757–1834): 141, 155, 166, 188–90, 202
Lamb, R.: 100, 125, 131, 133
Laurens, Henry: 188–90, 201, 203
Lee, Charles, General: 96, 107, 153, 159, 169, 172
—— R. H.: 107, 154
Leeward Islands: 212, 217, 218
Leslie, General: 137
Lexington: 73, 130, 152n, 161
Lindsay, Colin: 217
Lincoln, Benjamin, General: 129
Loan office: 55
Long Island: 98, 107, 121, 133, 173
Long, Robert, General: 93
Louis XVI (1754–93): 178
Louisiana: 221
Loyalists: 39, 41, 65, 74, 97, 101, 106, 117, 118, 165, 230, 232
Lyttelton, Lord (1709–73): 21

Mackenzie, Frederick, Colonel: 110, 111, 116, 119, 121, 125, 128, 211n., 137, 146
Maclean, Allan: 135
Madison, James (1751–1836): 80
Martinique: 215, 217
Maryland: 8, 11
Mason, William, Rev.: 187n
Massachusetts: 4, 7, 10, 12, 23, 28, 38, 51, 58, 64, 65, 68, 88, 185, 232
—— Act 1774: 23, 232
Mays, D. J.: 52, 156
Medows, William, Colonel (1738–1813): 216
Mercantilism: 52, 77: see Colonial system
Meredith, Sir W.: 83
Middleton, Charles: 207n
Molasses Act (1733): 6, 54
Monmouth Court House: 95, 159
Montgomery, Richard: 155

Moore, Sir John, General (1761–1809): 156, 157, 165
Morgan, Daniel: 130, 172
Morné Fortune: 217
Morris, Robert (1734–1806): 134
Morrison, S. E.: 14, 163
Mount Vernon: 70
Mulgrave, 2nd Lord (1744–92): 193
Murray, Capt. Sir James: 93, 98, 124, 133, 162
——, General: 127, 134
Mutiny Act: 64

Namier, Sir Lewis: 17, 78
Napoleon (1769–1821): 134, 221
Napier, Robert: 130
National Debt: 49, 224
Navigation Acts: 141, 221, 229, 235
——, 1650–96: 3, 10, 51, 54
Navy, British: 50, 103, 106, 108, 143–6, 172, 205 et seq., 215: see also Sea Power
Newark: 120
New England: 7; (paper money) 7, 8
Newfoundland: 8
New Hampshire: 58
New Jersey: 7, 12, 111, 113, 119, 135
Newport, R.I.: 172
New York: 7, 40, 64, 65, 98, 101, 111, 118, 126, 136, 172, 195, 206, 218
Nooth, J. M.: 121
Norfolk, Vir.: 71, 155
North, Frederick, 8th Lord, and 2nd Earl of Guilford (1732–92): 21, 24, 28–9, 45, 66, 67, 81, 83–4, 104, 116, 143, 147, 151, 176, 182, 204, 221
Northumberland, Duke of: see Earl Percy
North River: 169

Ohio Company: 47
Oliver, C. J.: 10
Oswald, Richard: 90

Page, John: 71
Paine, Thomas (1737–1809): 15, 71, 74
Paper Money Act, 1751: 7
Paris, Peace of, 1763: 1, 174
——, and Versailles, Peace of, 1783: 152n
Parker, Sir Peter, Admiral (1721–1811): 128, 145
——, Hyde, Admiral (1714–82): 218n

Parties, Political: 26, 221
Pearl: 217n
Peace Commission: 27, 31, 117, 119, 175, 193
Peerage in Colonies: 177–8
Pemberton, W. Baring: 151n
Pembroke, 10th Earl of, General (1734–94): 148
Pendleton, Edmund (1721–1803): 44, 59, 74, 155, 166
Penobscot Bay: 156
Pennsylvania: 11, 12, 40, 65, 118
Percy, Earl (2nd Duke of Northumberland, 1786): 98, 130, 167
Perkins, Simeon: 202
Perth Amboy: 133
Philadelphia: 40, 41, 70, 98, 100, 105, 134, 161, 195, 200
Pitt, William, 1st Earl of Chatham (1708–78): 36, 63, 78, 139, 154, 186
——, William, 'the Younger' (1759–1806): 75, 147, 224, 226, 233
Plymouth (New): 1
Pontiac Rising, 1763: 48
Population: 223
Portland, 3rd Duke of (1738–1809): 16, 24, 147, 149
Pownall, Thomas: 51, 66, 223
Portugal: 143
Prescot, Richard: 128
Prescott, Robert, General (1725–1816): 216
Price, Richard (1723–91): 79
Princeton: 97, 99, 112
Privy Council: 221
Proclamation of 1763: 2, 32, 45
—— of 1772: 46
—— of 1776: 119
Prohibitory Act, 1775: 74
Pulteney, William Johnstone (1729–1805): 81, 117, 178–81
——, George, Commodore: 178
Puritans: 14
Putnam, Isaac, General: 173

Quartering Act, 1766: 64
Quebec: 118, 171
—— Act, 1774: 32, 64, 69, 231

Rall, J. G., Colonel: 128
Randolph, John (1773–1833): 35
Rawdon, Francis, 1st Lord, 2nd Earl of

Mona and 1st Marquess of Hastings (1754–1826): 102, 108, 128
Reed, Douglas: 224
——, Joseph: 107
Revenue Acts, 1764–65: 56–7, 63, 67
Rhode Island: 12, 111, 137, 195, 220
Richmond, Sir H. W.: 49
Robertson, James, General: 117, 138, 140
Robinson, John (1739–1805): 116, 139
Rockingham, 2nd Marquess of (1730–82): 24, 36, 45, 59, 61, 62, 149, 186
Rodney, 1st Lord, Admiral (1719–92): 101, 108, 145
Roman Emperor: 211
Rosslyn, Earl of: *see* Wedderburn
Rush, Benjamin (1745–1813): 40, 173

Sackville, George, 1st Viscount (1716–85): 10, 96, 99, 104, 115, 121, 139, 140, 145, 176, 182, 198, 203, 206, 211
Saints, Battle of the: 146
St. Lucia: 143, 192–5, 199, 205, 206, 215, 217
Sandwich, 4th Earl of (1718–92): 101, 142, 144, 211, 236
Sandy Hook: 211
Saratoga: 100, 109, 131, 136, 173, 175; (Convention) 177
Savannah: 133
Savile, Sir George, Bart. (1726–84): 62, 147
Schuyler, Philip J. (1733–1804): 154, 173
Seabury, Samuel, Rev. (Westchester Farmer): 30
Sea power: 7, 9, 13, 31, 50, 136, 141–3, 234–5, 237: *see also* Navy
Sedgwick, R.: 16
Serle, Ambrose: 27, 124, 145, 148
Seven Years' War (1756–63): 1, 5, 7, 13, 43, 47, 96, 130, 145
Sharp, Granville (1735–1813): 80
Shelburne, 2nd Earl of, 1st Marquess of Lansdowne (1737–1808): 33, 60, 63, 85, 138, 149, 164, 227
Simcoe, J. G.: 132
Skenesborough: 105
Slavery: 14, 90, 221, 231, 233
Smith, Adam (1723–90): 3, 53, 227, 229
Sons of Liberty: 17
Spain: 142, 143, 164, 185, 187, 235, 237

Stafford, Marquess of: *see* Gower

Stamp Act, 1765: 7, 33, 34, 36, 38, 41; (tax) 55; 56, 87

Stedman, Charles (1753–1812), military historian: 165

Stuart, Charles, Colonel (1753–1801): 103, 111, 116, 121, 124, 128, 135, 209

Suffolk, 12th Earl of (1739–79): 183

Sugar Duties Act, 1764: 7, 54, 61

Sullivan, John, Brig.-Gen.: 171

Sydney, Viscount: *see* Thomas Townshend

Tarleton, Sir B., General (1754–1833): 95, 96

Taxation: 148, 233

Tea Act: 76

Thacher, James: 129

Throg's Neck: 98

Thurlow, Edward, 1st Lord (1731–1806): 176, 185

Ticonderoga: 74, 94, 131, 154, 169

Tobacco: 7, 47

Toynbee, Paget, Mrs.: 187n, 212n

Tobago: 227, 232

Townshend, Thomas, 1st Viscount Sydney (1733–1800): 84

——, Charles (1725–67): 38, 45, 58, 63, 66

Trade and Plantations, First Lord of, *see* list on p. 248

——, laws of: 7, 51–2; balance of: 5, 7, 8; general: 76–77, 141

—— and Navigation Acts: 3, 10, 31

Trenton: 99, 112, 120, 128, 172

Trevelyan, Sir George: 17

Tucker, Josiah, Dean: 15, 24

Turnbull, John: 57

Union Plan (1754): 13

United Empire Loyalists: *see* Loyalists

Valley Forge: 111, 120, 158, 160, 161, 165, 166

Vaughan, Sir John, General (*c.* 1748–95): 136 *see* Fort Montgomery

Venus: 214

Vermont: 220

Virginia: 2, 4, 7, 9, 11, 32, 47, 52, 56, 58 65, 70, 91, 118, 137, 140, 154, 155

Von Steuben, Baron: 158

Wallis, Samuel, Capt. (1728–95): 9

Walpole, Horace, 4th Earl of Orford (1717–97): 16, 29, 45, 63

Ward Artemus: 70

Washington, George (1732–99): 52, 59, 65, 70, 95, 97, 103, 112, 119, 134, 137, 140, 142, 146, 152n., 154, 160, 163, 169, 171, 173, 211, 222

Wavell, Lord, F.-M.: 134

Wayne, Anthony (1745–96): 173

Weazel: 217n

Wedderburn, Alexander, 1st Earl of Rosslyn (1733–1805): 22, 34, 176, 185, 196

West Indies: 4, 8, 46, 62, 126, 145, 211–13, 227

Weymouth, 3rd Viscount, 1st Marquess of Bath (1734–96): 183n, 192

Whateley, Thomas (d. 1772): 61

White Horse Tavern: 172

Whiteplains: 110, 158, 161

Wilmot, Chester: 223

Wilson, James: 79

Wolfe, James, General (1727–59): 135

Woodford, William, Colonel: 71, 155

Woollen Act (1699): 6

Yorktown: 129, 141, 152n., 170